Fast Cooking in a Slow Cooker Every Day of the Year

A Slow Cooker Vegetarian Cookbook

JoAnn Rachor

Family Health Publications, LLC
8777 Musgrove Hwy
Sunfield MI 48890
www.familyhealthpub.com

ISBN: 978-1-878726-26-1 (13 digit)
ISBN: 1-878726-26-9 (10 digit)

Photographer *David Sherwin*
Photo layout *Dexter Saddler*
Food stylist *JoAnn Rachor*
Thank you to *Pier 1 Imports* for donating many of the place settings.

Family Health Publications, LLC
8777 Musgrove Hwy
Sunfield MI 48890

800 488-3878 order line
www.familyhealthpub.com
joann@familyhealthpub.com

Library of Congress Control Number: 2005907617

Publisher's Cataloging-In-Publication Data
(Prepared by The Donohue Group, Inc.)

Rachor, JoAnn.
Fast cooking in a slow cooker every day of the year : a slow cooker vegetarian cookbook / by JoAnn Rachor.

p. : ill. ; cm.
ISBN: 978-1-878726-26-1
ISBN: 1-878726-26-9

1. Electric cookery, Slow. 2. Vegan cookery. 3. Low-fat diet--Recipes.
4. Low-cholesterol diet--Recipes. I. Title.

TX827 .R33 2005
641.5/636 2005907617

CONTENTS

Introduction • 6
How It All Began
Great Reasons for Using a Slow Cooker
Slow Cooker Tips
Extra Items for Extra Successful Slow Cookery
Definitions
Breakfasts • 12
Entrees • 25
Incredibly Delicious Bean Cuisine
Bean Cooking Tips
Photographs • 65
Vegetables • 81
Soups, Gravies and Sauces • 92
Breads • 104
Desserts • 125
Cooker Free Recipes • 136
Recipe Titles in the Photos • 139
"Tips" Index • 141
General Index • 142

RECIPES AT A GLANCE

Breakfasts 12
Cereal Cooking Chart-Small Amount 12
Cereal Cooking Chart-Medium Amount 13
Cereal Cooking Chart-Large Amount 14
Cereal Cooking Chart-1½ Qt Crock-Pot 15
"All Night" Slow Cooked Cereal 16
Corn Millet Porridge 17
Tropical Rice 18
Multi Grain Hot Cereal 19
Heart Healthy Baked Whole Grains 20
Baked Apples & Oats 21
Apple Crumble Crisp 22
Blueberry Crumble Crisp 22
Fruit Lasagna 23
Fruit Pizza 24

Entrees 25
Bean Cooking Chart 1 28
Bean Cooking Chart 2 29
Bean Cooking Chart 3 30
Bean Cooking Chart 4 31
Bean Chart 1½ Qt Rival Crock-Pot 32
Great! Great Northerns 33
Simple but Simply Delicious Beans 34
Sesame Tahini Creamy Beans 34
South of the Border Beans 35
Cuban Black Beans 36
Baked Beans 37
Mazidra 38
Instant! Slow Cooked Refried Beans 39
Haystacks 39
Millet Tomato Bake 40
Corn Tamale Casserole 41
Spanish Rice 42
Nutty Carrot Rice 43
Cashew Rice 44
Bread Dressing 45
Chickpea A La King 46
Chunky Fried Tofu Gravy & Rice 47
Pasta Fagioli 48
Pasta Alfredo 49
Easy Does It Spaghetti 50
Garden Style Spaghetti 51
Macaroni & Cheese #1 52
Macaroni & Cheese #2 53
Stuffed Shells 54
Vegetable Lasagna 55
Goulash 56
Grape Leaf Tofu Rolls 57
Collard Leaf Tofu Rolls 57
Tender Gluten 58
Barbecued Gluten 59
Gluten Cooked in Gravy 59
Roast Beef-less 59
Tortilla Bake 60
Pizza 61
Bean Burritos 62
Barbecued Sloppy Joes 62
Hot Sandwiches-Ready to Go! 62
Tofu Loaf 63
Sun Seed Roast 63
Harvest Nut Loaf 64
Lentil Loaf 64

Vegetables 81
Maple Almond Sweet Potatoes 81
Honey Coconutty Sweet Potatoes 82
Tangy Orange Sweet Potatoes 83
Baked Sweet Potatoes 84
Simple Sweet Potatoes 85
Baked Potatoes 84
Potato Salad 84
Rustic Potatoes 85
Old Fashion Scalloped Potatoes 86
Mashed Potatoes 87
Roasted Garlic 87
Roasted Onion Rings 87
Butternut, Acorn Squash or Pie Pumpkin 88
Roasted Herb Sweet Corn 88
Baked Spaghetti Squash 88
Roasted Corn on the Cob 88
Eggplant Garlic Bake 89
Greens with Veggies 90
Simply Beets 91
Lemon Beets 91

Soups, Gravies and Sauces 92
Harvest Vegetable Soup 92
Lima Bean Chowder 93
Cream of Tomato Vegetable Soup 94
Split Pea Chowder 95
Lentil Vegetable Soup 96
Chili 97
Bean Without the Bacon Soup 98
Potato Corn Chowder 99

Boca Beefless Stew 100
Cashew Gravy 101
Chicken Style Gravy 101
White Sauce 101
Cheese Sauce #1 102
Cheese Sauce #2 102
Spaghetti Sauce 103
Chunky Pine-Apple Sauce 103

Breads 104
Crusty Whole Wheat Bread 104
Flax Bread 105
Old World Black Bread 106
Whole Grain Rye Bread 107
Poppy Seed Bread 108
Oatmeal Raisin Bread 109
Whole Wheat Bread in a Can 110
Flax Bread in a Can 110
Old World Black Bread in a Can 111
Whole Grain Rye Bread in a Can 111
Poppy Seed Bread in a Can 112
Oatmeal Raisin Bread in a Can 112
Whole Wheat Rolls 113
Flax Rolls 113
Old World Black Rolls 114
Whole Grain Rye Rolls 114
Poppy Seed Rolls 115
Oatmeal Raisin Rolls 115
Focaccia 116
Pizza Crust 117
Personal Pizza Crust 118
Pock-et & Crock-it Sandwich 119
Melt in Your Mouth Sweet Rolls 120
Crunchy Fruit Roll 121
Oven Fresh Rolls & Bread 122
Garlic Bread 122
Pizza Rolls 122
Banana Bread in a Can 123
Date Nut Bread in a Can 123
Soy Corn Bread in a Can 124
Fruit & Nut Soy Corn Bread in a Can 124

Desserts 125
Date Filled Dream Bars 125
Polynesian Bars 125
Peanut Butter Flax Bars 126
Fudgy Carob Brownies 127
Coconut Crunch Banana Bars 128
Carob Clusters 129
"Chocolate" Covered Cherry Drops 129
Carob Pudding 130
Carob Hot Fudge Topping 130
Vanilla Pudding 131
Cheese Cake 131
Banana Cream Pie 131
Tapioca Rice Pudding 132
Pineapple Upside Down Cake 133
Fruit Upside Down Cake 133
Vanilla Ice Cream 134
Vanilla Mint Chip Ice Cream 135
Carob Mint Chip Ice Cream 135
Carob Ice Cream 135
Cherry Ripple Ice Cream 135
Lemon Sherbert 135
Rice Supreme Ice Cream 135
Maple Walnut Ice Cream 135
Caramel Nut Crunch Ice Cream 135

Cooker Free Recipes 136
Chicken Seasoning 136
Soy Sauce 136
Tofu Sour Cream 136
Chunky Fried Tofu 136
Garbanzomole 137
Garbanzo Tomato Salad 137
Blanched Almonds 137
Toasted Nuts & Seeds 137
Caramel Nut Crunch 137
Tofu Cream 138
Carob Mocha Frosting 138
Crumb Crust 138
Maple Vanilla Topping 138
Simple Fruit Topping 138

How It All Began

At the time of this writing I own 25 slow cookers. I could use a couple more but one has to make do. My poor husband had no idea what he was getting into when, 6 years ago, he suggested I write another cookbook. I was reluctant, but did think about it. I am interested in alternative cooking methods and I like to experiment. I thought about food drying, pressure cooking and slow cooking. I knew the least about slow cooking, but started looking at recipes. I found very few that were meat and dairy free. I started playing in the kitchen. For the last 5 years most of our cooked or baked food has come from a slow cooker. It seems almost anything can be prepared this way. As I cooked, I soon realized that all slow cookers are not created equally. They cook at different speeds. After making many of the same recipes over and over and over again, in different cookers, I decided I could separate cookers into 3 categories. I call them "Average", "Fast" and "Extra Fast" cookers. See page 25, #3, for more information. I am really excited about this way of cooking. I hope and pray you will find these recipes helpful in providing healthy, delicious and easy to prepare meals.

Great Reasons for Using a Slow Cooker

- A helpful time management tool. You can be away from the kitchen for several hours, come home, and have a delicious meal on the table in minutes. I have frequently come home from church, accompanied with a group of guests, and had dinner ready in less than 15 minutes.
- A cost-effective method for cooking. Slow cookers use very little electricity.
- Say good-bye to pasta water boiling over the pan, when cooking on the stove.
- No more constant stirring on the stove, and the food still sticking or burning.
- Great for taking food to potlucks, especially if oven space is limited.
- Use on a trip, when staying in a motel.
- Use camping, if you have electricity.
- When serving a buffet leave the cooker on low, or warm, throughout the meal.
- Use a lamp/appliance timer to cook any time, day or night. See page 11.
- Use an adapter to plug in the cooker while in a car or boat.
- Nutrients are preserved since no cooking water is thrown out when cooking vegetables, grains or pasta.
- Gives off little heat in the kitchen. Great way to cook on a hot summer day. To avoid even the small amount of heat from the cooker, let it cook in the garage, or on the porch.
- Use a cooker that has a removable crock for easier serving and cleaning.

Slow Cooker Tips

Safe Beginnings

- Start with clean utensils and a clean work area. Wash your hands before doing any food preparation.
- Perishable food should be fresh, refrigerated and with no signs of spoilage. For example, water packed tofu should be used by its expiration date and rinsed before using. Tofu should have no hint of a sour smell or any discoloration. Fresh vegetables should be without spoilage and washed before using.
- If meat has been handled, the utensils and work area should be washed with soap and water before cutting other food. This is a precaution, as the meat may have bacteria that could be transferred to the food being prepared for the slow cooker.
- A **lamp/appliance timer**, plugged into your cooker, is a help for planning the time you would like to have a meal ready to eat. However, for extra precaution, do not put

hot food in the cooker if it will be left several hours before the timer turns the cooker on. Nor should you leave the cooker several hours, before the timer turns it on, if your room temperature is quite warm.

- I have included some guidelines as to how far in advance you might choose to set a timer for the food to begin cooking. These are based on my experience. In the breakfast section, when using fruit and grain recipes, the time is up to 8 hours after putting the food in the cooker. With bean and vegetables recipes the time is 6 hours. With recipes containing tofu I recommend turning the cooker on within 4 hours after it is filled. These delayed times do *not* apply to meat based recipes found in other cookbooks.
- A slow cooker needs to be able to get hot enough to heat your food to a safe temperature. If you are in question, here is a simple test drive to ensure that your cooker is safe to use, and that it will get your food cooked in a reasonable amount of time. Fill your cooker with 2 quarts of water. Heat the cooker on low for 8 hours. Using a thermometer, quickly check the water temperature. Be quick, as the temperature will drop the longer the lid is off. The temperature should be 185°. A cooker with a higher temperature will usually cook your food faster. A cooker with a lower temperature will take longer to cook than what most recipes call for. There is also the risk that foods, particularly those high in protein, like tofu (or meat if that is used), might not cook safely if the cooker is too slow.

Cooking Tips & Principles

- **Your Cooker Temperature Temperament**: I have divided slow cookers into three main categories, "Average", "Fast" and "Extra Fast". This makes it easier to determine how long a recipe will take to cook. An easy way to determine the temperament, or speed, of your cooker is to cook a pound of beans on low. Choose a variety of beans, such as great northern, navy or pinto beans, from Bean Cooking Chart 1, page 28. Watch to see how long the beans take to get soft. I have found that most 6-7 quart cookers are "Extra Fast". There are occasional smaller cookers that are also "Extra Fast", but they are usually considered "Average" or "Fast".
- **Cookers Heat From The Sides**: Slow cookers are usually designed with the heat coming from coils in the sides of the metal shell. Generally heat does not come from the bottom. This is why you may notice a hot spot on the side, where the food is cooking more quickly, but you will not find it burning on the bottom.
- **Cooking Temperatures**: Cookers usually have two heat settings. Low reaches about 200°. High reaches about 300°. 140-160° is the temperature range for a cooker that has a warm, or serve, setting.
- **Lid Alternatives**: If you no longer have a lid check your sauce pan lids. One may fit. Otherwise, use aluminum foil. I frequently use foil, because with some recipes a lid will not fit, such as when baking a loaf of bread in a can, or baking a big, spaghetti squash. Tuck the foil around the top to get a tight fit. Regular foil is fine but heavy duty foil is very easy to handle to get a tight fit. Larger cookers may require two pieces of foil to completely cover the top.
- **Quick and Easy Clean Up**: Spraying a cooker with a food release cooking spray is helpful for clean up with some recipes. For other recipes, particularly those that start out with a high ratio of water, then get very thick, such as cooked cereal, I use liquid lecithin. If any food has stuck, it will wipe off. Soap and water removes the lecithin. See page 11 for more information.
- **Herbs**: When possible I prefer to add dried herbs at the end of the cooking. I crush them with my fingers, as one would

use a mortar and pestle. This releases an immediate flavor which is ideal when adding them at the end. Fresh herbs, finely chopped and added at the end, will also generally give more flavor.

- **Vegetables**: Cut root vegetables, such as white potatoes, sweet potatoes, beets, parsnips, rutabagas and carrots, into thin slices, or small, bite size pieces. They may also be shred in a food processor. They will cook faster and more evenly if prepared in one of these ways.
- **Vegetables**: There are some vegetables I generally do not use in a slow cooker, either because of their taste or color, after they have cooked several hours. I use little or none of some of the stronger, watery, type vegetables, such as broccoli, cauliflower and green pepper, unless they are lightly cooked ahead of time, then added during the last few minutes of cooking. Frozen peas give a pretty color and nice texture. Add them during the last few minutes, or at the end of the cooking. If added at the end, let sit 5 minutes before serving.
- **Vegetables**: Some vegetables may be prepared and kept on hand in the refrigerator. Peel and chop sweet potatoes, winter squash, onions or carrots. Keep in plastic bags for a few days. Peeled garlic may also be refrigerated in a bag for several days. Peeled, white potatoes, whole, sliced or chopped, should be covered with water or they will turn brown.
- **White Potatoes:** I cook white potatoes on high, as oppose to low, for a whiter color. This applies to baked, as well as chopped or sliced potatoes. Old Fashion Scalloped Potatoes, page 86, stay white when baked on low because of a little lemon juice in the recipe.
- **Sweet Potatoes or Yams**: I prefer to bake on high, as oppose to low, for a brighter, richer, orange color.
- **Brown Rice**: Regular, long or short grain, brown rice should be cooked by itself, or add a few other light, non-dominate, ingredients, such as the pineapple in Tropical Rice, page 18, or with seasonings, such as chopped onion. Do not add uncooked, regular rice with other heavier ingredients, such as uncooked, dried beans, or in a rice casserole. The rice will not completely cook. It stays crunchy. I do use regular, *cooked*, rice in recipes. See Spanish Rice, page 42, and Nutty Carrot Rice, page 43. Quick (instant) brown rice can be added cooked or uncooked to a variety of recipes.
- **Pasta**: Add *uncooked* pasta during the last 15-40 minutes of cooking to a lightly boiling sauce. If the cooker is on low, it should be turned to *high* when adding the pasta. Use pasta such as whole wheat, semolina or spelt. They contain gluten which is the protein part of the grain. Gluten free pasta will partially dissolve. Pasta in thicker pieces, such as macaroni, takes 40 minutes to cook. Spaghetti cooks in 35 minutes, flat noodles (i.e. egg noodles) take 15 minutes. Try other kinds of pasta. If you are ready to add the pasta but the sauce is not quite boiling, but is steaming hot, turn the cooker on high and add the pasta. If the sauce is not steaming, turn it on high, wait 30 minutes then check. If steaming, add the pasta.
- **Thickening**: When making a cheese sauce, gravy or other creamy, smooth recipes, I use quick or rolled oats, with the other blended ingredients, for a smooth texture. Thickeners, such as flour or cornstarch, will not give a smooth, attractive appearance after they have cooked for several hours. They may be used, although, at the end of the cooking. If you want your recipe thicker, turn the cooker on high. Stir in flour or cornstarch, that has been dissolved in a small amount of water. Cover and let cook for 15-30 minutes, until thickened.
- **Garnishing**: Garnish food at serving time for added eye appeal. Try items such as

chopped, green onions, fresh herbs, carrot curls, thinly sliced fresh spinach, cheese sauce, chopped or sliced tomatoes or olives.

- **Baking**: Make wonderful, moist, homemade breads, rolls, brownies, date bars, flax bars, apple crisp and more. Most yeast bread recipes that require kneading can be baked in a slow cooker. If the recipe has a significant amount of nuts, seeds and dried fruit, it may not rise very well. If it is a yeast raised, batter bread (meaning it is stirred instead of kneaded) it will probably fall before it thoroughly bakes unless it is a very thick batter, such as the Banana Bread in a Can, page 123.
- **Make A Note**: There are two kinds of notes you might want to make. 1st In order to keep track of your cooking time, put masking tape or a sticky note on your cooker, telling what time you turned it on. 2nd Keep track on the page of the recipe you are fixing, how long it takes to cook in *your* cooker.
- **No Peeking**: Avoid removing the lid during cooking. This causes heat to be lost, and the cooking time to increase several minutes, depending on how long the lid is off. You will need to look at the food when the time is approaching for it to be done. First, try twirling the lid, or shake the lid back and forth, without lifting. This will shake some of the condensation off the lid, making it easier to see the food. This works good if you are looking to see if the ingredients have come to a boil around the edges. Most of the time you will need to remove the lid to see if the food is done. Be quick.
- **Speed Up The Cooking**: Many recipes with a higher water portion, that are cooking on low, may be turned to high to speed up the cooking, if needed. Recipes, such as sauces, gravies, puddings and soups, are not likely to burn on high.
- **Sputtering**: Some liquid may sputter out from under the lid with recipes that have a large portion of water, like beans and soups. This is usually only seen when the recipe comes to a boil, as it is cooked on high, in a "Fast" or "Extra Fast" cooker. Simply lay a hand towel over the cooker. This will absorb the small amount of water that seeps out.
- **Make Ahead**: In many cases the preparation for an entire recipe, or most of it, may be done ahead of time and refrigerated. There will be a note concerning this in the "Tip" section of the recipes. It is called "Make Ahead". When all of the ingredients are cold, the cooking time is generally 15-60 minutes longer. The more watery the recipe the quicker it will warm after being refrigerated. Gravy, for example, that is blended, refrigerated, then cooked the next day, will only take about 15 additional minutes to cook. A thick recipe, such as Tofu Loaf, will take an extra 45-60 minutes to cook if cold. Letting any recipe sit out of the refrigerator for about 2 hours gives enough time to take the chill off. When this is done the cooking time will stay about the same as in the recipe.
- **Reheat On Another Day**: At times there is a note in the "Tip" section for recipes that can be cooked and refrigerated, then reheated in a slow cooker. This is convenient when taking a dish somewhere, such as a church dinner or family gathering. The reheating time is usually 2-3 hours on low. If that is too long of a time, once you are at the event, then heat the dish at home and then plug it in again after arriving at the location. It will usually be hot again in less than 30 minutes.
- **Adapting Your Recipes**: Would you like to adapt your favorite recipes to a slow cooker? It will often work. It may take more than one try. Keep the following ideas in mind. The Cooking Tips, in this section, will give you some slow cooker

principles. Also, try finding a similar recipe in this book. Note the yield, the size cooker being used, the cooking time, the quantity of vegetables, grains or liquid being used. Since a slow cooker looses less water through evaporation, as compared to when cooking on the stove, or baking, it usually needs less liquid in the recipe.

- **Evaporation in a Slow Cooker:** Compared to cooking on the stove or in the oven, slow cookers have little evaporation. But when comparing cookers with each other there is a difference. When cooking a recipe that has a significant portion of water, such as soup, gravy, or cereal, the yield may decrease by ¼-1 cup when cooking in an "Extra Fast" cooker as compared to an "Average" cooker. If the recipe seems too thick stir in a little water at the end of the cooking.
- **What Size Cooker Do You Have?:** Fill the cooker with water to where the lid sits. Most cookers hold 1-2 cups less than the size they are sold at. For example, a 5 qt. cooker may only hold 18 cups of water but there are 20 cups in 5 quarts.
- **1½ Quart Rival Crock-Pots**: These cookers do not have a high-low temperature setting. They seem to cook somewhere between high and low when compared to an "Average" cooker. They will do fine for any of the Smaller Recipes in this book where the yield is 3½ cups or less and where cooking on high isn't a part of the directions. The cooking time will need to be adjusted.
- **Programmable Cookers**: These cookers are set to cook a specific number of hours then automatically go to a warm setting. They are sometimes called "Smart Pots". They are fine, but many of my recipes are done at different times then the cooking times available on these pots. I make my own pot "smart" by using a lamp/appliance timer. See page 11 for more information.
- **Buy in Bulk & Save**: There are many ingredients that may be purchased in bulk but I would especially like to mention onion and garlic powder. They are available in approximately 16 oz. containers at a much cheaper price per ounce as compared to small jars of powders. It is best to store the powders, along with all of your other herbs and seasonings, in a dark cupboard, away from light and the heat of the stove. This will help preserve flavor and nutrition. It is also best not to measure out your seasonings over a hot, steaming, cooker as the moisture can cause them to clump and stick together. Another item I buy in bulk is baking yeast. It is available in 1-2# amounts and is a great deal cheaper than the little envelopes of yeast from the supermarket. When I open the yeast I store it in a jar and keep it in the freezer. It will keep a year, probably longer. These bulk ingredients may be found at warehouse grocery stores, restaurant supply stores, health food stores, and many supermarkets.
- **Measuring Spoons & Cups**: I am throwing this in because I learned this interesting tidbit while working on this book. I have several different manufacturers for my measuring spoons and measuring cups (from ⅛ cup to 8 cup measuring cups). Not only are slow cookers not created equally, neither are measuring spoons and cups. There can actually be quite a difference from one brand to another. This can make a difference in taste and consistency of a recipe. Hummm...
- **What Size Cooker To Get**: Now, one last tip, just my personal preference. If you ask me what size cooker I would get, if I didn't already own 25, I would probably want an oval, 6 quart. This way I could prepare most any recipe, including the kind that calls for a dish to be inserted inside the cooker for baking, such as dinner rolls. If I could have a second cooker (a reasonable request, don't you think), I would like a small, more narrow one, such as a 2½-4 quart cooker. I would be happy with these 2 cookers. Plus a lamp/appliance timer, of course.

Extra Items for Extra Successful Slow Cookery

Lamp/Appliance Timer: Would you like to prepare a recipe but not cook it quite yet? Maybe you are going to be gone all day and won't be back in time to turn off the cooker. A timer is a *very good friend* when using a slow cooker. Prepare the recipe, but instead of cooking immediately, plug the cooker into a lamp/ appliance timer. The timer may be set to begin cooking several hours later. Timers are easily available for under $15.00 in the electrical or hardware departments of many stores. See Safe Beginnings, page 6, for guidelines when using a timer with your cooker.

Liquid Lecithin: Is your recipe sticking to the sides of your cooker? Sticking can be a problem when cooking cereals, as well as a few other recipes. Try brushing or blotting the cooker with liquid lecithin. You can gather together a clump of plastic wrap, dip it into the lecithin, then blot the cooker. The method I prefer is to pour the lecithin into a jar with an opening wide enough to dip in a 1" paint brush. I use a brush to dab and blot ½-1 teaspoon of lecithin on the sides, as well as the edge around the bottom, of a *completely dry* cooker. This is where sticking is most likely to occur since the heating element is usually around the sides. The bottom is not too likely to have sticking, but it should be coated just in case. The lecithin only needs to cover where the food will be. Another advantage is that sometimes, when cooking cereal, a thin layer of cereal forms on the sides during the last part of the cooking. If lecithin has been used, this layer will easily come off. Stir it into the rest of the cereal where it will soften. Liquid lecithin is a very thick, sticky oil that comes from the soy bean. It stays on the cooker until washed off with soap and water. It is available at health food stores and some supermarkets.

Trivets: A trivet is a devise used to elevate a baking container so that it does not sit directly on the bottom of your cooker. Trivets are available in the houseware department of stores. You can probably find something at home that will work as a trivet. It may be made out of metal, such as a canning ring, jar lid or vegetable steamer; glass, such as a small plate; or hard plastic, such as a jar lid. These are short trivets, at times you will need a taller trivet. Some times one trivet may be stacked on another for a taller trivet.

Baking Containers: Several recipes are baked in a dish inside of a cooker. Depending on the recipe, a number of containers can be used. You are only limited by what you can fit into your cooker. Baking containers include: a glass or metal baking dish, a bread pan, ramakins, a canapé bread pan, an 8" round cake pan or spring form pan, smaller slow cooker crocks, a 28 oz. can, 46 oz. juice can or larger cans. Cans are able to fit in most any size cooker. Glass containers bake a little faster than metal.

Definitions

Yeast Flakes: Not the same as baking yeast, which is used for raising bread. Sold under names such as nutritional yeast flakes, food yeast, Red Star nutritional yeast and yeast flakes. Some brands of Brewers Yeast have a stronger flavor and will not taste as good in recipes.

Tofu: Tofu is available in two common forms of packaging. One is "water packed". This tofu needs refrigeration. If it is not used by the expiration date, take it out of its packaging and rinse it. If it does not smell sour then place it in a container, cover with water. Refrigerate. Change the water every day or two and your tofu will usually last a few weeks. The second common form of packaging is called "aseptic". This packaging protects the tofu from spoilage without refrigeration for several months, until it is opened. Refrigerate after opening. A common brand is Mori-Nu. Both kinds of tofu are found in the produce section of the grocery store.

Cereal Cooking Chart~Small Amount

CEREAL YIELD: APPROXIMATELY 2 CUPS	SIZE COOKER TO USE	CEREAL	WATER	AVERAGE COOKER*	FAST COOKER*	EXTRA FAST COOKER*	YOUR COOKER'S TIME
Steel Cut Oats (whole oats-called oat groats-cut into small pieces)	2-6 quarts	½ cup	2 cups	4¾-5¼ hours	4½-5 hours	3¼-3¾ hrs, use 2⅓ cups water	
Brown Rice (long or short grain)	2-6 quarts	½ cup	1⅔ cups	4½-5 hours	3¾-4¼ hours	3¼-3¾ hrs, use 2 cups water	
Quick (Instant) Brown Rice	2-6 quarts	¾ cup	¾ cup	1¾-2 hours	1¼-1½ hours, use 1 cup water	1-1¼ hours, use 1 cup water	
Toasted Brown Rice (see tip below for toasting the rice)	2-6 quarts	½ cup	1⅔ cups	4½-5 hours	3¾-4¼ hours	3¾-4¼ hrs, use 2 cups water	
Millet (small, round, yellow grain)	2-6 quarts	½ cup	1¾ cups	6-6½ hours	4¼-4¾ hrs, use 2¼ cups water	3¼-3¾ hrs, use 2¼ cups water	
Corn Meal (best if label says whole grain)	2-6 quarts	⅔ cup	2 cups	4¾-5¼ hours	4½-5 hrs, use 2⅓ cups water	3¾-4¼ hrs, use 2⅓ cups water	
Corn Grits (best if label says whole grain)	2-6 quarts	⅔ cup	2 cups	4¾-5¼ hours	4½-5 hrs, use 2⅓ cups water	3¾-4¼ hrs, use 2⅓ cups water	
Cracked Wheat (cut whole wheat, not Cream of Wheat)	2-6 quarts	⅔ cup	2 cups	4½-5 hours	4¼-4¾ hrs, use 2⅓ cups water	3¾-4¼ hrs, use 2⅓ cups water	
Hulled Barley (less refined than pearled barley)	2-6 quarts	½ cup	2 cups	4¾-5¼ hours	4½-5 hrs, use 2⅓ cups water	3¼-3¾ hrs, use 2⅓ cups water	
Oat Groats (whole oats with hull removed)	2-6 quarts	½ cup	2 cups	4¾-5¼ hours	4½-5 hrs, use 2⅓ cups water	3¼-3¾ hrs, use 2⅓ cups water	
Berries-Wheat, Rye... (whole grain, no hulls)	2-6 quarts	¾ cup	2 cups	5-5½ hours	4½-5 hours	4-4¼ hours	

ADDITIONAL INGREDIENT:	⅛-¼ teaspoon salt or as desired	
OPTIONAL INGREDIENTS:		
⅓ cup chopped, dried fruit or raisins	2-4 tablespoons raw, chopped nuts	¾ teaspoon vanilla

1st I recommend brushing or wiping the cooker with ½ teaspoon of liquid lecithin. This is optional, but makes clean up *quick* and *easy*. See page 11 for more information on lecithin.
2nd Stir the cereal, water and salt into the cooker. **Cook on low**. If the cereal has finished cooking, before it is time to eat, turn off the cooker; or, turn it to "warm" or "serve", if the cooker has that setting. Twenty minutes before eating turn the cooker on low and stir the cereal. Add a little water or milk if the cereal has gotten to thick.
3rd Stir the optional ingredients in at the end of the cooking. Let sit 5 minutes.

- *See page 25, #3, for a description of the 3 types of cookers.
- The cooker may be plugged into a lamp/appliance timer, page 11, to begin cooking up to 8 hours later.
- Toasted brown rice: Continually stir ¼-½" rice in a skillet 8-12 minutes, over medium low heat, until a light, golden brown. Do not use a nonstick skillet. Pour into a glass or metal bowl. Toast extra rice for later use.

Cereal Cooking Chart~Medium Amount

CEREAL YIELD: 4-5 CUPS	SIZE COOKER TO USE	CEREAL	WATER	AVERAGE COOKER*	FAST COOKER*	EXTRA FAST COOKER*	YOUR COOKER'S TIME
Steel Cut Oats (oat groats cut into small pieces)	2-7 quarts	1¼ cups	4 cups	7-7½ hours	5½-6 hours	4½-5 hours	
Brown Rice (long or short grain)	2-7 quarts	1 cup	3⅓ cups	7-7½ hours	5-5½ hours	4-4½ hours	
Quick (Instant) Brown Rice	2-7 quarts	1½ cups	1½ cups	2-2¼ hours	1½-1¾ hrs, use 1¾ cups water	1¼-1½ hrs, use 1¾ cups water	
Toasted Brown Rice (see tip below for toasting)	2-7 quarts	1 cup	2¾ cups	7-7½ hours	5-5½ hours	4-4½ hours	
Millet (small, round, yellow grain)	2-7 quarts	1 cup	3⅓ cups	7-7½ hours	5-5½ hours	4-4½ hours	
Corn Meal (best if label says whole grain)	2-7 quarts	1¼ cups	4 cups	6-6½ hours	4½-5 hours	3½-4 hours	
Corn Grits (best if label says whole grain)	2-7 quarts	1⅓ cups	4 cups	6-6½ hours	4½-5 hours	3½-4 hours	
Cracked Wheat (cut whole wheat not Cream of Wheat)	2-7 quarts	1⅓ cups	4 cups	6-6½ hours	4¼-4¾ hours	3¼-3¾ hours	
Hulled Barley (less refined than pearled barley)	2-7 quarts	1¼ cups	4 cups	7-7½ hours	5½-6 hours	4½-5 hours	
Oat Groats (whole oats with hull removed)	2-7 quarts	1 cup	3¾ cups	7-7½ hours	5½-6 hours	4½-5 hours	
Berries-Wheat, Rye... (whole grain, no hulls)	2-7 quarts	1½ cups	4 cups	7½-8 hours	6-6½ hours	5-5½ hours	

ADDITIONAL INGREDIENT:	¼-½ teaspoon salt or as desired	
OPTIONAL INGREDIENTS:		
¾ cup chopped, dried fruit or raisins	⅓-⅔ cup raw, chopped nuts	1½ teaspoons vanilla

1st I recommend brushing or wiping the cooker with ½-1 teaspoon of liquid lecithin. This is optional, but makes clean up *quick* and *easy*. See page 11 for more information on lecithin. Lecithin also helps, because a thin layer of cereal often forms on the cooker during the last part of the cooking. This can easily be removed and stirred into the cereal.

2nd Stir the cereal, water and salt into the cooker. **Cook on low**. If the cereal has finished cooking, before it is time to eat, turn off the cooker; or, turn it to "warm" or "serve", if the cooker has that setting. Twenty minutes before eating turn the cooker on low and stir the cereal. Add a little water or milk if the cereal has gotten to thick.

3rd Stir the optional ingredients in at the end of the cooking. Let sit 5 minutes.

Tips

- *See page 25, #3, for a description of the 3 types of cookers.
- The cooker may be plugged into a lamp/appliance timer, page 11, to begin cooking up to 8 hours later.
- Toasted brown rice: Continually stir ¼-½" of rice in a skillet for 8-12 minutes, over medium low heat, until a light, golden brown. Do not use a nonstick skillet. Pour into a glass or metal bowl to cool. Toast extra rice for later use.

Cereal Cooking Chart~Large Amount

CEREAL YIELD: 6-7 CUPS	SIZE COOKER TO USE	CEREAL	WATER	AVERAGE COOKER*	FAST COOKER*	EXTRA FAST COOKER*	YOUR COOK-ER'S TIME
Steel Cut Oats (oat groats cut into small pieces)	2½-7 quarts	1⅔ cups	6 cups	8½-9 hours	6½-7 hours	6-6½ hours	
Brown Rice (long or short grain)	2½-7 quarts	1½ cups	4¾ cups	8½-9 hours	6½-7 hrs, use 5 cups water	5-5½ hrs, use 5 cups water	
Quick (Instant) Brown Rice	2½-7 quarts	2 cups	2 cups	2¼-2½ hours	1¾-2 hrs, use 2¼ cups water	1¾ hours, use 2¼ cups water	
Toasted Brown Rice (see tip below for toasting the rice)	2½-7 quarts	1½ cups	4¾ cups	8½-9 hours	6½-7 hrs, use 5 cups water	5-5½ hrs, use 5 cups water	
Millet (small, round, yellow grain)	2½-7 quarts	1½ cups	5 cups	7-7½ hours	5½-6 hrs, use 5½ cups water	4½-5 hrs, use 5½ cups water	
Corn Meal (best if whole grain)	2½-7 quarts	1¾ cups	6 cups	7-7½ hours	5½-6 hours	5-5½ hours	
Corn Grits (best if whole grain)	2½-7 quarts	2 cups	6 cups	7-7½ hours	5½-6 hours	5-5½ hours	
Cracked Wheat (cut whole wheat not Cream of Wheat)	2½-7 quarts	2 cups	6 cups	7-7½ hours	5-5½ hours	4-4½ hours	
Hulled Barley (less refined than pearled barley)	2½-7 quarts	1⅔ cups	6 cups	8½-9 hours	6½-7 hours	6-6½ hours	
Oat Groats (whole oats with hull removed)	2½-7 quarts	1⅔ cups	6 cups	8½-9 hours	6½-7 hours	6-6½ hours	
Berries-Wheat, Rye... (whole grain, no hulls)	2½-7 quarts	2 cups	5½ cups	10-10½ hours	8-8½ hours	6½-7 hours	

ADDITIONAL INGREDIENT:	½-¾ teaspoon salt or as desired	
OPTIONAL INGREDIENTS:		
1 cup chopped, dried fruit or raisins	½-1 cup raw, chopped nuts	2 teaspoons vanilla

1st I recommend brushing or wiping the cooker with 1 teaspoon of liquid lecithin. This is optional, but makes clean up *quick* and *easy*. See page 11 for more information on lecithin. Lecithin also helps, because a thin layer of cereal often forms on the cooker during the last part of the cooking. This can easily be removed and stirred into the cereal.

2nd Stir the cereal, water and salt into the cooker. **Cook on low**. If the cereal has finished cooking, before it is time to eat, turn off the cooker; or, turn it to "warm" or "serve", if the cooker has that setting. Twenty minutes before eating turn the cooker on low and stir the cereal. Add a little water or milk if the cereal has gotten to thick.

3rd Stir the optional ingredients in at the end of the cooking. Let sit 5 minutes.

Tips

- *See page 25, #3, for a description of the 3 types of cookers.
- The cooker may be plugged into a lamp/appliance timer, page 11, to begin cooking up to 8 hours later.
- Toasted brown rice: Continually stir ¼-½" rice in a skillet 8-12 minutes, over medium low heat, until a light, golden brown. Do not use a nonstick skillet. Pour into a glass or metal bowl. Toast extra rice for later use.

Cereal Cooking Chart~Rival 1 ½ Quart Crock-Pot

This little cooker has no high/low heat setting. The temperature seems to usually run between high and low, when compared to an Average cooker.

CEREAL YIELD: APPROXIMATELY 2 CUPS	SIZE COOKER	AMOUNT OF CEREAL	AMOUNT OF WATER	SALT (use as desired)	TIME FOR COOKING	YOUR COOKER'S TIME
Steel Cut Oats (oat groat cut into small pieces)	1½ quarts	½ cup	2 cups	⅛-¼ teaspoon	4 hours	
Brown Rice (long or short grain)	1½ quarts	⅔ cup	2 cups	⅛-¼ teaspoon	4 hours	
Quick (Instant) Brown Rice	1½ quarts	¾ cup	¾ cup	⅛ teaspoon	1½-1¾ hours	
Toasted Brown Rice (see note below)	1½ quarts	½ cup	2 cups	⅛-¼ teaspoon	4 hours	
Millet (small, round, yellow grain)	1½ quarts	½ cup	2 cups	⅛-¼ teaspoon	4 hours	
Corn Meal (best if label says whole grain)	1½ quarts	⅔ cup	2 cups	⅛-¼ teaspoon	4 hours	
Corn Grits (best if label says whole grain)	1½ quarts	⅔ cup	2 cups	⅛-¼ teaspoon	4 hours	
Cracked Wheat (cut whole wheat, not Cream of Wheat)	1½ quarts	1 cup	2 cups	⅛-¼ teaspoon	4 hours	
Hulled Barley (less refined than pearled barley)	1½ quarts	½ cup	2 cups	⅛-¼ teaspoon	5 hours	
Oat Groats (whole oat with hull removed)	1½ quarts	½ cup	2 cups	⅛-¼ teaspoon	5 hours	
Berries-Wheat, Rye, Spelt... (whole grain, hulls removed)	1½ quarts	¾ cup	2 cups	⅛-¼ teaspoon	6 hours	

OPTIONAL INGREDIENTS:		
⅓ cup chopped, dried fruit or raisins	2-4 tablespoons raw, chopped nuts	¾ teaspoon vanilla

1st I recommend brushing or wiping the cooker with ½ teaspoon of liquid lecithin. This is optional, but makes clean up *quick* and *easy*. See page 11 for more information on lecithin. Lecithin also helps, because a thin layer of cereal often forms on the cooker during the last part of the cooking. This can easily be removed and stirred into the cereal.

2nd Stir the cereal, water and salt into the cooker and cook. If the cereal has finished cooking, but it is not time to eat, unplug the cooker. Plug it back in 15 minutes before eating and stir. Add a little water or milk if the cereal has become too thick.

3rd Stir the optional ingredients in at the end of the cooking. Let sit 5 minutes.

Tips

- See page 25, #3, for more tips on cooking cereals.
- Portions may be increased. Use 3 cups of water and increase the cereal accordingly.
- The cooker may be plugged into a lamp/appliance timer, page 11, to begin cooking up to 8 hours later.
- Toasted brown rice: Continually stir ¼-½" of rice in a skillet for 8-12 minutes, over medium low heat, until the rice has a light, golden brown color. Do not use a nonstick skillet. Immediately pour the rice into a glass or metal bowl to cool. Extra rice may be toasted and stored for later use.

"All Night" Slow Cooked Cereal

This method requires a cooker that has a setting called "warm" or "serve". It is a lower temperature than "low".

1st Refer to the cereal cooking charts on pages 12-15. Choose the amount of cereal you would like to cook.
2nd I recommend brushing or wiping the cooker with ½-1 teaspoon of liquid lecithin. This is optional, but makes clean up *quick* and *easy*. See page 11 for a description of lecithin and how to apply it. Lecithin also helps, because a thin layer of cereal often forms on the cooker during the last part of the cooking. This can easily be removed and stirred into the rest of the cereal.
3rd Stir the ingredients into the cooker. Cook on high. Cooking on high is temporary. The goal is for the water to *just barely* begin to boil, in *some* places, around the edges of the cooker. (Do not wait for the water to boil all around the edges.) At this time, turn the cooker down to "warm" or "serve". After a few minutes you will notice that the cereal has begun to swell to the top of the water, or nearly so. It is best not to lift the lid at any time. Naturally, Average Cookers take longer than Fast or Extra Fast Cookers to come to this *very* light boil around the edges. The chart below applies to all types of cookers.

RECIPE SIZE	LENGTH OF COOKING TIME ON HIGH FOR ANY SIZE POT
Cooked Cereal~Small Amount, pg 12	1-1¾ hours
Cooked Cereal~Medium Amount, pg 13	1¼-2 hours
Cooked Cereal~Large Amount, pg 14	1¼-2¼ hours

Tips

- Cereals may be left on warm for at least 10 hours. If you find your cereal burned on the side in the morning, it is most likely that it was left on high too long the night before.
- If using the optional ingredients, listed in the cereal cooking charts, they should be stirred in at the end of the cooking and left to sit a few minutes for the dried fruit to soften.
- Make a note on this page of what cereal you prepared, and how long it took for your cooker to just barely begin to boil.

Corn Millet Porridge

Smaller Recipe		Larger Recipe
YIELD: 3 cups COOKER SIZE: 1½-5 qt.	INGREDIENTS	YIELD: 6 cups COOKER SIZE: 2½-7 qt.

1st I recommend brushing or wiping the cooker with ½-1 teaspoon of liquid lecithin. This is optional, but makes clean up *quick* and *easy*. See page 11 for a description of lecithin and how to apply it. Stir together the following ingredients into the cooker and cook.

Smaller Recipe	Ingredient	Larger Recipe
3 cups	water	6 cups
¼ cup + 2 tablespoons	millet	¾ cup
⅓ cup	whole grain corn meal	⅔ cup
¼ + ⅛ teaspoon	salt	¾ teaspoon

2nd Turn off the cooker. Stir in the following ingredients. Let sit 5 minutes for the dates to soften.

Smaller Recipe	Ingredient	Larger Recipe
½ cup	chopped dates	1 cup
¼ cup	coconut	½ cup

3rd Serve as is, or with a milk, such as soy milk.

COOKING TIME ON LOW:

Average Cooker: Smaller Recipe 6-6½ hours OR Larger Recipe 6½-7 hours

Fast Cooker: Smaller Recipe 4¼-4¾ hours OR Larger Recipe 5½-6 hours

Extra Fast Cooker: Smaller Recipe 4-4½ hours OR Larger Recipe 5-5½ hours

(See page 25, #3, for an explanation of the 3 types of cookers.)

Tip

- The cooker may be plugged into a lamp/appliance timer, page 11, to begin cooking up to 8 hours later.

Tropical Rice

Smaller Recipe YIELD: 3½ cups COOKER SIZE: 1½-4 qt.	INGREDIENTS	Larger Recipe YIELD: 6¾ cups COOKER SIZE: 3-6 qt.

1st Stir the following ingredients into the cooker and cook.

Smaller Recipe	Ingredients	Larger Recipe
1½ cups	water	2¾ cups
1 cup	unsweetened, crushed pineapple	1 (20 oz. can)
½ cup	unsweetened pineapple juice	¾ cup
½ cup	brown rice or if using quick (instant) rice see tip below	1 cup
¼ cup	raw, chopped, sliced or slivered almonds	½ cup
½ teaspoon	salt	1 teaspoon

2nd Turn off the cooker. Stir in the following ingredients. Let sit 5 minutes for the dried fruit to soften.

Smaller Recipe	Ingredients	Larger Recipe
½ cup	chopped, dried fruit or raisins	1 cup
1 teaspoon	vanilla	1½ teaspoons

3rd Serve as is, or with soy milk. Stir in a little additional water, pineapple juice or soy milk if the cereal is too thick.

COOKING TIME ON LOW FOR REGULAR BROWN RICE:

Average Cooker: Smaller Recipe 5¼-5¾ hours OR Larger Recipe 8-8½ hours

Fast Cooker: Smaller Recipe 4-4½ hours OR Larger Recipe 6-6½ hours

Extra Fast Cooker: Smaller Recipe 3¾-4¼ hours OR Larger Recipe 5-5½ hours

(See page 25, #3, for an explanation of the 3 types of cookers.)

COOKING TIME ON LOW FOR QUICK (INSTANT) BROWN RICE (see below for the amount of rice to use):

Average Cooker: Smaller Recipe 2½-3 hours OR Larger Recipe 3¼-3¾ hours

Fast Cooker: Smaller Recipe 2-2½ hours OR Larger Recipe 2¾-3¼ hours

Extra Fast Cooker: Smaller Recipe 1½-2 hours OR Larger Recipe 2¼-2¾ hours

(See page 25, #3, for an explanation of the 3 types of cookers.)

Tips

- Quick (instant) brown rice may replace regular brown rice. Use ¾ cup for the Smaller Recipe or 1½ cups for the Larger Recipe. See the Cooking Time chart above for Quick Brown Rice.
- The cooker may be plugged into a lamp/appliance timer, page 11, to begin cooking up to 8 hours later.

Multi Grain Hot Cereal

Smaller Recipe		Larger Recipe
YIELD: 3 cups COOKER SIZE: 1½-5 qt.	INGREDIENTS	YIELD: 6 cups COOKER SIZE: 2½-7 qt.

1st I recommend brushing or wiping the cooker with ½-1 teaspoon of liquid lecithin. This is optional, but makes clean up *quick* and *easy*. See page 11 for a description of lecithin and how to apply it. Stir together the following ingredients into the cooker and cook.

Smaller Recipe	Ingredient	Larger Recipe
3 cups	water	6 cups
½ cup	whole grain berries i.e. wheat, rye, spelt, kamut	1 cup
¼ cup	rolled, flaked cereal i.e. oats, barley, rye, wheat	½ cup
¼ cup	millet or brown rice	½ cup
¼ teaspoon	salt	½ teaspoon

2nd Turn off the cooker. Stir in the following ingredients. Let sit 5 minutes for the dried fruit to soften.

Smaller Recipe	Ingredient	Larger Recipe
½ cup	chopped, dried fruit or raisins	1 cup
¼-½ cup	chopped, raw nuts or coconut	½-1 cup

3rd Serve as is, or with a milk, such as soy milk, or with a fruit sauce such as apple sauce. See photo on page 67.

COOKING TIME ON LOW:

Average Cooker: Smaller Recipe 7½-8 hours OR Larger Recipe 9-9½ hours

Fast Cooker: Smaller Recipe 6-6½ hours OR Larger Recipe 7½-8 hours

Extra Fast Cooker: Smaller Recipe 5-5½ hours OR Larger Recipe 6½-7 hours

(See page 25, #3, for an explanation of the 3 types of cookers.)

Tips

- Experiment with other cereal combinations.
- The cooker may be plugged into a lamp/appliance timer, page 11, to begin cooking up to 8 hours later.

Heart Healthy Baked Whole Grains

Smaller Recipe		Larger Recipe
YIELD: 3 cups COOKER SIZE: 1½-6 qt.	INGREDIENTS	YIELD: 6 cups COOKER SIZE: 5-7 qt.

1st I recommend brushing or wiping the cooker with ½-1 teaspoon of liquid lecithin. This is optional, but makes clean up *quick* and *easy*. See page 11 for a description of lecithin and how to apply it. Stir together the following ingredients into the cooker and bake.

Smaller Recipe	Ingredient	Larger Recipe
2 cups	soy, rice or nut milk	4 cups
½ cup	rolled oats, rolled barley, rolled wheat or a combination	1 cup
½ cup	chopped dates or other dried fruit	1 cup
⅓ cup	chopped, raw nuts or coconut	⅔ cup
1	sliced banana, optional	1-2
¼ cup	quick (instant) brown rice	½ cup
¾ teaspoon	vanilla, cherry or almond flavoring	1½ teaspoons
¼ teaspoon	salt	½ teaspoon

2nd Serve as is, or with a milk, such as soy milk, or with a fruit sauce, such as apple sauce.

BAKING TIME ON LOW:

Average Cooker: Smaller Recipe 3½-4 hours OR Larger Recipe 4-4½ hours

Fast Cooker: Smaller Recipe 2¾-3¼ hours OR Larger Recipe 3¼-3¾ hours

Extra Fast Cooker: Smaller Recipe 1¾-2¼ hours OR Larger Recipe 3-3½ hours

(See page 25, #3, for an explanation of the 3 types of cookers.)

Tips

- The cooker may be plugged into a lamp/appliance timer, page 11, to begin cooking up to 8 hours later.
- Bake in a Dish Inside the Cooker: Mix together the Smaller Recipe. Spray a dish that will hold at least 3½ cups with a food release cooking spray. Make sure the dish will fit easily into a 5-7 quart cooker. (Some 4½ quart oval cookers may also be used.) This is important, as the dish will be hot when being removed. Fill the dish with the recipe. Cover with foil. Place the dish on a trivet, such as a canning ring or jar lid, inside the cooker. See page 11 for more ideas for trivets. Bake for 5 hours in an Extra Fast Cooker. If using a Fast or Average Cooker then add 30-60 minutes.

Baked Apples & Oats

Smaller Recipe		Larger Recipe
YIELD: 3¼ cups COOKER SIZE: 1½-5 qt.	INGREDIENTS	YIELD: 6½ cups COOKER SIZE: 3½-7 qt.

1st I recommend brushing or wiping the cooker with ½-1 teaspoon of liquid lecithin. This is optional, but makes clean up *quick* and *easy*. See page 11 for a description of lecithin and how to apply it. Stir together the following ingredients in a mixing bowl; then pour into the cooker and bake.

Smaller Recipe	Ingredients	Larger Recipe
1¾ cups	apple juice or water	3½ cups
1½ cups	sliced or chopped apples	3 cups
1 cup	quick or rolled oats	2 cups
½ cup	quick (instant) brown rice	1 cup
½ cup	chopped, dried fruit or raisins	1 cup
¼ cup	chopped, raw nuts	½ cup
¼ teaspoon	salt	½ teaspoon

2nd Serve as is, or with a milk, such as soy milk, or with a fruit sauce, such as apple sauce.

BAKING TIME ON LOW:

Average Cooker: Smaller Recipe 5-5½ hours OR Larger Recipe 7-7½ hours

Fast Cooker: Smaller Recipe 4-4½ hours OR Larger Recipe 5-5½ hours

Extra Fast Cooker: Smaller Recipe 3-3½ hours OR Larger Recipe 4-4½ hours

(See page 25, #3, for an explanation of the 3 types of cookers.)

Tips

- The cooker may be plugged into a lamp/appliance timer, page 11, to begin cooking up to 8 hours later.
- Bake in a Dish Inside the Cooker: Mix together the Smaller Recipe. Spray a dish that will hold at least 3½ cups with a food release cooking spray. Make sure the dish will fit easily into a 5-7 quart cooker. (Some 4½ quart oval cookers may also be used.) This is important, as the dish will be hot when being removed. Fill the dish with the recipe. Cover with foil. Place the dish on a trivet, such as a canning ring or jar lid, inside the cooker. See page 11 for more ideas for trivets. Bake for 5 hours in an Extra Fast Cooker. If using a Fast or Average Cooker, then add 30-60 minutes.

Apple Crumble Crisp

Smaller Recipe		Larger Recipe
YIELD: 6 cups COOKER SIZE: 3½-5 qt.	INGREDIENTS	YIELD: 8 cups COOKER SIZE: 4½-7 qt.

1st Place the following sliced apples in the cooker. Stir in the cornstarch. Sprinkle the dried fruit on top of the apples.

8 cups	peeled and sliced apples	10-11 cups
1½ tablespoons	cornstarch	2 tablespoons
⅔ cup	chopped, dried fruit	¾ cup

2nd Blend the oats in the following table in a blender into a coarse flour.

1¾ cups	quick oats	2 cups

3rd Mix the following ingredients in a mixing bowl, along with the blended oats.

2¾ cups	quick oats	3½ cups
½ teaspoon	salt	½ teaspoon

4th Stir together the following ingredients. Stir and toss them with the oats to thoroughly coat the oats. Sprinkle over the apples. Cover the cooker with a hand towel that has not been washed with fabric softener (the smell may permeate the topping) or, cover with 2 layers of paper towels. Cover with the lid. Bake until the crust is lightly browned.

3 tablespoons	honey	¼ cup
2½ tablespoons	mild tasting olive oil or canola oil	3 tablespoons

5th Serve as is, or with a milk, such as soy milk.

BAKING TIME ON LOW:

Average Cooker: Smaller Recipe 5½-6 hours OR Larger Recipe 6½-7 hours

Fast Cooker: Smaller Recipe 4-4½ hours OR Larger Recipe 4½-5 hours

Extra Fast Cooker: Smaller Recipe 3½-4 hours OR Larger Recipe 4-4½ hours

(See page 25, #3, for an explanation of the 3 types of cookers.)

Tip

- The cooker may be plugged into a lamp/appliance timer, page 11, to begin cooking up to 8 hours later.

Blueberry Crumble Crisp

Replace the apples with the same amount of frozen blueberries. Thaw and drain the berries then add the same amount of cornstarch and dried fruit as listed above. Follow the remaining directions as above. (Fresh blueberries are too juicy for this recipe.) See photo on page 67.

Fruit Lasagna

Smaller Recipe		Larger Recipe
YIELD: 5½ cups COOKER SIZE: 3½-5 qt.	INGREDIENTS	YIELD: 11 cups COOKER SIZE: 5-7 qt.

1st Boil the noodles for 5 minutes. I find them easier to handle if they are in 6-9" pieces. Smaller pieces work fine as well. Lay the cooked noodles in a single layer on a cookie sheet covered with wax paper. There are 4 layers of noodles in the recipe, so divide the noodles into 4 fairly equal portions. Note: The noodles may be refrigerated for later use. Single layers of noodles and wax paper may be stacked on top of each other.

Smaller Recipe	Ingredient	Larger Recipe
¼#	lasagna noodles, preferably whole wheat	½#

2nd Mix together the following ingredients.

Smaller Recipe	Ingredient	Larger Recipe
2¾ cups	applesauce	5½ cups
1 cup	chopped dates	2 cups
¾ cup	chopped, sliced or slivered, raw almonds	1½ cups
½ teaspoon	salt	1 teaspoon

3rd Prepare the apple slices in the following table. Spread ¾ cup of the applesauce mixture in the cooker for the Smaller Recipe. Use 1¼ cups for the Larger Recipe. Top with one of the four portions of noodles. Follow with the same amount of applesauce mixture, then add the apple slices. For the apples, use ½ cup for the Smaller Recipe, or 1 cup for the Larger Recipe. Continue by adding the same portions of noodles, applesauce mixture, apples, noodles, applesauce mixture, apples, etc. Use the remaining apples just before the final layer of noodles. The last portion of noodles should be covered with the remaining applesauce mixture.

Smaller Recipe	Ingredient	Larger Recipe
1½ cups	peeled, sliced apples	3 cups

4th Sprinkle on the following coconut. Bake until bubbly, and apples are tender.

Smaller Recipe	Ingredient	Larger Recipe
2 tablespoons	coconut	3 tablespoons

5th Let sit 10 minutes, then serve.

BAKING TIME ON LOW:

Average Cooker: Smaller Recipe 4-4½ hours OR Larger Recipe 5-5½ hours

Fast Cooker: Smaller Recipe 3½-4 hours OR Larger Recipe 4½-5 hours

Extra Fast Cooker: Smaller Recipe 3¼-3¾ hours OR Larger Recipe 4-4½ hours

(See page 25, #3, for an explanation of the 3 types of cookers.)

Tips

- The cooker may be plugged into a lamp/appliance timer, page 11, to begin cooking up to 8 hours later.
- Make Ahead: Prepare Steps 1 and 2, then refrigerate. The recipe may also be assembled in the slow cooker crock and refrigerated until ready to bake. In either case add about 20-30 minutes to the baking time unless the recipe sits out at least 2 hours before turning on the cooker.
- Bake in a Dish Inside the Cooker: Spray a 6½x8½" glass dish or 8" round cake pan with a food release cooking spray. Assemble the Smaller Recipe, breaking the noodles to fit. Place the dish on a trivet in an oval 6-7 qt. cooker. Bake 4½ hours on low in an Extra Fast Cooker. Increase the baking time 30-60 minutes if using a Fast or Average Cooker.

Fruit Pizza or Personal Fruit Pizza or Pita Fruit Pizza

Smaller Recipe		Larger Recipe
YIELD: 1 pizza COOKER SIZE: size of crust	INGREDIENTS	YIELD: 1 pizza COOKER SIZE: size of crust

1st Using a pre-baked crust, add the following ingredients. Place the pizza into the cooker. For the pita bread or the personal pizza, use the Smaller Recipe.

Smaller Recipe	Personal Pizza Crust pg 118, or Pita Bread, or Pizza Crust pg 117	Larger Recipe
⅓-½ cup	applesauce	½-⅔ cup
¼ cup	chopped, dried fruit	⅓ cup
2-3 tablespoons	chopped, raw nuts	4-5 tablespoons

2nd The pizza is ready to bake, or add any of the following optional ingredients, then bake.

	Add one of the following or a combination:	
	replace the applesauce with one of the jams below	
	spread peanut butter on the crust before the applesauce	
	sprinkle with coconut or sesame seeds before baking	
	try other favorite toppings	
	top with slices of fresh fruit after baking	
	sprinkle with Caramel Nut Crunch, pg 137, after baking	

3rd Ready to serve. See photo on page 79.

COOKING TIME ON LOW:
Average Cooker: 1½ hours
Fast Cooker: 1¼ hours
Extra Fast Cooker: 1-1¼ hours
(See page 25, #3, for an explanation of the 3 types of cookers.)

Tip
- The cooker may be plugged into a lamp/appliance timer, page 11, to begin cooking up to 8 hours later.

Date Pineapple Jam
1½ cups chopped dates
¾ cup pineapple juice
¾ cup crushed pineapple
1 teaspoon vanilla
Lightly boil the dates and juice in a covered sauce pan for 5-10 minutes, until the dates are soft. Stir in the pineapple and vanilla. Mash with a fork, or potato masher, or blend smooth in a blender.

Dried Fruit Jam
1¼ cups chopped dried fruit
1 cup water or fruit juice
Lightly boil the ingredients in a covered sauce pan for 5-10 minutes, until the dried fruit is soft. Mash the fruit with a fork, or potato masher, or blend smooth in the blender.
Variations for the dried fruit jam:
- Combine equal amounts of dates and apricots with pineapple juice.
- Add ¼ teaspoon coriander and 1 teaspoon vanilla to prune or date jam after it is cooked.

Incredibly Delicious Bean Cuisine

This is one of the most important sections of this book. Beans are a valuable addition to our diet. They are a good source of protein, B vitamins, phytochemicals, fiber and more. They contain soluble fiber which helps to lower cholesterol. I have spent many hours experimenting in different cookers with several hundred pounds of these incredibly delicious morsels.

1. Sorting Beans
2. Soaking Beans
3. Temperature Temperament- Do you have an "Average", "Fast" or "Extra Fast" Cooker?
4. What Size Cooker Do You Have?
5. Lamp/Appliance Timer
6. Cooking with Salt
7. How Much Salt and Oil to Add
8. Cooking Old Beans
9. Water Sputtering from Lid
10. Not Home-But Beans are Done!
11. Are Beans Well Cooked?
12. Reheating Beans
13. Ways to Use Leftovers
14. Oops! 'xcuse Me-Gas Problem
15. Measuring Beans
16. Buying in Bulk
17. Dried, Instant, Refried Beans

Bean Cooking Tips

1. Sort through dried beans, looking for small clumps of dirt and stones. Cover beans with water, rinse, then drain.

2. Beans are now ready to cook or they may be soaked in water before cooking. Soaking has been shown to make the beans easier to digest for many individuals.
If beans are to be soaked, put them in a bowl. Add 4 cups of water for ½# of beans, or 8 cups of water for 1# of beans. Let soak at least 8 hours. Drain off the water. Now they are ready to be cooked.

3. Not all slow cookers are created equally. Some are faster than others. I have tested lots of slow cookers; I own 25 myself (well, some people buy shoes)! Any way, I have been able to consistently divide most cookers into 3 categories, based on how quickly they cook. The categories are: "*Average*" cookers, "*Fast*" cookers, and "*Extra Fast*" cookers. If you do my simple test, it will take the guess work out of how long it takes to cook a large variety of recipes. **So, if you are not sure how fast your cooker operates, you can easily learn this by cooking a pound of dried beans on low, then comparing the cooking time of your beans with the cooking time from the bean cooking chart on page 28.** Be sure you use one of the bean varieties listed in the chart, such as great northern, navy or pinto beans. *Watch to see when they are soft.* Most 6-7 qt. cookers seem to be "Extra Fast", as well as are some occasional smaller cookers. There are also the occasional "*Slow*" slow cookers. These will take a few hours longer than "*Average*" cookers. I would recommend that if this is what you have that you replace it.
Don't let these time variations discourage you.

You can quickly learn your pot's temperature temperament, then make great meals and know when they will be done!

4. If you are not sure what size cooker you have then fill your cooker with water to the edge where the lid rests. Most cookers hold 1-2 cups less than the size they are sold at. For example, a 5 qt. may hold 18 cups but there are 20 cups in 5 quarts.

5. A Lamp/Appliance Timer is a wonderful addition to making your slow cooking completely convenient and adaptable to your schedule. Place all of the ingredients into the cooker, but instead of cooking immediately, plug the cooker into a timer, then plug the timer into an electrical outlet. Set the timer to begin cooking several hours later. See page 11 for more information on timers.

6. Salt may be added at the beginning of the cooking. I have not found that it lengthens the cooking time. If you are using tomatoes, or sugar of any kind, add these after the beans are cooked. Otherwise they may interfere with beans getting soft.

7. Add 1½ teaspoons, or less, of salt per pound of beans. Not using any salt is also an option. Add 1 tablespoon, or less, of olive oil. The oil is optional, but gives a very good flavor. I especially like using extra virgin olive oil with beans because of the flavor. Studies show olive oil, a monounsaturated fat, may reduce the risk of coronary heart disease as well as have other health benefits when used in moderation.

8. If you have had your beans for more than about 2 years, they may take longer to cook. I have had soy beans that I have kept for several years that did not get soft after 24 hours of cooking.

9. *"Fast"* and *"Extra Fast"* cookers tend to sputter, especially when cooking beans on high. Some water may splatter out from under the lid when the cooker comes to a boil. Simply lay a hand towel over the lid to absorb the small amount of water.

10. If you are cooking beans on low in an *"Average"* cooker and are not available to turn off the cooker when the beans are done, they may be left on for an additional 2-3 hours. If you are cooking beans on low in a *"Fast"* or *"Extra Fast"* cooker, then add an extra cup of water at the beginning of the cooking, if you know they are going to be left on an extra 2-3 hours.

11. Beans should be cooked until very soft. Well cooked beans are easier to digest then firm or crunchy beans.

12. Previously cooked beans may be reheated on low. This will take 2-3 hours, depending on the volume being reheated. This is especially convenient when taking a bean dish for a meal after church, or to other group functions. Another option is to reheat the beans in the cooker before going to a function, then plugging it in as soon as arriving. Usually they will be quite hot if plugged in again for about 30 minutes before the meal.

Slow Cooker
Temperature Temperament

If you do this simple test it will take the guess work out of how long it takes to cook a large variety of recipes. See page 25, #3.

13. Ways to use leftover beans besides simply reheating them include: sprinkling on salads, adding to a gravy or sauce being served over vegetables, pasta or rice, adding to soups or chowders, mashed with seasonings such as onion and garlic powder or Baked Garlic, page 87, and used as a spread for bread or chips.

14. If it seems hard to digest beans, noticed by gas and stomach cramping, here are some tips: Soak the beans before cooking (see page 25, #2). Cook until very soft. Chew beans to a cream before swallowing. Eat beans daily, maybe only ¼ cup a day for several days, then gradually increase the amount. This may help adjust the bacteria in the stomach which will in turn make digestion easier.

15. There are 2½-2¾ cups of most dried beans in a pound. When cooked, they yield 6-7 cups. 1 cup of dried beans equals about 2½ cups cooked.

16. If beans are bought in bulk, try bagging some of them in ½# or 1# amounts so that they are ready to use.

17. Now to close, you may remember, at the beginning of this article, that I stated that I have cooked several hundred pounds of beans in preparation for this cookbook. Did you wonder what I did with *that* many beans? (Besides taking them to church dinners, family dinners, serving them to guests and eating them almost daily!) Well, if you were to look into my pantry you would see several gallons of beans that I have dried in my food dryer. This is great! You can buy dried, instant, refried beans, but you can make your own so much cheaper. This is how I do it. Drain the beans in a colander after they are cooked, then mash and refrigerate them. Chill them so that they become quite stiff. My food dryer has mesh linings that I can lay on the drying trays. This is a small mesh, like window screen. I drop small chucks of mashed beans, ¼-½" high, on the trays, then dry. Leave space for air to circulate between the chunks of mashed beans. If your food dryer does not have mesh liners you can make your own from hardware cloth. It looks similar to window screen but is not treated with aluminum as is window screen. It is available at hardware stores. I fill only 2-3 trays of beans at a time to ensure they dry before they develop a sour smell and spoil. Drying takes about 12 hours. My dryer has a temperature gauge. I turn it all the way up. After the beans are completely dry, let them cool. Store in jars. Rehydrate the beans on the stove or in a slow cooker. See Instant! Slow Cooked Refried Beans, page 39, to prepare the beans in your slow cooker. If cooking on the stove: Bring 2 cups of water to a boil. Stir in 2 cups dried beans. Lightly boil 10 minutes, stirring occasionally. Add more water if needed. Remove from the heat, uncover and let sit 5 minutes. This will give you about 2 cups of beans. Other seasonings may be stirred in with the beans, such as onion and garlic powder. For several pages of ideas on drying meals for traveling, camping or a quick meal at home, order my cookbook, Of These Ye May Freely Eat.

Bean Cooking Chart 1

1# Dried Beans NOT Soaked and Cooked on LOW   Yield: 6-7 cups

Sort through the beans, looking for small clumps of dirt and stones. Cover the beans with water, rinse and drain, then empty into the cooker. Add the amount of water recommended in the following chart for your type of cooker. ***See page 25, #3, for a description of the 3 types of cookers**. Add the optional ingredients if using. Cook until the beans are very soft. Add more water toward the end of the cooking if needed, or, if the beans are too watery, use a large spoon to drain off some of the water at the end of the cooking. If desired, the cooker may be plugged into a lamp/appliance timer, page 25, #4, to begin cooking up to 6 hours later. See Bean Cooking Tips, page 25, for more helpful suggestions.

Variety of Beans 1# (2½-2¾ cups) Size cooker: 3½-7 qt.	Average Cooker* Water & Cooking Time on Low	Fast Cooker* Water & Cooking Time on Low	Extra Fast Cooker* Water & Cooking Time on Low	Your Slow Cooker Time on Low
Great Northern Beans	5 cups & 9-9½ hours	5 cups & 7½-8 hours	5½ cups & 6½-7 hours	
Navy Beans	5 cups & 9-9½ hours	5½ cups & 8-8½ hours	5½ cups & 6½-7 hours	
Pinto Beans	5 cups & 9-9½ hours	5½ cups & 8-8½ hours	5½ cups & 6½-7 hours	
Black (Turtle) Beans	Not recommended	5¾ cups & 9-9½ hours	6 cups & 8-8½ hours	
Lima Beans	5 cups & 9-9½ hours	5½ cups & 8-8½ hours	5½ cups & 6½-7 hours	
Kidney Beans	5 cups & 10½-11 hours	5½ cups & 8-8½ hours	5½ cups & 6½-7 hours	
Lentils	5 cups & 8-8½ hours	5½ cups & 7-7½ hours	5½ cups & 6-6½ hours	
Garbanzos (Chickpeas)	Not recommended	6 cups & 9½-10 hours	6 cups & 7½-8 hours	
Soy Beans	Not recommended	Not recommended	Not recommended	

Optional ingredients for 1# of beans: Amount you are using:

Extra Virgin Olive Oil	1 tablespoon or less	
Salt	1½ teaspoons or less	

½# Dried Beans NOT Soaked and Cooked on LOW   Yield: 3-3½ cups

Variety of Beans ½# (1¼-1⅓ cups) Size cooker: 2-6 qt.	Average Cooker* Water & Cooking Time on Low	Fast Cooker* Water & Cooking Time on Low	Extra Fast Cooker* Water & Cooking Time on Low	Your Slow Cooker Time on Low
Great Northern Beans	2½ cups & 6½-7 hours	2½ cups & 4½-5 hours	2¾ cups & 3½-4 hours	
Navy Beans	2¾ cups & 9-9½ hours	2¾ cups & 6-6½ hours	2¾ cups & 5½-6 hours	
Pinto Beans	2½ cups & 9-9½ hours	2¾ cups & 5½-6 hours	2¾ cups & 4-4½ hours	
Black (Turtle) Beans	Not recommended	3¾ cups & 8-8½ hours	3¾ cups & 7-7½ hours	
Lima Beans	2½ cups & 9-9½ hours	2¾ cups & 5½-6 hours	2¾ cups & 4-4½ hours	
Kidney Beans	2¾ cups & 10-10½ hours	2¾ cups & 5½-6 hours	2¾ cups & 4-4½ hours	
Lentils	2¾ cups & 5½-6 hours	2¾ cups & 3-3½ hours	2¾ cups & 3-3½ hours	
Garbanzos (Chickpeas)	Not recommended	2¾ cups & 5½-6 hours	2¾ cups & 4½-5 hours	
Soy Beans	Not recommended	Not recommended	Not recommended	

Optional ingredients for ½# of beans: Amount you are using:

Extra Virgin Olive Oil	1½ teaspoons or less	
Salt	¾ teaspoon or less	

Bean Cooking Chart 2

1# Dried Beans NOT Soaked and Cooked on HIGH Yield: 6-7 cups

Sort through the beans, looking for small clumps of dirt and stones. Cover the beans with water, rinse and drain, then empty into the cooker. Add the amount of water recommended in the following chart for your type of cooker. ***See page 25, #3, for a description of the 3 types of cookers**. Add the optional ingredients if using. Cook until the beans are very soft. Add more water toward the end of the cooking if needed, or, if the beans are too watery, use a large spoon to drain off some of the water at the end of the cooking. If desired, the cooker may be plugged into a lamp/appliance timer, page 26, #4, to begin cooking up to 6 hours later. See Bean Cooking Tips, page 25, for more helpful suggestions.

Variety of Beans 1# (2½-2¾ cups) Size cooker: 3½-7 qt.	Average Cooker* Water & Cooking Time on High	Fast Cooker* Water & Cooking Time on High	Extra Fast Cooker* Water & Cooking Time on High	Your Slow Cooker Time on High
Great Northern Beans	5 cups & 5-5½ hours	5½ cups & 4-4½ hours	5¾ cups & 3-3½ hours	
Navy Beans	5 cups & 5½-6 hours	5½ cups & 5-5½ hours	5¾ cups & 4-4½ hours	
Pinto Beans	5 cups & 5½-6 hours	5½ cups & 5-5½ hours	5¾ cups & 4-4½ hours	
Black (Turtle) Beans	5 cups & 6-6½ hours	5½ cups & 5½-6 hours	5¾ cups & 5-5½ hours	
Lima Beans	5 cups & 5½-6 hours	5½ cups & 5-5½ hours	5¾ cups & 4-4½ hours	
Kidney Beans	5 cups & 5½-6 hours	5½ cups & 5-5½ hours	5¾ cups & 4-4½ hours	
Lentils	5 cups & 5-5½ hours	5½ cups & 4-4½ hours	5½ cups & 3-3½ hours	
Garbanzo (Chickpeas)	5 cups & 5½-6 hours	5½ cups & 5-5½ hours	5¾ cups & 4-4½ hours	
Soy Beans	5¾ cups & 10-10½ hours	6 cups & 9-9½ hours	6 cups & 8-8½ hours	

Optional ingredients for 1# of beans: Amount you are using:

Extra Virgin Olive Oil	1 tablespoon or less	
Salt	1½ teaspoons or less	

½# Dried Beans NOT Soaked and Cooked on HIGH Yield: 3-3½ cups

Variety of Beans ½# (1¼-1⅓ cups) Size cooker: 2-6 qt.	Average Cooker* Water & Cooking Time on High	Fast Cooker* Water & Cooking Time on High	Extra Fast Cooker* Water & Cooking Time on High	Your Slow Cooker Time on High
Great Northern Beans	2½ cups & 3½-4 hours	3 cups & 3½-4 hours	3 cups & 3-3½ hours	
Navy Beans	2¾ cups & 3½-4 hours	3 cups & 3½-4 hours	3 cups & 3½-4 hours	
Pinto Beans	2¾ cups & 3½-4 hours	3 cups & 3½-4 hours	3 cups & 3¼-3¾ hours	
Black (Turtle) Beans	2¾ cups & 4½-5 hours	3 cups & 4-4½ hours	3 cups & 3½-4 hours	
Lima Beans	2¾ cups & 3½-4 hours	3 cups & 3½-4 hours	3 cups & 3-3½ hours	
Kidney Beans	2¾ cups & 4-4½ hours	3 cups & 3½-4 hours	3 cups & 3-3½ hours	
Lentils	2¾ cups & 2½-3 hours	2¾ cups & 2-2½ hours	2¾ cups & 1¾-2 hours	
Garbanzo (Chickpeas)	3 cups & 4-4½ hours	3 cups & 4-4½ hours	3 cups & 4-4½ hours	
Soy Beans	3½ cups & 8-8½ hours	4 cups & 7½-8 hours	4 cups & 6-6½ hours	

Optional ingredients for ½# of beans: Amount you are using:

Extra Virgin Olive Oil	1½ teaspoons or less	
Salt	¾ teaspoon or less	

Bean Cooking Chart 3

1# Dried Beans SOAKED and Cooked on LOW   Yield: 6-7 cups

Sort through the beans, looking for small clumps of dirt and stones. Cover the beans with water, rinse then drain. Soak 1# of beans in 8 cups of water for at least 8 hours. Or, for the bottom chart, soak ½# of beans in 4 cups of water for at least 8 hours. Drain the beans then add them to the cooker along with the amount of water recommended in the following chart for your type of cooker. ***See page 25, #3, for a description of the 3 types of cookers**. Add the optional ingredients if using. Cook until the beans are very soft. Add more water toward the end of the cooking if needed, or, if the beans are too watery, use a large spoon to drain off some of the water at the end of the cooking. If desired, plug the cooker into a lamp/appliance timer, page 26, #4, to begin cooking up to 6 hours later. See Bean Cooking Tips, page 25, for more helpful suggestions.

Variety of Beans 1# (2½-2¾ cups) Size cooker: 3½-7 qt.	Average Cooker* Water & Cooking Time on Low	Fast Cooker* Water & Cooking Time on Low	Extra Fast Cooker* Water & Cooking Time on Low	Your Slow Cooker Time on Low
Great Northern Beans	3½ cups & 8-8½ hours	3½ cups & 7-7½ hours	3½ cups & 5-5½ hours	
Navy Beans	3½ cups & 8½-9 hours	3¾ cups & 8-8½ hours	3¾ cups & 6-6½ hours	
Pinto Beans	3½ cups & 8½-9 hours	3¾ cups & 7-7½ hours	3¾ cups & 5½-6 hours	
Black (Turtle) Beans	3½ cups & 12-12½ hours	3¾ cups & 8-8½ hours	3¾ cups & 7-7½ hours	
Lima Beans	3½ cups & 8½-9 hours	3¾ cups & 8-8½ hours	3¾ cups & 5½-6 hours	
Kidney Beans	3½ cups & 8½-9 hours	3¾ cups & 8-8½ hours	3¾ cups & 5½-6 hours	
Garbanzo (Chickpeas)	3½ cups & 9-9½ hours	3¾ cups & 8-8½ hours	3¾ cups & 7-7½ hours	
Soy Beans	Not recommended	5 cups & 12-14 hours	5 cups & 11-12 hours	

Optional ingredients for 1# of beans: Amount you are using:

Extra Virgin Olive Oil	1 tablespoon or less	
Salt	1½ teaspoons or less	

½# Dried Beans SOAKED and Cooked on LOW   Yield: 3-3½ cups

Variety of Beans ½# (1¼-1⅓ cups) Size cooker: 2-6 qt.	Average Cooker* Water & Cooking Time on Low	Fast Cooker* Water & Cooking Time on Low	Extra Fast Cooker* Water & Cooking Time on Low	Your Slow Cooker Time on Low
Great Northern Beans	1¾ cups & 6-6½ hours	2½ cups & 5-5½ hours	2½ cups & 4½-5 hours	
Navy Beans	2 cups & 6-6½ hours	2½ cups & 5-5½ hours	2¾ cups & 4½-5 hours	
Pinto Beans	2 cups & 6-6½ hours	2½ cups & 5-5½ hours	2¾ cups & 4½-5 hours	
Black (Turtle) Beans	1¾ cups & 12-12½ hours	2½ cups & 8-8½ hours	2¾ cups & 6-6½ hours	
Lima Beans	2 cups & 6-6½ hours	2½ cups & 5-5½ hours	2½ cups & 3½-4 hours	
Kidney Beans	2 cups & 6-6½ hours	2½ cups & 5-5½ hours	2¾ cups & 4½-5 hours	
Garbanzo (Chickpeas)	2 cups & 7-7½ hours	2½ cups & 6-6½ hours	2¾ cups & 4½-5 hours	
Soy Beans	Not recommended	2½ cups & 12-14 hours	3 cups & 11-12 hours	

Optional ingredients for ½# of beans: Amount you are using:

Extra Virgin Olive Oil	1½ teaspoons or less	
Salt	¾ teaspoon or less	

Bean Cooking Chart 4

1# Dried Beans SOAKED and Cooked on HIGH Yield 6-7 cups

Sort through the beans, looking for small clumps of dirt and stones. Cover the beans with water, rinse then drain. Soak 1# of beans in 8 cups of water for at least 8 hours. Or, for the bottom chart, soak ½# of beans in 4 cups of water for at least 8 hours. Drain the beans then add them to the cooker along with the amount of water recommended in the following chart for your type of cooker. ***See page 25, #3, for a description of the 3 types of cookers**. Add the optional ingredients if using. Cook until the beans are very soft. Add more water toward the end of the cooking if needed, or, if the beans are too watery, use a large spoon to drain off some of the water at the end of the cooking. If desired, plug the cooker into a lamp/appliance timer, page 26, #4, to begin cooking up to 6 hours later. See Bean Cooking Tips, page 25, for more helpful suggestions.

Variety of Beans 1# (2½-2¾ cups) Size cooker: 3½-7 qt.	Average Cooker* Water & Cooking Time on High	Fast Cooker* Water & Cooking Time on High	Extra Fast Cooker* Water & Cooking Time on High	Your Slow Cooker Time on High
Great Northern Beans	3½ cups & 4½-5 hours	3¾ cups & 4-4½ hours	3¾ cups & 3-3½ hours	
Navy Beans	3½ cups & 4½-5 hours	3¾ cups & 4-4½ hours	3¾ cups & 3-3½ hours	
Pinto Beans	3½ cups & 4½-5 hours	3¾ cups & 4-4½ hours	3¾ cups & 3-3½ hours	
Black (Turtle) Beans	3½ cups & 4½-5 hours	3¾ cups & 4-4½ hours	3¾ cups & 3-3½ hours	
Lima Beans	3½ cups & 3½-4 hours	3¾ cups & 3-3½ hours	3¾ cups & 2½-3 hours	
Kidney Beans	3½ cups & 4½-5 hours	3¾ cups & 4-4½ hours	3¾ cups & 3-3½ hours	
Garbanzo (Chickpeas)	3½ cups & 4½-5 hours	3¾ cups & 4-4½ hours	3¾ cups & 3-3½ hours	
Soy Beans	3½ cups & 8-8½ hours	4 cups & 7-7½ hours	4 cups & 6-6½ hours	

Optional ingredients for 1# of beans:		Amount you are using:
Extra Virgin Olive Oil	1 tablespoon or less	
Salt	1½ teaspoons or less	

½# Dried Beans SOAKED and Cooked on HIGH Yield: 3-3½ cups

Variety of Beans ½# (1¼-1⅓ cups) Size cooker: 2-6 qt.	Average Cooker* Water & Cooking Time on High	Fast Cooker* Water & Cooking Time on High	Extra Fast Cooker* Water & Cooking Time on High	Your Slow Cooker Time on High
Great Northern Beans	2 cups & 4-4½ hours	2¼ cups & 3-3½ hours	2½ cups & 2½-3 hours	
Navy Beans	2 cups & 4½-5 hours	2¼ cups & 3-3½ hours	2¾ cups & 3-3½ hours	
Pinto Beans	2 cups & 4½-5 hours	2¼ cups & 3-3½ hours	2½ cups & 3-3½ hours	
Black (Turtle) Beans	2¼ cups & 6-6½ hours	3 cups & 6-6½ hours	3 cups & 5½-6 hours	
Lima Beans	2 cups & 4-4½ hours	2¼ cups & 3-3½ hours	2½ cups & 3-3½ hours	
Kidney Beans	2 cups & 4-4½ hours	2¼ cups & 3-3½ hours	2½ cups & 3-3½ hours	
Garbanzo (Chickpeas)	2¼ cups & 4-4½ hours	2¼ cups & 3½-4 hours	2½ cups & 3½-4 hours	
Soy Beans	2½ cups & 6-6½ hours	3 cups & 5½-6 hours	3 cups & 5-5½ hours	

Optional ingredients for ½# of beans:		Amount you are using:
Extra Virgin Olive Oil	1½ teaspoons or less	
Salt	¾ teaspoon or less	

Beans Not Soaked-1 ½ Quart Rival Crock-Pot

This cooker has no high/low setting. The temperature seems to be between high and low, compared to an Average cooker.

Sort through ½# of beans (1¼-1⅓ cups) looking for small clumps of dirt and stones. Rinse and drain the beans, then empty into the cooker. Add the amount of water recommended in the chart. Add the optional ingredients if using. Cook until the beans are very soft. Add more water toward the end of the cooking if needed, or, if the beans are too watery, use a large spoon to drain off some of the water at the end of the cooking. If desired, plug the cooker into a lamp/appliance timer, page 26, #4, to begin cooking up to 6 hours later.

Variety of Beans (½#)	Water & Cooking Time	Your Slow Cooker Time
Great Northern Beans	3 cups & 8-8½ hours	
Navy Beans	3½ cups & 9½-10 hours	
Pinto Beans	3 cups & 8-8½ hours	
Black (Turtle) Beans	3½ cups & 10-10½ hours	
Lima Beans	2¾ cups & 7½-8 hours	
Kidney Beans	3 cups & 7½-8 hours	
Lentils	2¾ cups & 5-5½ hours	
Garbanzo (Chickpeas)	3½ cups 10-10½ hours	
Soy Beans	3¾ cups & 13-13½ hours	

Optional ingredients for ½# of beans: Amount you are using:

Extra Virgin Olive Oil	1½ teaspoons or less	
Salt	¾ teaspoon or less	

Beans Soaked-1 ½ Quart Rival Crock-Pot

This cooker has no high/low setting. The temperature seems to be between high and low, compared to an Average cooker.

Sort through ½# of beans, (1¼-1⅓ cups) looking for small clumps of dirt and stones. Cover the beans with water, rinse then drain. Soak the beans in 4 cups of water for at least 8 hours. Drain then add them, along with the amount of water recommended in the following chart, to the cooker. Add the optional ingredients if using. Cook until the beans are very soft. Add more water toward the end of the cooking if needed, or, if the beans are too watery use a spoon to drain off some of the water at the end of the cooking. If desired, plug the cooker into a lamp/appliance timer, page 26, #4, to begin cooking up to 6 hours later.

Variety of Beans (½#)	Water & Cooking Time	Your Slow Cooker Time
Great Northern Beans	1¾ cups & 5½-6 hours	
Navy Beans	1¾ cups & 7-7½ hours	
Pinto Beans	1¾ cups & 5½-6 hours	
Black (Turtle) Beans	2 cups & 10-10½ hours	
Lima Beans	1¾ cups & 5½-6 hours	
Kidney Beans	1¾ cups & 5½-6 hours	
Lentils	Soaking not needed	
Garbanzo (Chickpeas)	1¾ cups 5½-6 hours	
Soy Beans	2¼ cups & 11-11½ hours	

Optional ingredients for ½# of beans: Amount you are using:

Extra Virgin Olive Oil	1½ teaspoons or less	
Salt	¾ teaspoon or less	

Great! Great Northerns

Smaller Recipe		Larger Recipe
YIELD: approx. 3 cups COOKER SIZE: 1½-6 qt.	INGREDIENTS	YIELD: approx. 6 cups COOKER SIZE: 3½-7 qt.

1ST Sort through the beans, looking for small clumps of dirt and stones. Cover the beans with water, rinse then drain. Next, choose how you would like to cook the beans. They may be cooked on high or low. They may be soaked ahead of time, or not soaked. See the Bean Cooking Charts, pages 28-32, to choose the method right for you and your cooker. For example, if you want to cook great northern beans on low without soaking them, then see page 28. If you have an Average Cooker and are cooking the Larger Recipe, then you will cook the beans in 5 cups of water for 9-9½ hours. Add the following ingredients with the beans and water, and cook until the beans are very soft.

Smaller Recipe	Ingredient	Larger Recipe
see Bean Cooking Charts	water	see Bean Cooking Charts
1¼-1⅓ cups or ½#	dried great northern beans or other white beans	1# or 2½-2¾ cups
½ cup	chopped onion	1 cup
1½ teaspoons	extra virgin olive oil, optional, but great taste	1 tablespoon
¼ + ⅛ teaspoon	salt	¾ teaspoon

2nd Pre-measure the following dry ingredients into a small dish. Stir them into the cooker, along with the spinach. Turn off the cooker and let sit 5 minutes.

Smaller Recipe	Ingredient	Larger Recipe
1 tablespoon	onion powder	2 tablespoons
2¼ teaspoons	McKay's Chicken Seasoning or Chicken Seasoning, pg 136	1½ tablespoons
½ teaspoon	garlic powder	1 teaspoon
½ cup	finely chopped, fresh spinach, optional	1 cup

3rd Ready to serve.

COOKING TIME:

See Bean Cooking Charts, pages 28-32, to determine the cooking time.

Tips
- See page 25 for additional Bean Cooking Tips.
- The cooker may be plugged into a lamp/appliance timer, page 26, #4, to begin cooking up to 6 hours later.
- Reheat on Another Day: Reheat on low about 2 hours for the Smaller Recipe or 2½-3 hours for the Larger Recipe.

Simple but Simply Delicious Beans

Smaller Recipe		Larger Recipe
YIELD: approx. 3 cups COOKER SIZE: 1½-6 qt.	INGREDIENTS	YIELD: approx. 6 cups COOKER SIZE: 3½-7 qt.

1st Sort through the beans, looking for small clumps of dirt and stones. Cover the beans with water, rinse then drain. Next, choose how you would like to cook the beans. They may be cooked on high or low. They may be soaked ahead of time or not soaked. See the Bean Cooking Charts, pages 28-32, to choose the method right for you and your cooker. For example, if you want to cook great northern beans on low without soaking them, then see page 28. If you have an Average Cooker and are cooking the Larger Recipe, then you will cook the beans in 5 cups of water for 9-9½ hours. Add the following ingredients with the beans and water, and cook until the beans are very soft.

Smaller Recipe	Ingredient	Larger Recipe
see Bean Cooking Charts	water	see Bean Cooking Charts
1¼-1⅓ cups or ½#	dried great northern, navy or your favorite beans	1# or 2½-2¾ cups
1½ teaspoons	extra virgin olive oil, optional, but great taste	1 tablespoon
¾ teaspoon	salt	1½ teaspoons

2nd Crush the basil in the following table between your fingers. Crushing the basil releases more immediate flavor, which is ideal for brief cooking. Pre-measure the following dry ingredients into a small dish. Stir them into the cooker. Turn off the cooker and let sit 5 minutes.

Smaller Recipe	Ingredient	Larger Recipe
2 tablespoons	yeast flakes, pg 10, optional	¼ cup
1½ teaspoons	onion powder	1 tablespoon
1 teaspoon	garlic powder	2 teaspoons
½ teaspoon	basil	1 teaspoon

3rd Ready to serve.

COOKING TIME:

See Bean Cooking Charts, pages 28-32, to determine the cooking time.

Tips

- See page 25 for additional Bean Cooking Tips.
- The cooker may be plugged into a lamp/appliance timer, page 26, #4, to begin cooking up to 6 hours later.
- Reheat on Another Day: Reheat on low about 2 hours for the Smaller Recipe or 2½-3 hours for the Larger Recipe.

Sesame Tahini Creamy Beans

Leave out the oil. Stir in tahini with the seasonings at the end of the cooking. (Tahini is similar to peanut butter but is made from sesame seeds.) Add 2 tablespoons for the Smaller Recipe, or ¼ cup for the Larger Recipe.

South of the Border Beans

Smaller Recipe		Larger Recipe
YIELD: approx. 3 cups COOKER SIZE: 1½-6 qt.	INGREDIENTS	YIELD: approx. 6 cups COOKER SIZE: 3½-7 qt.

1st Sort through the beans, looking for small clumps of dirt and stones. Cover the beans with water, rinse then drain. Next, choose how you would like to cook the beans. They may be cooked on high or low. They may be soaked ahead of time or not soaked. See the Bean Cooking Charts, pages 28-32, to choose the method right for you and your cooker. For example, if you want to cook great northern beans on low without soaking them, then see page 28. If you have an Average Cooker and are cooking the Larger Recipe, then you will cook the beans in 5 cups of water for 9-9½ hours. Add the following ingredients with the beans and water, and cook until the beans are very soft.

see Bean Cooking Charts	water	see Bean Cooking Charts
1¼-1⅓ cups or ½#	dried great northern beans, navy or your favorite beans	1# or 2½-2¾ cups
½ cup	chopped onion	1 cup
1½ teaspoons	extra virgin olive oil, optional, but great taste	1 tablespoon
¾ teaspoon	salt	1½ teaspoons

2nd Crush the basil in the following table between your fingers. Crushing the basil releases more immediate flavor, which is ideal for brief cooking. Stir all of the following ingredients into the cooker. Turn off the cooker and let sit 5 minutes.

3 tablespoons	tomato paste	⅓ cup
½ cup	sliced or chopped, black olives	1 cup
1-2 tablespoons	finely chopped, fresh cilantro	2-3 tablespoons
3 cloves	minced garlic	5-6 cloves
¾ teaspoon	ground cumin	1½ teaspoons
½ teaspoon	basil	1 teaspoon

3rd Ready to serve.

COOKING TIME:

See Bean Cooking Charts, pages 28-32, to determine the cooking time.

Tips

- See page 25 for additional Bean Cooking Tips.
- The cooker may be plugged into a lamp/appliance timer, page 26, #4, to begin cooking up to 6 hours later.
- Reheat on Another Day: Reheat on low about 2 hours for the Smaller Recipe or 2½-3 hours for the Larger Recipe.

Cuban Black Beans

Smaller Recipe		Larger Recipe
YIELD: approx. 3 cups COOKER SIZE: 1½-6 qt.	INGREDIENTS	YIELD: approx. 6 cups COOKER SIZE: 3½-7 qt.

1st Sort through the black beans, looking for small clumps of dirt and stones. Cover the beans with water, rinse then drain. Next, choose how you would like to cook the beans. They may be cooked on high or low. They may be soaked ahead of time or not soaked. See the Bean Cooking Charts, pages 28-32, to choose the method right for you and your cooker. For example, if you want to cook the beans on low without soaking them, then see page 28. If you have an Fast Cooker and are cooking the Larger Recipe, then you will cook the beans in 5½ cups of water for 8½-9 hours. Add the following ingredients with the beans and water, and cook until the beans are very soft.

Smaller Recipe	Ingredient	Larger Recipe
see Bean Cooking Charts	water	see Bean Cooking Charts
1¼-1⅓ cups or ½#	dried black beans	1# or 2½-2¾ cups
¾ cup	chopped onion	1½ cups
1 tablespoon	extra virgin olive oil, optional, but great taste	2 tablespoons
¾ teaspoon	salt	1½ teaspoons

2nd Pre-measure the following dry ingredients into a small dish. Stir all of the following ingredients into the cooker. Turn off the cooker and let sit 5 minutes.

Smaller Recipe	Ingredient	Larger Recipe
2 tablespoons	lemon juice	¼ cup
1-2 tablespoons	finely chopped, fresh cilantro, optional	2-4 tablespoons
1 tablespoon	onion powder	2 tablespoons
1½ teaspoons	Bragg Liquid Aminos	1 tablespoon
3 cloves	minced garlic	5-6 cloves
1 teaspoon	ground cumin	2 teaspoons
¾ teaspoon	garlic powder	1½ teaspoons

3rd Ready to serve. Serve as is or over brown rice. See photo on page 66.

COOKING TIME:

See Black Beans in the Bean Cooking Charts, pages 28-32, to determine the cooking time.

Tips
- See page 25 for additional Bean Cooking Tips.
- The cooker may be plugged into a lamp/appliance timer, page 26, #4, to begin cooking up to 6 hours later.
- Reheat on Another Day: Reheat on low about 2 hours for the Smaller Recipe or 2½-3 hours for the Larger Recipe.

Baked Beans

Smaller Recipe		Larger Recipe
YIELD: approx. 3¼ cups COOKER SIZE: 1½-6 qt.	INGREDIENTS	YIELD: approx. 6½ cups COOKER SIZE: 3½-7 qt.

1st Sort through the beans, looking for small clumps of dirt and stones. Cover the beans with water, rinse then drain. Next, choose how you would like to cook the beans. They may be cooked on high or low. They may be soaked ahead of time or not soaked. See the Bean Cooking Charts, pages 28-32, to choose the method right for you and your cooker. For example, if you want to cook navy beans on low without soaking them, then see page 28. If you have an Average Cooker and are cooking the Larger Recipe, then you will cook the beans in 5 cups of water for 9-9½ hours. Add the following ingredients with the beans and water, and cook until the beans are very soft.

Smaller Recipe	Ingredient	Larger Recipe
see Bean Cooking Charts	water	see Bean Cooking Charts
1¼-1⅓ cups or ½#	dried navy, great northern or soy beans	1# or 2½-2¾ cups
½ cup	chopped onion	1 cup
1½ teaspoons	extra virgin olive oil, optional, but great taste	1 tablespoon
¾ teaspoon	salt	1½ teaspoons

2nd Pre-measure the following dry ingredients into one small dish and the wet ingredients into another dish. Stir them into the cooker. Turn off the cooker and let sit 5 minutes.

Smaller Recipe	Ingredient	Larger Recipe
3 tablespoons	tomato paste	⅓ cup
2 tablespoons	sucanat, cane juice crystals, fructose, brown sugar or honey	¼ cup
4½ teaspoons	lemon juice	3 tablespoons
1 tablespoon	molasses	2 tablespoons
1 tablespoon	onion powder	2 tablespoons
1 teaspoon	garlic powder	2 teaspoons
⅛ teaspoon	Hickory Seasoning Liquid Smoke, optional	¼ teaspoon

3rd Ready to serve. See photo on page 68.

COOKING TIME:

See Bean Cooking Charts, pages 28-32, to determine the cooking time.

Tips

- See page 25 for additional Bean Cooking Tips.
- The cooker may be plugged into a lamp/appliance timer, page 26, #4, to begin cooking up to 6 hours later.
- Reheat on Another Day: Reheat on low about 2 hours for the Smaller Recipe or 2½-3 hours for the Larger Recipe.

Mazidra

Smaller Recipe		Larger Recipe
YIELD: 6¼ cups COOKER SIZE: 2½-5 qt.	INGREDIENTS	YIELD: 10 cups COOKER SIZE: 3½-7 qt.

1st Stir the following ingredients into the cooker and cook until the lentils are soft.

Smaller Recipe	Ingredients	Larger Recipe
2¾ cups	water	4½ cups
1½ cups	lentils	2 cups
1 cup	chopped onion	1½ cups
1 tablespoon	extra virgin olive oil, optional but great taste	1½ tablespoons
¾ teaspoon	salt	1¼ teaspoons

2nd Crush the basil in the following table between your fingers. Crushing the basil releases more immediate flavor, which is ideal for brief cooking. Stir all of the following ingredients into the cooker. Turn off the cooker and let 5 minutes.

Smaller Recipe	Ingredients	Larger Recipe
14.5 oz. can or 1¾ cups	chopped or diced, canned tomatoes with juice	2½ cups
⅓ cup	tomato paste	½ cup
2	minced garlic cloves	4
1 tablespoon	lemon juice	1½ tablespoons
2 teaspoons	onion powder	1 tablespoon
¾ teaspoon	basil	1¼ teaspoons

3rd Ready to serve. Serve as is or over brown rice. See photo on page 76.

COOKING TIME ON LOW:

Average Cooker: Smaller Recipe 5½-6 hours OR Larger Recipe 8-8½ hours

Fast Cooker: Smaller Recipe 4-4½ hours OR Larger Recipe 7-7½ hours

Extra Fast Cooker: Smaller Recipe 3-3½ hours OR Larger Recipe 6-6½ hours

COOKING TIME ON HIGH:

Average Cooker: Smaller Recipe 2½-3 hours OR Larger Recipe 5-5½ hours

Fast Cooker: Smaller Recipe 2¼-2½ hours OR Larger Recipe 4-4½ hours

Extra Fast Cooker: Smaller Recipe 2-2¼ hours OR Larger Recipe 3-3½ hours

(See page 25, #3, for an explanation of the 3 types of cookers.)

Tips

- See page 25 for additional Bean Cooking Tips.
- The cooker may be plugged into a lamp/appliance timer, page 26, #4, to begin cooking up to 6 hours later.
- Reheat on Another Day: Reheat on low about 2 hours for the Smaller Recipe or 2½-3 hours for the Larger Recipe.

Instant! Slow Cooked Refried Beans

Smaller Recipe		Larger Recipe
YIELD: 2½ cups COOKER SIZE: 1½-5 qt.	INGREDIENTS	YIELD: 5 cups COOKER SIZE: 2½-7 qt.

1st Stir together the following ingredients in the cooker. Cook until steaming hot. You may see a light boiling in a few places around the edges. (The beans are available at health food stores, restaurant supply stores and online.)

Smaller Recipe	Ingredients	Larger Recipe
3 cups	dried, instant, refried beans	6 cups
2¼ cups	water	4½ cups
1 tablespoon	onion powder, optional	2 tablespoons
1 teaspoon	garlic powder, optional	2 teaspoons
1 teaspoon	ground cumin, optional	2 teaspoons

2nd May add 1 or 2 cloves of minced garlic at the end. A little more water may be stirred in at the end of cooking if needed. If a thick consistency is preferred let the beans sit for a few minutes, uncovered, after cooking.

COOKING TIME ON LOW:

Average Cooker: Smaller Recipe 2-2¼ hours OR Larger Recipe 2¾-3 hours

Fast Cooker: Smaller Recipe 1¾-2 hours OR Larger Recipe 2¼-2½ hours

Extra Fast Cooker: Smaller Recipe 1-1¼ hour OR Larger Recipe 1¾-2 hours

(See page 25, #3, for an explanation of the 3 types of cookers.)

Tips

- The cooker may be plugged into a lamp/appliance timer, page 26, #4, to begin cooking up to 6 hours later.
- If you dry your own mashed, cooked beans in a food dryer they may be substituted for the beans in this recipe. See Bean Cooking Tips, page 27, #16, for more information on drying your home cooked beans. Increase the water to 2½ cups for the Smaller Recipe or 5 cups for the Larger Recipe.

Haystacks

This is a quick, easy, delicious meal. Most everything can be done in advance. Haystacks can be prepared with a variety of items. Choose what you like. Prepare this recipe on your plate in a layered manner. Usually, for the first layer, is brown rice or corn chips, such as oil free, baked chips. Next is a layer of beans, usually partially mashed, such as pintos, red beans, black beans, navy or great northern beans. The Instant! Slow Cooked Refried Beans, see recipe above, works great for this. (If needed, add a little water to the cooked beans so that they will spread easily.) From here you add fresh vegetables, such as, alfalfa sprouts, chopped lettuce, tomatoes, and onion. Top with Cheese Sauce, page 102, Tofu Sour Cream, page 136, and/or an avocado spread, such as Garbanzomole, page 137. And there you have your creative, one of a kind, masterpiece! See photo on page 69.

Millet Tomato Bake

Smaller Recipe YIELD: 3½ cups COOKER SIZE: 5-7 qt.	INGREDIENTS	Larger Recipe YIELD: 5½ cups COOKER SIZE: 6-7 qt.

1st This recipe cooks the most evenly if it is baked in a dish inside a slow cooker. Blend the following ingredients until smooth in a blender, then pour into a mixing bowl.

Smaller Recipe	Ingredients	Larger Recipe
¾ cup	canned tomato juice	1 cup
½ cup	onion, cut in chunks	¾ cup
¼ cup	raw cashews or almonds	⅓ cup

2nd Rinse the blender with the juice in the following ingredients, then add to the mixing bowl. Stir in the remaining ingredients. Choose a glass or metal baking dish that will hold at least 4 cups for the Smaller Recipe, or 6 cups for the Larger Recipe. Make sure the dish will fit easily into the cooker. This is important, as the dish will be hot when being removed. There are some oval 4½ qt. cookers that will easily hold a dish containing the Smaller Recipe. Spray the dish with a food release cooking spray. Pour the ingredients into the dish, and cover with foil. Place the dish on a trivet inside the cooker. See page 11 for what can be used for a trivet. Bake until thick and the millet is soft.

Smaller Recipe	Ingredients	Larger Recipe
1¼ cups	canned tomato juice	2 cups
½ cup	cooked, drained garbanzo beans or beans of choice	1 cup
½ cup	sliced, black olives	1 cup
½ cup	uncooked millet	¾ cup
½ teaspoon	thyme	¾ teaspoon
½ teaspoon	marjoram	¾ teaspoon

3rd Ready to serve. See photo on page 73.

BAKING TIME ON LOW:

Average Cooker: Smaller Recipe 5-5½ hours OR Larger Recipe 5½-6 hours

Fast Cooker: Smaller Recipe 4½-5 hours OR Larger Recipe 5-5½ hours

Extra Fast Cooker: Smaller Recipe 4-4½ hours OR Larger Recipe 4½-5 hours

(See page 25, #3, for an explanation of the 3 types of cookers.)

Tips

- The cooker may be plugged into a lamp/appliance timer, page 26, #4, to begin cooking up to 6 hours later.
- Make Ahead: Prepare Step 1. Combine with ingredients in Step 2, except for the millet, thyme, and marjoram. Refrigerate in a storage container. Add the millet and herbs when preparing to bake. Add 20-30 minutes to the baking time, unless waiting at least 2 hours before baking, to take the chill off the food.

Corn Tamale Casserole

Smaller Recipe		Larger Recipe
YIELD: 3¼ cups COOKER SIZE: 1½-4 qt.	INGREDIENTS	YIELD: 6½ cups COOKER SIZE: 2½-5 qt.

1st I recommend brushing or wiping the cooker with ½-1 teaspoon of liquid lecithin. This is optional, but makes clean up *quick and easy*. See page 11 for more information on liquid lecithin. If not using lecithin, then spray the cooker with a food release cooking spray. Sauté the following onion in the oil for a few minutes until soft.

Smaller Recipe	Ingredient	Larger Recipe
¾ cup	chopped onion	1½ cups
1 tablespoon	olive oil	2 tablespoons

2nd Stir together the sautéed onion with the following ingredients in a mixing bowl, then pour into the cooker.

Smaller Recipe	Ingredient	Larger Recipe
¾ cup	corn meal, preferably whole grain	1½ cups
¾ cup + 2 tablespoons	tomato sauce	15 oz. can
¾ cup + 2 tablespoons	cooked, drained great northern beans or beans of choice	1¾ cups or 15 oz. can
¾ cup	salt free, drained, canned or frozen corn	1½ cups
⅓ cup	water	⅔ cup
¼ cup	chopped or sliced, black olives	½ cup
2	minced garlic	4
½ teaspoon	ground cumin	1 teaspoon

3rd Sprinkle on the tomatoes, then the olives, and bake until lightly browned around the edges.

Smaller Recipe	Ingredient	Larger Recipe
½ cup	chopped or diced, canned tomatoes, drained	½ cup
¼-½ cup	chopped or sliced, black olives	¼-½ cup

4th Ready to serve. May sprinkle with fresh parsley before serving. See photo on page 78.

BAKING TIME ON LOW:

Average Cooker: Smaller Recipe 5-5½ hours OR Larger Recipe 5½-6 hours

Fast Cooker: Smaller Recipe 3¾-4¼ hours OR Larger Recipe 4½-4¾ hours

Extra Fast Cooker: Smaller Recipe 3-3½ hours OR Larger Recipe 3¼-3¾ hours

(See page 25, #3, for an explanation of the 3 types of cookers.)

Tips

- The cooker may be plugged into a lamp/appliance timer, page 26, #4, to begin cooking up to 6 hours later.
- Make Ahead: Prepare Step 1. Combine with ingredients in Step 2, except for adding the corn meal. Refrigerate in a storage container until ready to bake. Assemble the recipe when preparing to bake. Add 20-40 minutes to the baking time, unless waiting at least 2 hours before baking, to take the chill off the food.
- Bake in a Dish Inside the Cooker: This is my favorite way to prepare this recipe. Spray with a food release cooking spray, a glass or metal dish that will hold at least 3½ cups for the Smaller Recipe, or 6½ cups for the Larger Recipe. Make sure the dish will fit easily into the cooker. This is important as the dish will be hot when being removed. Add the ingredients and cover with foil. Place the dish on a trivet in the cooker. See page 11 for what can be used for a trivet. Bake on low in an Extra Fast Cooker for 4½-5 hours for the Smaller Recipe, or 5-5½ hours, for the Larger Recipe. Otherwise, add 30-60 minutes for a Fast or Average Cooker.

Spanish Rice

Smaller Recipe YIELD: 4½ cups COOKER SIZE: 1½-5 qt.	INGREDIENTS	Larger Recipe YIELD: 6½ cups COOKER SIZE: 2½-6 qt.

1st Spray the cooker with a food release cooking spray. Stir together the following ingredients in a mixing bowl then add to the cooker and bake.

Smaller Recipe	Ingredients	Larger Recipe
2 cups	cooked, brown rice	3 cups
1 cup	cooked, drained garbanzo beans or beans of choice	1¾ cups or 15 oz. can
1 cup	chopped or diced, canned tomatoes with juice	1¾ cups or 14.5 oz. can
1 cup	browned, crumbled vegetarian burger, opt., see note below	1¾ cups
¾ cup	sliced, black olives	6 oz. can
¾ cup	finely chopped onion	1 cup
⅓ cup	tomato paste	½ cup
2	minced garlic	3
1 teaspoon	basil	1½ teaspoons
⅛ teaspoon	salt	¼ teaspoon

2nd Ready to serve. May garnish with parsley before serving. See photo on page 68.

BAKING TIME ON LOW:

Average Cooker: Smaller Recipe 4-4½ hours OR Larger Recipe 5-5½ hours

Fast Cooker: Smaller Recipe 3-3½ hours OR Larger Recipe 4-4½ hours

Extra Fast Cooker: Smaller Recipe 2½-3 hours OR Larger Recipe 3¼-3¾ hours

(See page 25, #3, for an explanation of the 3 types of cookers.)

Note: Vegetarian burger may come from a variety of sources:

- If using a commercial frozen patty, such as vegan Boca Burgers or Morningstar patties or commercial, canned patties, such as from Cedar Lake or Loma Linda, they should be browned then crumbled. Commercial ground burger is also available canned or frozen. Follow package directions for browning.
- Try your favorite homemade gluten recipe, or the Tender Gluten, page 58. Cut it into very small pieces or chop in a food processor.

Tips

- The cooker may be plugged into a lamp/appliance timer, page 26, #4, to begin cooking up to 6 hours later.
- Make Ahead: Prepare Step 1. Refrigerate in a storage container until ready to bake. Add 20-40 minutes to the baking time, unless waiting at least 2 hours before baking, to take the chill off the food.
- Bake in a Dish Inside the Cooker: Spray, with a food release cooking spray, a glass or metal dish that will hold at least 4½ cups for the Smaller Recipe, or 7 cups for the Larger Recipe. Make sure the dish will fit easily into the cooker. This is important as the dish will be hot when being removed. Add the ingredients and cover with foil. Place the dish on a trivet in the cooker. See page 11 for what can be used for a trivet. Bake on low in an Extra Fast Cooker for 4½-5 hours for the Smaller Recipe, or 5½-6 hours for the Larger Recipe. Otherwise, add 30-60 minutes for a Fast or Average Cooker.
- Reheat on Another Day: Reheat on low about 2 hours for the Smaller Recipe or 2½-3 hours for the Larger Recipe.

Nutty Carrot Rice

Smaller Recipe		Larger Recipe
YIELD: 3¼ cups COOKER SIZE: 1½-4 qt.	INGREDIENTS	YIELD: 5½ cups COOKER SIZE: 3½-6 qt.

1st I recommend brushing or wiping the cooker with ½-1 teaspoon of liquid lecithin. This is optional, but makes clean up *quick and easy*. See page 11 for a description of lecithin and how to apply it. If not using lecithin, then spray the cooker with a food release cooking spray. Stir together the following ingredients in a mixing bowl.

Smaller Recipe	Ingredient	Larger Recipe
¾ cup	chopped onion	1¼ cups
⅓ cup	peanut butter or almond butter	⅔ cup
1 teaspoon	thyme	1¾ teaspoons
1 teaspoon	salt	1½ teaspoons

2nd Stir in the rice then the carrots. Pat down the ingredients into the cooker. If possible, use a fork to pull the ingredients away from the sides ¼". Bake until the carrots are tender.

Smaller Recipe	Ingredient	Larger Recipe
2⅔ cups	cooked, brown rice	4½ cups
1½ cups	shredded carrots	2½ cups

3rd Ready to serve.

BAKING TIME ON LOW:

Average Cooker: Smaller Recipe 5-5½ hours OR Larger Recipe 5¾-6¼ hours

Fast Cooker: Smaller Recipe 4-4½ hours OR Larger Recipe 4½-5 hours

Extra Fast Cooker: Smaller Recipe 3½-4 hours OR Larger Recipe 4-4½ hours

(See page 25, #3, for an explanation of the 3 types of cookers.)

Tips

- The cooker may be plugged into a lamp/appliance timer, page 26, #4, to begin cooking up to 6 hours later.
- Make Ahead: Prepare Steps 1 and 2. Refrigerate in a storage container until ready to bake. Add 20-40 minutes to the baking time, unless waiting at least 2 hours before baking, to take the chill off the food.
- Bake in a Dish Inside the Cooker: Spray, with a food release cooking spray, a glass or metal dish that will hold at least 3½ cups for the Smaller Recipe, or 6 cups for the Larger Recipe. Make sure the dish will fit easily into the cooker. This is important as the dish will be hot when being removed. Add the ingredients and cover with foil. Place the dish on a trivet in the cooker. See page 11 for what can be used for a trivet. Bake on low for 4½-5 hours for the Smaller Recipe, or 5½-6 hours for the Larger Recipe, if using an Extra Fast Cooker. Otherwise, add 30-60 minutes for a Fast or Average Cooker.

Cashew Rice

Smaller Recipe		Larger Recipe
YIELD: 3½ cups COOKER SIZE: 1½-5 qt.	INGREDIENTS	YIELD: 7 cups COOKER SIZE: 3-7 qt.

1st I recommend brushing or wiping the cooker with ½-1 teaspoon of liquid lecithin. This is optional, but makes clean up *quick and easy*. See page 11 for more information on liquid lecithin. Blend the following ingredients until smooth in a blender, then pour into the cooker.

Smaller	Ingredient	Larger
⅓ cup	raw cashews	⅔ cup
⅓ cup	water	⅔ cup

2nd Rinse the blender with the water in the following table. Add to the cooker.

Smaller	Ingredient	Larger
1⅓ cups	water	2⅔ cups

3rd Stir the remaining ingredients into the cooker. Cook until the rice is soft.

Smaller	Ingredient	Larger
⅓ cup	chopped, raw nuts, i.e. cashews, almonds, walnuts	⅔ cup
1 cup	uncooked quick (instant) brown rice	2 cups
4½ teaspoons	McKay's Chicken Seasoning or Chicken Seasoning, pg 136	3 tablespoons
2 teaspoons	onion powder	1½ tablespoons
1 tablespoon	chopped, fresh cilantro, optional	2 tablespoons
¼ teaspoon	salt	½ teaspoon
⅛ teaspoon	turmeric	¼ teaspoon

4th Stir in the peas. Cover and continue to cook 5 minutes.

Smaller	Ingredient	Larger
½ cup	frozen green peas	1 cup

5th Ready to serve.

BAKING TIME ON LOW:

Average Cooker: Smaller Recipe 1¾-2 hours OR Larger Recipe 2¼-2½ hours

Fast Cooker: Smaller Recipe 1¼-1½ hours OR Larger Recipe 2-2¼ hours

Extra Fast Cooker: Smaller Recipe 1-1¼ hours OR Larger Recipe 1¾-2 hours

(See page 25, #3, for an explanation of the 3 types of cookers.)

Tips

- The cooker may be plugged into a lamp/appliance timer, page 26, #4, to begin cooking up to 6 hours later.
- Make Ahead: Prepare Steps 1 and 2, then refrigerate. Mix ingredients in Step 3, except for the cilantro, in a storage container. Combine when ready to bake.

Bread Dressing

Smaller Recipe		Larger Recipe
YIELD: 5 cups COOKER SIZE: 2-4½ qt.	INGREDIENTS	YIELD: 7 cups COOKER SIZE: 5-6½ qt.

1st Sauté the following ingredients about 10 minutes on medium heat, until the onion and celery are soft.

1 cup	chopped onion	1½ cups
1 cup	chopped celery	1½ cups
2 tablespoons	olive oil	3 tablespoons

2nd Turn off the heat. Stir the following ingredients into the sauce pan.

1 cup	chopped, raw nuts, i.e. walnuts, pecans, cashews or almonds	1¼ cups
½ cup	water	¾ cup
¼ cup	yeast flakes, pg 10	½ cup
1 tablepoon	cornstarch	1½ tablespoons
1 tablespoon	onion powder	1½ tablespoons
1 teaspoon	garlic powder	1½ teaspoons
½ teaspoon	basil	¾ teaspoon
½ teaspoon	marjoram	¾ teaspoon
¼ teaspoon	rosemary	½ teaspoon
¼ teaspoon	thyme	½ teaspoon
¼ teaspoon	sage	½ teaspoon
¼ teaspoon	salt	¼ + ⅛ teaspoon

3rd Stir the following bread cubes in with the ingredients in the sauce pan. Spray the cooker with a food release cooking spray. Firmly pat the dressing into the cooker. Cover with a hand towel that has not been washed with fabric softener (the smell may permeate the dressing), or cover with 2 layers of paper towels. Cover with the lid. Cook until lightly browned on the edges.

6 cups	whole grain bread, cut into ½x½" cubes	9 cups

4th Serve as is, or with a gravy or white sauce, such as on page 101.

BAKING TIME ON LOW:

Average Cooker: Smaller Recipe 4-4¼ hours OR Larger Recipe 4¾-5 hours

Fast Cooker: Smaller Recipe 3-3¼ hours OR Larger Recipe 3¾-4 hours

Extra Fast Cooker: Smaller Recipe 1½-1¾ hours OR Larger Recipe 2-2¼ hours

(See page 25, #3, for an explanation of the 3 types of cookers.)

Tips

- The cooker may be plugged into a lamp/appliance timer, page 26, #4, to begin cooking up to 6 hours later.
- Make Ahead: Prepare Step 1 and refrigerate. Combine Step 2, except the water, in a storage container. Cube the bread and store in a plastic bag.
- While sautéing the vegetables you may add chopped water chestnuts, red pepper or pimento, or mushrooms .

Chickpea A La King

Smaller Recipe YIELD: 3¼ cups COOKER SIZE: 1½-4½ qt.	INGREDIENTS	Larger Recipe YIELD: 6½ cups COOKER SIZE: 2½-7 qt.

1st Blend the following ingredients in a blender for 2 minutes, until very smooth. Pour into the cooker.

Smaller Recipe	Ingredient	Larger Recipe
½ cup	water	1 cup
¼ cup	raw cashews	½ cup
¼ cup	quick or rolled oats	½ cup
1 tablespoon	McKay's Chicken Seasoning or Chicken Seasoning, pg 136	2 tablespoons
½ teaspoon	salt	1 teaspoon
1/16 teaspoon	turmeric, for color	⅛ teaspoon

2nd Rinse the blender with the water in the following ingredients. Add to the cooker. Stir the remaining following ingredients into the cooker. Cook until the carrots are tender crisp. The sauce should be boiling in various places around the edges of the cooker and thickened throughout.

Smaller Recipe	Ingredient	Larger Recipe
1 cup	water	2 cups
1 cup	shredded carrots	2 cups
1 cup	cooked, drained, garbanzo beans	1¾ cups or 15 oz. can
¼ cup	chopped onion	½ cup

3rd Stir in the peas. Turn off the cooker and let sit 5 minutes.

Smaller Recipe	Ingredient	Larger Recipe
1 cup	frozen peas	2 cups

4th Ready to serve. Serve over rice, potatoes, toast, cous cous or other pasta. See photo on page 72.

COOKING TIME IF COOKING ON LOW:

Average Cooker: Smaller Recipe 5-5½ hours OR Larger Recipe 6-6½ hours

Fast Cooker: Smaller Recipe 4¼-4¾ hours OR Larger Recipe 4¾-5¼ hours

Extra Fast Cooker: Smaller Recipe 3¾-4¼ hours OR Larger Recipe 4¼-4¾ hours

COOKING TIME IF COOKING ON HIGH:

Average Cooker: Smaller Recipe 2½-3 hours OR Larger Recipe 3-3½ hours

Fast Cooker: Smaller Recipe 2-2½ hours OR Larger Recipe 2½-3 hours

Extra Fast Cooker: Smaller Recipe 1¾-2¼ hours OR Larger Recipe 2¼-2¾ hours

(See page 25, #3, for an explanation of the 3 types of cookers.)

Tips

- For a quick preparation use 2 cups of frozen, mixed vegetables in place of the carrots, onion and peas for the Smaller Recipe, or 4 cups for the Larger Recipe. Cook the vegetables. Add at Step 3, in place of the peas.
- Use other varieties of cooked beans or use Chunky Fried Tofu, page 136, in place of the garbanzo beans.
- The cooker may be plugged into a lamp/appliance timer, page 26, #4, to begin cooking up to 6 hours later.
- Make Ahead: Prepare Step 1, add the water from Step 2, then refrigerate. Combine the vegetables in Step 2 and refrigerate in a storage container. Combine when ready to cook. Add 20-30 minutes to cooking time, unless waiting at least 2 hours before cooking, to take the chill off the ingredients. May also prepare ahead what the gravy will be served over.
- Reheat on Another Day: Reheat on low about 1½-2 hours for the Smaller Recipe, or 2½-3 hours for the Larger Recipe. Add the peas at the end in order for them to remain a bright green color.

Chunky Fried Tofu Gravy & Rice

Smaller Recipe		Larger Recipe
YIELD: 3½ cups COOKER SIZE: 1½-4½ qt.	INGREDIENTS	YIELD: 7 cups COOKER SIZE: 3-7 qt.

1st Blend the following ingredients in a blender for 2 minutes, until very smooth. Pour into the cooker.

Smaller Recipe	Ingredient	Larger Recipe
½ cup	water	1 cup
¼ cup + 2 tablespoons	raw cashews	¾ cup
3 tablespoons	quick or rolled oats	⅓ cup
1 tablespoon	onion powder	2 tablespoons
1 tablespoon	yeast flakes, pg 10, optional	2 tablespoons
1¼ teaspoons	salt	2½ teaspoons
½ teaspoon	garlic powder	1 teaspoon
⅛ teaspoon	turmeric, for color	¼ teaspoon

2nd Rinse the blender with the water in the following table. Add to the cooker. Cook until the sauce is boiling in various places around the edges of the cooker and thickened throughout.

Smaller Recipe	Ingredient	Larger Recipe
1½ cups	water	3 cups

3rd Stir the following into the cooker. Turn off the cooker and let sit 5 minutes.

Smaller Recipe	Ingredient	Larger Recipe
2 cups or ½#	frozen vegetables i.e. brussel sprouts or broccoli, cooked	4 cups or 1#
½-1 recipe	Chunky Fried Tofu, pg 136	1 recipe

4th Serve over rice, potatoes, corn grits, toast, cous cous or other pasta. See photo on back cover.

COOKING TIME IF COOKING ON LOW:

Average Cooker: Smaller Recipe 4-4½ hours OR Larger Recipe 4¼-4¾ hours

Fast Cooker: Smaller Recipe 3¼-3¾ hours OR Larger Recipe 4-4½ hours

Extra Fast Cooker: Smaller Recipe 2¾-3¼ hours OR Larger Recipe 3½-4 hours

COOKING TIME IF COOKING ON HIGH:

Average Cooker: Smaller Recipe 1¾-2¼ hours OR Larger Recipe 2¼-2¾ hours

Fast Cooker: Smaller Recipe 1½-2 hours OR Larger Recipe 1¾-2¼ hours

Extra Fast Cooker: Smaller Recipe 1¼-1¾ hours OR Larger Recipe 1½-2 hours

(See page 25, #3, for an explanation of the 3 types of cookers.)

Tips

- The cooker may be plugged into a lamp/appliance timer, page 26, #4, to begin cooking up to 6 hours later.
- Make Ahead: Prepare Step 1, add the water from Step 2, then refrigerate. Combine the vegetables and tofu in Step 3 and refrigerate in a storage container until ready to add to the cooked gravy. Add 20-30 minutes to cooking time, unless waiting at least 2 hours before cooking, to take the chill off the ingredients. May also prepare ahead what the gravy will be served over.
- Reheat on Another Day: Reheat on low about 1½-2 hours for the Smaller Recipe, or 2½-3 hours for the Larger Recipe. Add the vegetables at the end of the reheating.

Pasta Fagioli

Smaller Recipe		Larger Recipe
YIELD: 3 cups COOKER SIZE: 2-4 qt.	INGREDIENTS	YIELD: 7 cups COOKER SIZE: 3½-7 qt.

1st Sort through the beans, looking for small clumps of dirt and stones. Cover the beans with water, rinse then drain. Stir the following ingredients into the cooker. Cook on low until the beans are soft.

Smaller Recipe	Ingredients	Larger Recipe
1½ cups	water	3 cups
¾ cup + 2 tablespoons	dried navy beans	1⅔ cups
½ cup	chopped onion	1 cup
½ cup	chopped celery	1 cup
½ cup	sliced, black olives	1 cup
1½ teaspoons	extra virgin olive oil, optional, but great taste	1 tablespoon
¼ + ⅛ teaspoon	salt	¾ teaspoon

2nd Crush the basil in the following table between your fingers. Crushing the basil releases more immediate flavor, which is ideal for brief cooking. Stir the following ingredients in the cooker. Turn off the cooker.

Smaller Recipe	Ingredients	Larger Recipe
½ cup	frozen green peas	1 cup
1 tablespoon	finely chopped, fresh parsley or spinach, optional	2 tablespoons
4 teaspoons	McKay's Chicken Seasoning or Chicken Seasoning pg 136	2 tablespoons + 2 tsp.
¼ teaspoon	basil	½ teaspoon

3rd Cook the macaroni in the following table on the stove while the beans are cooking. Stir the macaroni in the cooker. Let sit 5 minutes.

Smaller Recipe	Ingredients	Larger Recipe
¾ cup + 2 tablespoons	uncooked macaroni, preferably whole wheat	1¾ cups

4th Ready to serve. If the recipe is too thick add ¼-½ cup of water.

COOKING TIME ON LOW:

Average Cooker: Smaller Recipe 7½-8 hours OR Larger Recipe 8½-9 hours

Fast Cooker: Smaller Recipe 5-5½ hours OR Larger Recipe 6-6½ hours

Extra Fast Cooker: Smaller Recipe 4-4½ hours OR Larger Recipe 5-5½ hours

(See page 25, #3, for an explanation of the 3 types of cookers.)

Tips

- The cooker may be plugged into a lamp/appliance timer, page 26, #4, to begin cooking up to 6 hours later.
- Make Ahead: Prepare and refrigerate the onion, celery and olives in Step 1. Cook and refrigerate the macaroni in Step 3. Assemble when ready to cook.
- Reheat on Another Day: Stir in a small amount of water if needed. Reheat on low about 2-2½ hours for the Smaller Recipe, or 3-3½ hours for the Larger Recipe. Add the peas and parsley at the end of the reheating for a brighter green color.

Pasta Alfredo

Smaller Recipe		Larger Recipe
YIELD: 4¼ cups COOKER SIZE: 2-4 qt.	INGREDIENTS	YIELD: 8½ cups COOKER SIZE: 3-7 qt.

1st Blend the following ingredients in a blender for 2 minutes, until very smooth. Pour into the cooker.

½ cup	water	1 cup
⅓ cup	raw cashews or blanched (white) almonds, pg 137	⅔ cup
3 tablespoons	quick or rolled oats	⅓ cup
3 tablespoons	yeast flakes, pg 10	⅓ cup
3 tablespoons	lemon juice	⅓ cup
1½ teaspoons	onion powder	1 tablespoon
1¼ teaspoons	salt	2½ teaspoons
1 teaspoon	garlic powder	2 teaspoons
1/16 teaspoon	turmeric, for color	⅛ teaspoon

2nd Rinse the blender with the water in the following table. Add to the cooker. Add the remaining following ingredients. Cook until the sauce is lightly boiling in a few places around the edges of the cooker.

2½ cups	water	5 cups
¾ cup	shredded or thinly chopped or sliced carrots	1½ cups
½ cup	chopped onion	1 cup
½ cup	sliced, black olives	1 cup

3rd Turn on high. Stir in the noodles. Cook for 15 minutes.

¼# or approx. 2¾ cups	uncooked flat noodles (egg-free egg noodles), i.e. whole wheat	½# or approx. 5½ cups

4th Turn off the cooker. Stir in the spinach. Let sit 5 minutes.

½ cup	finely chopped, fresh spinach	1 cup

5th Ready to serve. See photo on page 69.

COOKING TIME FOR SAUCE TO COME TO A LIGHT BOIL IF COOKING ON LOW:

Average Cooker: Smaller Recipe 5½-6 hours OR Larger Recipe 7½-8 hours

Fast Cooker: Smaller Recipe 3¾-4¼ hours OR Larger Recipe 4¼-4¾ hours

Extra Fast Cooker: Smaller Recipe 3¼-3¾ hours OR Larger Recipe 4-4½ hours

COOKING TIME FOR SAUCE TO COME TO A LIGHT BOIL IF COOKING ON HIGH:

Average Cooker: Smaller Recipe 1¾-2 hours OR Larger Recipe 3½-4 hours

Fast Cooker: Smaller Recipe 1½-2 hours OR Larger Recipe 2½-3 hours

Extra Fast Cooker: Smaller Recipe 1¼-1¾ hours OR Larger Recipe 2¼-2¾ hours

(See page 25, #3, for an explanation of the 3 types of cookers.)

Tips

- The cooker may be plugged into a lamp/appliance timer, page 26, #4, to begin cooking up to 6 hours later.
- Make Ahead: Prepare Step 1, add the water from Step 2 and refrigerate. Prepare and refrigerate the carrots, onion and olives in Step 2. Measure the noodles. Assemble when ready to cook.

Easy Does It Spaghetti

Smaller Recipe		Larger Recipe
YIELD: 4½ cups with burger COOKER SIZE: 2-5 qt.	INGREDIENTS	YIELD: 9 cups with burger COOKER SIZE: 3½-7 qt.

1st Stir the following ingredients into the cooker. Cook until lightly boiling in a few places around the edges.

1¼ cups	spaghetti sauce	2½ cups
1½ cups	water	3 cups
⅓ cup	tomato paste	6 oz. can or ⅔ cup

2nd Break the spaghetti into thirds. This makes it easier to add. After the sauce has begun to lightly boil, stir in the spaghetti. This should be done quickly but thoroughly, in order to retain heat in the sauce. When adding the spaghetti, stir it well so that it will not stick together while cooking. Turn the cooker on *high*. Cook 35 minutes. (If using an "average cooker" on low and it is not boiling at all after the time listed below, but it is steaming hot, turn it on high and add the spaghetti. If it is not steaming, turn it on high and wait about 30 minutes for it to get steaming hot then add the spaghetti.)

4 oz. or ¼#	uncooked spaghetti, preferably whole wheat	½# or 8 oz.

3rd Prepare the burger following the directions below. Stir in after the spaghetti is cooked. Turn off the cooker.

1 cup	browned, crumbled vegetarian burger, opt. see tip below	2 cups

4th Stir the ingredients, making sure none of the spaghetti is sticking together. Let sit 5-10 minutes, uncovered, for the sauce to thicken. Serve as is, or with a cheese sauce, such as on page 102.

COOKING TIME FOR SAUCE TO COME TO A LIGHT BOIL IF COOKING ON LOW:

Average Cooker: Smaller Recipe 8-8½ hours OR Larger Recipe 9-9½ hours

Fast Cooker: Smaller Recipe 4¾-5¼ hours OR Larger Recipe 5½-6 hours

Extra Fast Cooker: Smaller Recipe 4¼-4¾ hours OR Larger Recipe 5-5½ hours

COOKING TIME FOR SAUCE TO COME TO A LIGHT BOIL IF COOKING ON HIGH:

Average Cooker: Smaller Recipe 2¼-2¾ hours OR Larger Recipe 2½-3 hours

Fast Cooker: Smaller Recipe 2-2½ hours OR Larger Recipe 2¼-2¾ hours

Extra Fast Cooker: Smaller Recipe 1¾-2¼ hours OR Larger Recipe 1¾-2¼ hours

(See page 25, #3, for an explanation of the 3 types of cookers.)

Tips

Vegetarian burger may come from a variety of sources:

- If using a commercial frozen patty, such as vegan Boca Burgers or Morningstar patties or commercial canned patties, such as from Cedar Lake or Loma Linda, they should be browned then crumbled. Commercial ground burger is also available canned or frozen. Follow package directions for browning.
- Try your homemade gluten recipe or the Tender Gluten, page 58. Cut it into small pieces or chop in a food processor. Meatballs, such as Tender Gluten Meatballs, page 58, may be added after the spaghetti is cooked.
- May also use Soy Curls or Soy Add-Ums. These are a dried textured vegetable protein products (TVP). Add 1 cup of the TVP with ¾ cup water and ¼ teaspoon salt for the Smaller Recipe, or 2 cups of the TVP with 1½ cups water and ½ teaspoon salt for the Larger Recipe. Add to the cooker when adding the spaghetti.
- The cooker may be plugged into a lamp/appliance timer, page 26, #4, to begin cooking up to 6 hours later.
- Reheat on Another Day: Stir in ½-1½ cups of water depending on how much spaghetti is being reheated. Heat 4-6 cups of spaghetti 2-2½ hours on low. Heat 8-13 cups 3½-4 hours on low.

Garden Style Spaghetti

Smaller Recipe		Larger Recipe
YIELD: 6½ cups with burger COOKER SIZE: 2½-5 qt.	INGREDIENTS	YIELD: 13 cups with burger COOKER SIZE: 3½-7 qt.

1st Stir the following ingredients into the cooker. Cook until lightly boiling in a few places around the edges. Carrots take the longest to cook so cut them small. A food processor works great for carrots and onions.

Smaller Recipe	Ingredients	Larger Recipe
2½ cups	water	5 cups
1 cup	finely chopped carrots	2 cups
¾ cup + 2 tablespoons	chopped or diced, canned tomatoes with juice	14.5 oz. can or 1¾ cups
¾ cup	chopped onion	1½ cups
⅔ cup or 6 oz. can	tomato paste	12 oz. can or 1⅓ cups
1 tablespoon	cane juice crystals, sucanat, fructose, sugar or honey	2 tablespoons
1 teaspoon	salt	2 teaspoons

2nd Break the spaghetti into thirds. This makes it easier to add. Prepare the burger. See page 50 , Easy Does It Spaghetti, for burger options. Pre measure the following herbs into a dish, then add after the sauce has begun to lightly boil. This should be done quickly but thoroughly. Stir the spaghetti well so that it does not stick together while cooking. Turn the cooker on *high*. Cook 35 minutes. (If you are using an "average cooker" on low and it is not boiling after the time listed below, but it is steaming hot, turn it on high and add the spaghetti. If it is not steaming, turn it on high and wait for about 30 minutes for it to get steaming hot, then add the spaghetti.)

Smaller Recipe	Ingredients	Larger Recipe
4 oz. or ¼#	uncooked spaghetti, preferably whole wheat	½# or 8 oz.
1 cup	browned, crumbled vegetarian burger, opt. see tip on pg 50	2 cups
¾ teaspoon	basil	1½ teaspoons
½ teaspoon	marjoram	1 teaspoon
¼ teaspoon	oregano	½ teaspoon

3rd Turn off the cooker. Stir the ingredients, making sure none of the spaghetti is sticking together. If you would like an extra hint of flavor, mince 2 or 3 cloves of garlic and fresh herbs, such as basil, to add at this time. Let sit 5-10 minutes, uncovered, for the sauce to thicken. Serve as is, or with Cheese Sauce, page 102. See photo on page 75.

COOKING TIME FOR SAUCE TO COME TO A LIGHT BOIL IF COOKING ON LOW:
Average Cooker: Smaller Recipe 7-7½ hours OR Larger Recipe 7½-8 hours
Fast Cooker: Smaller Recipe 4½-5 hours OR Larger Recipe 5½-6 hours
Extra Fast Cooker: Smaller Recipe 4-4½ hours OR Larger Recipe 5-5½ hours
COOKING TIME FOR SAUCE TO COME TO A LIGHT BOIL IF COOKING ON HIGH:
Average Cooker: Smaller Recipe 2¾-3¼ hours OR Larger Recipe 3½-4 hours
Fast Cooker: Smaller Recipe 2½-3 hours OR Larger Recipe 3¼-3¾ hours
Extra Fast Cooker: Smaller Recipe 2-2½ hours OR Larger Recipe 3-3½ hours
(See page 25, #3, for an explanation of the 3 types of cookers.)

Tips
- The cooker may be plugged into a lamp/appliance timer, page 26, #4, to begin cooking up to 6 hours later.
- Make Ahead: Mix together all but the water in Step 1 and refrigerate. Prepare burger and measure pasta.
- Reheat on Another Day: Stir in ½-1½ cups of water depending on how much spaghetti is being reheated. Heat 4-6 cups of spaghetti 2-2½ hours on low. Heat 8-13 cups 3½-4 hours on low.

Macaroni & Cheese #1

Smaller Recipe		Larger Recipe
YIELD: 4 cups COOKER SIZE: 2-4½ qt.	INGREDIENTS	YIELD: 8 cups COOKER SIZE: 3½-7 qt.

1st Blend the following ingredients in a blender for 1 minute, until very smooth. Pour into the cooker.

Smaller Recipe	Ingredient	Larger Recipe
½ cup	water	1 cup
½ cup	quick or rolled oats	1 cup
⅓ cup	yeast flakes, pg 10	⅔ cup
¼ cup	pimento	½ cup or 4 oz.
3 tablespoons	lemon juice	⅓ cup
1 tablespoon	onion powder	2 tablespoons
1¼ + ⅛ teaspoons	salt	2¾ teaspoons

2nd Rinse the blender with the water in the following table. Add to the cooker. Add the oil. Cook until boiling in a few places around the edges. (The oil is stirred in so that the blender won't be oily. This makes for quicker cleaning of the blender.)

Smaller Recipe	Ingredient	Larger Recipe
2¾ cups	water	5⅓ cups
3 tablespoons	mild tasting olive oil or canola oil	⅓ cup

3rd Stir in the macaroni. This should be done quickly but thoroughly, in order to retain heat in the sauce. Turn the cooker on *high*. Cook for 40 minutes. (If you are using an "average cooker" on low, and it is not boiling after the time listed below, but is steaming hot, turn it on high and add the macaroni. If it is not steaming, turn it on high and wait for about 30 minutes for it to get steaming hot, then add the macaroni.)

Smaller Recipe	Ingredient	Larger Recipe
1½ cups	uncooked macaroni, preferably whole wheat	3 cups

4th Turn off the cooker. Thoroughly stir the ingredients with a fork, making sure none of the macaroni is sticking together. Let sit 10 minutes, uncovered, for the cheese to thicken. See photo on page 73.

COOKING TIME FOR SAUCE TO COME TO A LIGHT BOIL IF COOKING ON LOW:

Average Cooker: Smaller Recipe 5-5½ hours OR Larger Recipe 6½-7 hours

Fast Cooker: Smaller Recipe 4¼-4¾ hours OR Larger Recipe 4½-5 hours

Extra Fast Cooker: Smaller Recipe 4-4½ hours OR Larger Recipe 4¼-4¾ hours

COOKING TIME FOR SAUCE TO COME TO A LIGHT BOIL IF COOKING ON HIGH:

Average Cooker: Smaller Recipe 2½-3 hours OR Larger Recipe 4-4½ hours

Fast Cooker: Smaller Recipe 2-2½ hours OR Larger Recipe 2¼-2¾ hours

Extra Fast Cooker: Smaller Recipe 1¾-2¼ hours OR Larger Recipe 2-2½ hours

(See page 25, #3, for an explanation of the 3 types of cookers.)

Tips

- The cooker may be plugged into a lamp/appliance timer, page 26, #4, to begin cooking up to 6 hours later.
- Make Ahead: Prepare Step 1 and refrigerate. Measure pasta. Assemble when ready to cook.
- Reheat on Another Day: Heat 4-6 cups of macaroni & cheese 2-2½ hours on low. Heat 8-12 cups 3½-4 hours on low. Stir in ½-1½ cups of water at the beginning or while reheating to make the sauce more smooth.

Macaroni & Cheese #2

Smaller Recipe		Larger Recipe
YIELD: 3¾ cups COOKER SIZE: 2-4½ qt.	INGREDIENTS	YIELD: 7½ cups COOKER SIZE: 3½-7 qt.

1st Blend the following ingredients in a blender for 2 minutes, until very smooth. Pour into the cooker.

Smaller Recipe	Ingredients	Larger Recipe
½ cup	water	1 cup
½ cup	raw cashews or blanched (white) almonds, pg 137	1 cup
⅓ cup	yeast flakes, pg 10	⅔ cup
¼ cup	quick or rolled oats	½ cup
¼ cup	pimento	½ cup or 4 oz.
3 tablespoons	lemon juice	⅓ cup
1 tablespoon	onion powder	2 tablespoons
1 teaspoon	garlic powder	2 teaspoons
1⅛ teaspoons	salt	2¼ teaspoons

2nd Rinse the blender with the water in the following table. Add to the cooker. Cook until the sauce is lightly boiling in a few places around the edges of the cooker.

Smaller Recipe	Ingredients	Larger Recipe
2½ cups	water	5 cups

3rd Stir in the macaroni. This should be done quickly but thoroughly, in order to retain heat in the sauce. Turn the cooker on *high* and cook 40 minutes. (If you are using an "average cooker" on low, and it is not boiling after the time listed below, but is steaming hot, turn it on high and add the macaroni. If it is not steaming, turn it on high and wait for about 30 minutes for it to get steaming hot, then add the macaroni.)

Smaller Recipe	Ingredients	Larger Recipe
1¼ cups	uncooked macaroni, preferably whole wheat	2½ cups

4th Turn off the cooker. Thoroughly stir the ingredients with a fork, making sure none of the macaroni is sticking together. Let sit 10 minutes, uncovered, for the cheese to thicken.

COOKING TIME FOR SAUCE TO COME TO A LIGHT BOIL IF COOKING ON LOW:

Average Cooker: Smaller Recipe 5-5½ hours OR Larger Recipe 7½-8 hours

Fast Cooker: Smaller Recipe 3½-4 hours OR Larger Recipe 5-5½ hours

Extra Fast Cooker: Smaller Recipe 2½-3 hours OR Larger Recipe 4½-5 hours

COOKING TIME FOR SAUCE TO COME TO A LIGHT BOIL IF COOKING ON HIGH:

Average Cooker: Smaller Recipe 2-2½ hours OR Larger Recipe 4¼-4¾ hours

Fast Cooker: Smaller Recipe 2-2½ hours OR Larger Recipe 3-3½ hours

Extra Fast Cooker: Smaller Recipe 1¾-2¼ hours OR Larger Recipe 2½-3 hours

(See page 25, #3, for an explanation of the 3 types of cookers.)

Tips

- The cooker may be plugged into a lamp/appliance timer, page 26, #4 to begin cooking up to 6 hours later.
- Make Ahead: Prepare Step 1 and refrigerate. Measure pasta. Assemble when ready to cook.
- Reheat on Another Day: Heat 4-6 cups of macaroni & cheese 2-2½ hours on low. Heat 8-12 cups 3½-4 hours on low. Stir in ½-1½ cups of water at the beginning or while reheating to make the sauce more smooth.

Stuffed Shells

Smaller Recipe Cooker Size: 2½-4½ qt. Yield: 8-13	INGREDIENTS	Larger Recipe Cooker Size: 5-7 qt. Yield: 14-18 shells

1st Boil the shells for 4 minutes then drain. The cooked shells may be used now or refrigerated for later use.

Smaller	Ingredient	Larger
8-13	jumbo stuffing shells, preferably whole wheat	14-18

2nd Blend smooth the following ingredients in a blender. (If you happen to be using Mori Nu tofu, in a 12.3 oz. box, it contains 1½ cups of tofu).

Smaller	Ingredient	Larger
¾ cup	firm or extra firm tofu	1½ cups
¼ cup	raw cashews	½ cup
1 tablespoon	lemon juice	2 tablespoons
1 tablespoon	water	2 tablespoons

3rd Mix the following ingredients with the blended ingredients. The Smaller Recipe will fill about 15 shells, the Larger about 30. Fill the shells until the edges at the top are touching or slightly overlapped.

Smaller	Ingredient	Larger
½ of a 10 oz. box	thawed (with juice squeezed out), frozen spinach, optional	10 oz. box
¾ cup	mashed, firm or extra firm tofu	1½ cups
1½ teaspoons	onion powder	1 tablespoon
1½ teaspoons	dried parsley	1 tablespoon
1½ teaspoons	cane juice crystals, sucanat, fructose, honey or sugar	1 tablespoon
1 teaspoon	salt	2 teaspoons
1 teaspoon	basil	2 teaspoons
½ teaspoon	garlic powder	1 teaspoon

4th Stir the following ingredients in the cooker. Place the shells in the sauce. They will be covered, or mostly covered, with the sauce. Cook until bubbly.

Smaller	Ingredient	Larger
2¼ cups	spaghetti sauce	2¾ cups
½ cup	water	¾ cup

5th Let sit 5 minutes. Serve as is, or open the shells and add a small amount of leftover tofu mixture for a pretty garnish. The leftover tofu makes a delicious sandwich filling or use in a number of other ways such as on baked potatoes, crackers, or as a stuffing in fresh tomatoes. See photo on page 67.

COOKING TIME ON LOW:

Average Cooker: Smaller Recipe OR Larger Recipe 3¼-3½ hours

Fast Cooker: Smaller Recipe OR Larger Recipe 2¾-3 hours

Extra Fast Cooker: Smaller Recipe OR Larger Recipe 2½-2¾ hours

(See page 25, #3, for an explanation of the 3 types of cookers.)

Tips

- The cooker may be plugged into a lamp/appliance timer, page 26, #4, to begin cooking up to 4 hours later.
- Make Ahead: Prepare Steps 1-3. Refrigerate until ready to cook. Even if the shells are not stuffed they may be cooked ahead and refrigerated. Prepare the tofu filling, as well, and refrigerate.

Vegetable Lasagna

Smaller Recipe		Larger Recipe
Cooker Size: 3½-5 qt. Yield: 5¼ cups	INGREDIENTS	Cooker Size: 5-7 qt. Yield: 10½ cups

1st Boil the noodles for 5 minutes. I find them easier to handle if they are in 6-9" pieces. Smaller pieces work fine as well. Lay all the cooked noodles in a single layer on a cookie sheet covered with wax paper. There are 4 layers of noodles in the recipe, so divide the noodles into 4 fairly equal portions. Note: The noodles may also be refrigerated for later use. Single layers of noodles and wax paper may be stacked on top of each other.

Smaller	Ingredient	Larger
¼#	uncooked lasagna noodles, preferably whole wheat	½#

2nd (For the Larger Recipe reserve ¼ cup of the olives in the following table for garnish.) Mix together the following ingredients. (If you happen to be using Mori Nu tofu, in a 12.3 oz. box, it contains 1½ cups of tofu).

Smaller	Ingredient	Larger
¾ cup	mashed, firm or extra firm tofu	1½ cups
½ cup	sliced, black olives	6 oz. can
½ of a 10 oz. box	thawed (with juice squeezed out), frozen spinach	10 oz. box
1 tablespoon	lemon juice	2 tablespoons
1½ teaspoons	onion powder	1 tablespoon
1 teaspoon	garlic powder	2 teaspoons
⅛ teaspoon	salt	¼ teaspoon

3rd Spread ½ cup of the following spaghetti sauce in the cooker for the Smaller Recipe. Use 1 cup for the Larger Recipe. Top with one of the four portions of noodles. Follow with the same amount of spaghetti sauce then add the tofu mixture. For the tofu mixture, use ⅓ cup for the Smaller Recipe, or ¾ cup for the Larger Recipe. Continue by adding the same portions of noodles, spaghetti sauce, tofu mixture, noodles, spaghetti sauce, tofu mixture, etc. After the last portion of noodles, top with the remaining sauce and the remaining tofu mixture.

Smaller	Ingredient	Larger
2½ cups	spaghetti sauce	5 cups

4th Add the cheese, then sprinkle on the olives. Bake until bubbly around the edges.

Smaller	Ingredient	Larger
½-¾ cup	Cheese Sauce, pg 102 or commercial, shredded, veggie cheese	1-1½ cups
¼ cup	sliced, black olives	¼ cup (reserved from above)

5th Let sit 10 minutes, then serve. See photo on bake cover.

BAKING TIME ON LOW:

Average Cooker: Smaller Recipe 5-5½ hours OR Larger Recipe 5½-6 hours

Fast Cooker: Smaller Recipe 4-4½ hours OR Larger Recipe 5-5½ hours

Extra Fast Cooker: Smaller Recipe 3¼-3¾ hours OR Larger Recipe 4½-5 hours

(See page 25, #3, for an explanation of the 3 types of cookers.)

Tips

- The cooker may be plugged into a lamp/appliance timer, page 26, #4, to begin cooking up to 4 hours later.
- Make Ahead: Prepare Steps 1 and 2, then refrigerate. Or, assemble the recipe in the slow cooker crock and refrigerated until ready to bake. In either case add about 20-40 minutes to the cooking time unless the recipe sits out at least 2 hours before turning on the cooker.
- Bake in a Dish Inside the Cooker: Choose a dish, such as an 8" round cake pan, that will fit on a trivet in a 6-7 qt. cooker. Spray with a food release cooking spray. Assemble the Smaller Recipe, breaking the noodles to fit. Bake 5 hours on low in an Extra Fast Cooker. Add 30-60 minutes if baking in a Fast or Average Cooker.

Goulash

Smaller Recipe		Larger Recipe
YIELD: 3½ cups COOKER SIZE: 1½-4 qt.	INGREDIENTS	YIELD: 7 cups COOKER SIZE: 3½-7 qt.

1st Bring the water in the following table to a boil. Cook the macaroni 10 minutes, then drain.

Smaller Recipe	Ingredient	Larger Recipe
2 cups	water	4 cups
¾ cup	uncooked macaroni, preferably whole wheat	1½ cups

2nd There are several options for the vegetarian burger in the following table. Commercial frozen patties, such as vegan Boca Burgers or Morningstar patties or commercial canned patties, such as from Cedar Lake or Loma Linda may be used. They should be browned, then crumbled by hand or chopped in a food processor. Commercial ground burger is also available canned or frozen. Follow the package directions for browning. Or, try your favorite homemade gluten recipe or the Tender Gluten, page 58. Chop it in a food processor. Mix the burger with the following ingredients, then gently stir in the macaroni. Empty into a cooker and cook until bubbly.

Smaller Recipe	Ingredient	Larger Recipe
1½ cups	browned, crumbled, vegetarian burger	3 cups
¾ cup + 2 tablespoons	tomato sauce	1¾ cups or 15 oz. can
¾ cup + 2 tablespoons	chopped or diced, canned tomatoes with juice	1¾ cups or 14.5 oz. can
¾ cup	cooked, drained, kidney beans	1¾ cups or 15 oz. can
½ cup	chopped onion	1 cup
¼ cup	tomato paste	½ cup
1½ tablespoons	cornstarch	3 tablespoons

3rd May garnish with sliced green onion, then serve. See photo on page 72.

COOKING TIME ON LOW:

Average Cooker: Smaller Recipe 3-3½ hours OR Larger Recipe 3½-4 hours

Fast Cooker: Smaller Recipe 2-2½ hours OR Larger Recipe 2½-3 hours

Extra Fast Cooker: Smaller Recipe 1½-2 hours OR Larger Recipe 2-2½ hours

(See page 25, #3, for an explanation of the 3 types of cookers.)

Tips

- The cooker may be plugged into a lamp/appliance timer, page 26, #4, to begin cooking up to 6 hours later.
- Make Ahead: Prepare Step 1, then mix with ingredients in Step 2. Refrigerate in a storage container until ready to cook. Add 20-40 minutes to the cooking time, unless waiting at least 2 hours before cooking to take the chill off the food.
- Reheat on Another Day: Heat the Smaller Recipe on low 2-2½ hours, or 3-3½ hours for the Larger Recipe.

Grape Leaf Tofu Rolls

Smaller Recipe		Larger Recipe
YIELD: 8 pieces COOKER SIZE: 2-5 qt.	INGREDIENTS	YIELD: 16 pieces COOKER SIZE: 5-7 qt.

1st Rinse the tofu, then press it firmly but gently between paper towels. Cut the tofu into 16 pieces. This is done by cutting it into quarters then cutting each quarter into 4 pieces. Set the tofu pieces on paper towel, cover with paper towel, then gently press to get out more of the water.

7-8 oz.	firm or extra firm, water packed tofu	14-16 oz.

2nd Spray a nonstick skillet with a food release cooking spray. Preheat on medium heat. Mix the following ingredients in a small bowl. Lightly pat all sides of the tofu in the mixture. Set the tofu on the hot skillet, then sprinkle on the remaining yeast flake mixture. Fry tofu on 4 sides until golden brown, 3-4 minutes on each side.

2 tablespoons	yeast flakes, pg 10	¼ cup
1 teaspoon	onion powder	2 teaspoons
½ teaspoon	garlic powder	1 teaspoon
⅛ teaspoon	salt	¼ teaspoon

3rd Find grape leaves at some specialty food stores and health food stores. They are canned in a salt brine. Cut off the stems. Place a tofu cube in the center, at the bottom of a leaf. Roll up once. Fold the sides of the leaf toward the center, over the tofu. Continue to roll. Two small leaves may be over lapped to serve as one.

8	grape leaves	16

4th Place the rolls in *one* layer in the cooker. Mix together the following, then drizzle over the rolls and cook.

1 cup	water	2 cups
1 tablespoon	lemon juice	2 tablespoons

5th Serve as is, or with Tofu Sour Cream, page 136, or Cheese Sauce page 102. See photo on page 80.

COOKING TIME ON LOW: (Cook one hour less if using collard leaves.)

Average Cooker: Smaller Recipe OR Larger Recipe 7½ hours

Fast Cooker: Smaller Recipe OR Larger Recipe 7 hours

Extra Fast Cooker: Smaller Recipe OR Larger Recipe 7 hours

(See 25, #3, for an explanation of the 3 types of cookers.)

Tips
- The cooker may be plugged into a lamp/appliance timer, page 26, #4, to begin cooking up to 4 hours later.
- Make Ahead: Prepare Steps 1-3. Refrigerate until ready to cook.
- Unused grape leaves may be drained and frozen in bags. Freeze in amounts that are likely to be used at one time.

Collard Leaf Tofu Rolls

Cut off the stalk. Leaves should be 8-12". Steam 2 minutes, until bright green and limp. Cut out ¾ or more of the middle rib that runs up the middle of the leaves. This is for easy rolling. Over lap the two cut sides ½" where the rib was removed. Place the tofu in the center at the bottom. Roll the tofu up 1 or 2 times, then fold the sides of the leaf over the tofu and continue to roll. Ragged ends at the tip may be cut off. Leaves may be patched if there is not quite enough to roll. Add ½ teaspoon of salt in the water for the Smaller Recipe and 1 teaspoon of salt for the Larger. Cook 1 hour less then if using grape leaves.

Tender Gluten

Smaller Recipe		Larger Recipe
YIELD: 4 cups COOKER SIZE: 2-4 qt.	INGREDIENTS	YIELD: 8 cups COOKER SIZE: 3½-7 qt.

1st Mix the following ingredients. (If using Mori Nu tofu, in a 12.3 oz. box, it contains 1½ cups of tofu).

Smaller Recipe	Ingredient	Larger Recipe
¾ cup	mashed, firm or extra firm tofu	1½ cups
¼ cup	quick or rolled oats, or raw wheat germ	½ cup
3 tablespoons	water	⅓ cup
2 tablespoons	yeast flakes, pg 10	¼ cup
2 tablespoons	Bragg Liquid Aminos, soy sauce or Soy Sauce, pg 136	¼ cup
1 tablespoon	onion powder	2 tablespoons
1½ teaspoons	basil	1 tablespoon
1 teaspoon	garlic powder	2 teaspoons
¾ teaspoon	sage	1½ teaspoons

2nd Mix in half of the flour in the following table, then add the remaining flour. Knead for a minute to mix well.

Smaller Recipe	Ingredient	Larger Recipe
1 cup	gluten flour	2 cups

3rd Choose *one* of the following gluten preparations:

- Meatballs- Pinch off 1½ tablespoons of dough, roll into a ball. Proceed to Step 4 for browning. Yield: 33 meatballs for the Larger Recipe. See photo on page 69, 75 and front cover.
- Patties- Pinch off 2 tablespoons of dough. Flatten into patties ¼" thick. Proceed to Step 4 for browning. Yield: 25 patties for the Larger Recipe.
- Strips- Make patties. After browning (Step 4), cut patties into 4-6 strips. Strips are ready for Step 5.

4th Browning: Spray a nonstick skillet with a food release cooking spray. Preheat on medium-low heat.

- Meatballs- Brown for 4-5 minutes on 4 sides.
- Patties- Brown on each side 5-7 minutes.

5th Choose one of the three following methods for cooking the gluten:

Method One: Tender Gluten Cooked in Broth

1st Stir together the following ingredients in the cooker. Add the gluten and cook. See the cooking time chart on the next page. The gluten may be served in the broth, but this method is more intended for adding the gluten to another recipe. See Serving Ideas below.

Smaller Recipe	Ingredient	Larger Recipe
2¼ cups	water	4½ cups
1½ tablespoons	Bragg Liquid Aminos, soy sauce or Soy Sauce, pg 136	3 tablespoons
1 tablespoon	yeast flakes, pg 10	2 tablespoons
1½ teaspoons	onion powder	1 tablespoon
1 teaspoon	garlic powder	2 teaspoons

Serving Ideas: Drain and use as is, or chop in a food processor. •With spaghetti •In a sandwich •Cut into pieces or strips and added to dishes such as soups, pasta, potatoes, rice •Serve with your favorite sauce or gravy •When chopped in a food processor it will look like ground burger for goulash, sloppy joes, on pizza, etc.

Method Two: Barbecued Gluten

1st Stir the following ingredients in the cooker. Add the gluten and cook. See the cooking time chart below.

Smaller Recipe		Larger Recipe
1¾ cups	water	3¼ cups
½ cup	chopped onion	1 cup
½ cup	tomato paste	1 cup
¼ cup + 2 tablespoons	lemon juice	¾ cup
¼ cup	sucanat, cane juice crystals, honey, fructose or sugar	½ cup
1 tablespoon	olive oil	2 tablespoons
1 tablespoon	molasses	2 tablespoons
1½ teaspoons	onion powder	1 tablespoon
1 teaspoon	garlic powder	2 teaspoons
1 teaspoon	salt	2 teaspoons

Method Three: Tender Gluten Cooked in Gravy

1st Blend the following ingredients with ½ cup of the water for the Smaller Recipe, or 1 cup for Larger Recipe. Add to the cooker. Rinse the blender with the remaining water. Add to the cooker with the gluten, stir then cook.

Smaller Recipe		Larger Recipe
3¼ cups	water	6½ cups
¼ cup + 2 tablespoons	raw cashews	¾ cup
¼ cup	quick or rolled oats	½ cup
2 tablespoons	Bragg Liquid Aminos, soy sauce or Soy Sauce, pg 136	¼ cup
1 tablespoon	onion powder	2 tablespoons
1 tablespoon	yeast flakes, pg 10	2 tablespoons
1 teaspoon	garlic powder	2 teaspoons
½ teaspoon	Hickory Seasoning Liquid Smoke, optional	1 teaspoon
⅛ teaspoon	salt	¼ teaspoon

COOKING TIME: (Reduce cooking time by 30 minutes if using the Smaller Recipe)

Average Cooker: 9 hours on Low OR 5 hours on High

Fast Cooker: 8½ hours on Low OR 4½ hours on High

Extra Fast Cooker: 8 hours on Low OR 4½ hours on High

(See 25, #3, for an explanation of the 3 types of cookers.)

Tips

- The cooker may be plugged into a lamp/appliance timer, page 26, #4, to begin cooking up to 4 hours later.
- Make Ahead: Gluten may be frozen or refrigerated after the browning stage, Step 4, until ready to cook.
- Reheat on Another Day: Reheat any of the three cooking methods, on low, about 2 hours for the Smaller Recipe, or 3 hours for the Larger Recipe.

Roast Beef-less

Divide the Smaller Recipe of dough into 2 balls, or 4 balls for the Larger Recipe. Spray a nonstick skillet with a food release cooking spray. Brown the balls on medium low heat 4-5 minutes at a time, turning 6 times. Cook in the Broth, page 58. Let the gluten cool, then slice in very thin slices. Serve in a sandwich or with gravy. Sliced Roast Beef-less may be reheated the next day with leftover gravy in a slow cooker. See photo on page 66.

Tortilla Bake

Smaller Recipe		Larger Recipe
YIELD: 4 cups COOKER SIZE: 2½-7 qt.	INGREDIENTS	YIELD: 8 cups COOKER SIZE: 3½-7 qt.

1st Stir together the following spaghetti sauce mixture.

Smaller Recipe	Ingredients	Larger Recipe
½ cup + 2 tablespoons	spaghetti sauce	1¼ cups
¼ cup	your favorite cheese sauce or Cheese Sauce, pg 102	½ cup

2nd Mix together the following tofu mixture. (If you happen to be using Mori Nu tofu, in a 12.3 oz. box, it contains 1½ cups of tofu).

Smaller Recipe	Ingredients	Larger Recipe
¾ cup	mashed, firm or extra firm tofu	1½ cups
½ cup	sliced or chopped, black olives	1 cup
1 tablespoon	lemon juice	2 tablespoons
1½ teaspoons	onion powder	1 tablespoon
1 teaspoon	garlic powder	2 teaspoons

3rd Spray the cooker with a food release cooking spray. Pour ¼ cup of the spaghetti sauce mixture in the middle of the cooker. (This applies to both the Smaller and Larger Recipe.) Lay one tortilla in the cooker. It may be torn to fit if necessary. If pieces are torn off they should be put in the cooker first, followed by the one full piece. Gently press down on the tortilla to spread the sauce out a little. Next spread on ¼ cup of the spaghetti sauce mixture. Follow with ½ cup of the tofu mixture then another tortilla. Continue the layering process.

After the 2nd tortilla (for the Smaller Recipe) or the 5th tortilla (for the Larger Recipe) spread the remaining tofu mixture. Top with the final tortilla and spread with the remaining spaghetti sauce mixture.

Smaller Recipe	Ingredients	Larger Recipe
3	8-8½" tortillas, preferably whole wheat	6

4th Top with the following olives and bake.

Smaller Recipe	Ingredients	Larger Recipe
¼ cup	sliced or chopped, black olives	¼ cup

5th Slice and serve.

BAKING TIME ON LOW:

Average Cooker: Smaller Recipe 3-3½ hours OR Larger Recipe 4-4½ hours

Fast Cooker: Smaller Recipe 2¼-2¾ hours OR Larger Recipe 3-3½ hours

Extra Fast Cooker: Smaller Recipe 1¾-2¼ hours OR Larger Recipe 2¼-2¾ hours

(See 25, #3, for an explanation of the 3 types of cookers.)

Tips

- The cooker may be plugged into a lamp/appliance timer, page 26, #4, to begin cooking up to 4 hours later.
- Make Ahead: Prepare Steps 1 and 2. Refrigerate in separate containers until ready to bake.

Pizza or Personal Pizza or Pita Pizza

Smaller Recipe		Larger Recipe
YIELD: 1 pizza COOKER SIZE: fit the crust	INGREDIENTS	YIELD: 1 pizza COOKER SIZE: fit the crust

1st Using a pre-baked crust or a whole wheat pita bread, add the following ingredients, then place the crust into the cooker. For the pita bread or the personal pizza use the Smaller Recipe.

Smaller Recipe	Personal Pizza Crust pg 118, or Pita Bread, or Pizza Crust pg 117	Larger Recipe
¼ cup	spaghetti sauce	⅓ cup
2-4 tablespoons	Cheese Sauce, pg 102, or commercial, shredded veggie cheese	¼-⅓ cup

2nd The pizza is ready to bake or sprinkle on any of the following optional ingredients then bake.

2-4 tablespoons	Add one of the following or a combination:	⅓ cup
	chopped or sliced, black olives	
	browned, crumbled, vegetarian burger	
	chopped onion	
	chopped or sliced, seeded tomato	
	other favorite toppings	

3rd Ready to serve. See photo on page 70.

BAKING TIME ON LOW:

Average Cooker: Smaller Recipe or Larger Recipe 1½ hours

Fast Cooker: Smaller Recipe or Larger Recipe 1¼ hours

Extra Fast Cooker: Smaller Recipe or Larger Recipe 1-1¼ hours

(See page 25, #3, for an explanation of the 3 types of cookers.)

Tip

- The cooker may be plugged into a lamp/appliance timer, page 26, #4, to begin cooking up to 6 hours later.

Bean Burritos

YIELD: varies	COOKER SIZE: any size

1st Use whole wheat tortillas at room temperature. If using an 8" tortilla, spread ⅓-½ cup of mashed beans or refried beans in a strip, on the bottom half of the tortilla. (May add seasonings to the beans such as minced onion or garlic, onion or garlic powder, or cumin.) Do not spread the beans all the way to the edges. Fold the right and left edges over the filling, toward the center. Fold the bottom edge toward the center and gently roll until the tortilla is completely wrapped around the filling. Spray the cooker with a food release cooking spray. Lay the burritos side by side, and on top of each other, in the cooker. Cover and heat. Serve as is, or with Tofu Sour Cream, page 136, Cheese Sauce, page 102, or warm spaghetti sauce.

WARMING TIME ON LOW:
(Time is for 6-8 burritos. If doing more or less adjust the time 15-30 minutes.)
Average Cooker: 2-2¼ hours
Fast Cooker: 1½-1¾ hours
Extra Fast Cooker: 1¼-1½ hours
(See page 25, #3, for explanation of 3 types of cookers.)

Barbecued Sloppy Joes

YIELD: varies	COOKER SIZE: any size

1st Prepare the Barbecued Gluten, page 59. Chop in a food processor. Stir in any remaining Barbecue Sauce. Heat on the stove, microwave or in a slow cooker. A slow cooker will take about 2 hours, on low, to heat 4 cups, or 3 hours on low, to heat 8 cups. Serve in a whole grain bun. See photo on page 68.

Hot Sandwiches-Ready to Go!

YIELD: varies	COOKER SIZE: any size

1st The sandwich possibilities are endless! Make them for 1 or 2, or for a crowd. Here are a few ideas...

(1) Use Barbecued Sloppy Joes, above, or make a sandwich spread. A spread can be made by crumbling patties or a loaf, i.e. Harvest Nut Loaf, page 64. Moisten it with spaghetti sauce and a cheese sauce, i.e. page 102, along with finely chopped onion. Spread on a whole grain hamburger bun, English muffin, pita bread, sliced bread, or dinner roll. A tortilla works great. See tip in following column on how to wrap a tortilla.

(2) Use burgers, patties (homemade or commercially available), or sliced loaf. Wait to add condiments, like ketchup or cheese sauce, until time to eat. Place in a whole grain hamburger bun, English muffin, pita bread, sliced bread, or dinner roll. Wrapping in a tortilla gives more options. For a tortilla, cut the burger, or loaf, to fit for wrapping. Add ketchup and/or cheese sauce and onion. See tip below on how to wrap a tortilla.

(3) Place vegetarian hotdogs in whole grain hotdog buns. Wait to add condiments when preparing to eat. If heating the hotdog in a tortilla, the condiments may be wrapped with the hotdog before heating.

(4) Peanut butter and jelly sandwiches, warmed in the cooker, are delicious. Try your favorite nut butter, along with a juice sweetened jam, honey, or a dried fruit jam, such as on page 24. May also add chopped dried fruit. Spread on a whole grain bagel, hamburger bun, English muffin, pita bread, sliced bread, dinner roll, or wrap in a tortilla. See tip below on how to wrap a tortilla.

(5) Prepare a trail mix with chopped nuts, chopped, dried fruit, and carob chips. Wrap in a tortilla. See tip below on how to wrap a tortilla. Warm. Serve as is, or with Tofu Cream, page 136.

2nd Place sandwiches side by side, or on top of each other, in a paper lunch bag. Close the bag. Pat 2-3 teaspoons of water around the outside of the bag. Place the bag in the cooker.

WARMING TIME ON LOW: (For ½-¾ full lunch bag. Reduce time about 15 minutes if bag is only ¼ full.)
Average Cooker: 1¾-2 hours
Fast Cooker: 1¼-1½ hours
Extra Fast Cooker: 1-1¼ hours
(See page 25, #3, for explanation of 3 types of cookers.)

Tip on rolling a tortilla:
If using a tortilla, the ends need to be closed to keep the filling in the wrap. Place the filling on the bottom half of the tortilla. Do not spread all the way to the edges. Fold the right and left edges over the filling, toward the center. Fold the bottom edge toward the center. Gently roll until the tortilla is completely wrapped around the filling.

Tofu Loaf

YIELD: 3 cups	COOKER SIZE: depends on the size baking dish being used

1st Stir together the following ingredients in a mixing bowl. (If you happen to be using Mori Nu tofu, in a 12.3 oz. box, it contains 1½ cups of tofu.)

1½ cups	mashed, firm or extra firm tofu
¾ cup	chopped walnuts or pecans
2 tablespoons	onion powder
2 tablespoons	Bragg Liquid Aminos or soy sauce
1 teaspoon	sage
1 teaspoon	basil

2nd Coarsely crush the cereal in a food processor or put it in a plastic bag and crush with a rolling pin. Break slices of bread and blend in a blender or food processor. Stir with the ingredients in the mixing bowl.

2 cups	dry flake cereal, i.e. Total
2 cups	whole grain bread crumbs

3rd Spray with a food release cooking spray, a dish that will hold 3½ cups or more. It may be glass or metal, such as a flat bottom rectangle or round baking dish or a bread pan. Make sure the dish will fit easily into the cooker. This is important, as the dish will be hot when being removed. Firmly pack the mixture into the dish. Cover with foil. Place the dish in the cooker on a trivet, such as a canning ring or something taller if needed. See page 11 for more trivet ideas. Bake until golden brown. Remove from cooker. Remove foil. Let sit 10 minutes. Serve as is, or with a gravy, spaghetti sauce, Cheese Sauce, page 102, Tofu Sour Cream, page 136, or ketchup. After the loaf is chilled it is more firm and may be sliced for sandwiches. See photo on back cover.

BAKING TIME ON LOW:
Average Cooker: 5¾-6 hours
Fast Cooker: 5½-5¾ hours
Extra Fast Cooker: 5¼-5½ hours
(See page 25, #3, for explanation of 3 types of cookers.)

Tips

- The cooker may be plugged into a lamp/appliance timer, page 26, #4, to begin cooking up to 4 hours later.
- Make Ahead: Prepare Steps 1 and 2. Follow Step 3 but refrigerate the baking dish with the recipe in it until ready to bake. Add 45-60 minutes to the baking time, unless waiting at least 2 hours before baking to take the chill off the ingredients.

Sun Seed Roast

YIELD: 3 cups	COOKER SIZE: depends on the size baking dish being used

1st Stir together the following ingredients in a mixing bowl. (If you happen to be using Mori Nu tofu, in a 12.3 oz. box, it contains 1½ cups of tofu.)

1½ cups	mashed, firm or extra firm tofu
1¼ cups	rolled oats
½ cup	raw sunflower seeds or chopped nuts
½ cup	uncooked, quick (instant) brown rice
¼ cup	yeast flakes
¼ cup	water
2 teaspoons	onion powder
1 teaspoon	salt
1 teaspoon	thyme

2nd Spray with a food release cooking spray, a dish that will hold 3½ cups or more. It may be glass or metal, such as a flat bottom rectangle or round baking dish or a bread pan. Make sure the dish will fit easily into the cooker. This is important, as the dish will be hot when being removed. Pat down the mixture into the dish and cover with foil. Place the dish in the cooker on a trivet, such as a canning ring or something taller if needed. See page 11 for more trivet ideas. Bake until golden brown. Remove from cooker. Remove foil. Let sit 10 minutes to become more firm. Serve as is, or with a gravy, spaghetti sauce, Cheese Sauce, page 102, Tofu Sour Cream, page 136, or ketchup. After the loaf is chilled it is more firm and may be sliced for sandwiches. See photo on page 65.

BAKING TIME ON LOW:
Average Cooker: 5-5½ hours
Fast Cooker: 4¾-5 hours
Extra Fast Cooker: 4½-4¾ hours
(See page 25, #3, for explanation of 3 types of cookers.)

Tips

- The cooker may be plugged into a lamp/appliance timer, page 26, #4, to begin cooking up to 4 hours later.
- Make Ahead: Prepare Step 1. Follow Step 2 but refrigerate the baking dish with the recipe in it until ready to bake. Add 45-60 minutes to the baking time, unless waiting at least 2 hours before baking to take the chill off the ingredients.

Harvest Nut Loaf

YIELD: 3 cups	COOKER SIZE: depends on the size baking dish being used

1ST Stir together the following ingredients in a mixing bowl.

1 cup	chopped onion
1 cup	chopped celery
¾ cup	chopped walnuts or pecans
⅓ cup	whole wheat flour
1½ teaspoons	basil
½ teaspoon	salt
½ teaspoon	sage

2nd Break slices of bread and blend in a blender or food processor. Stir into the mixing bowl with the rice.

1½ cups	whole grain bread crumbs
1 cup	cooked rice

3rd Spray with a food release cooking spray, a dish that will hold 4 cups or more. It may be glass or metal, such as a flat bottom rectangle or round baking dish or a bread pan. Make sure the dish will fit easily into the cooker. This is important, as the dish will be hot when being removed. Firmly pack the mixture into the dish. Cover with foil. Place the dish on a trivet, such as a canning ring or jar lid, in the cooker. See page 11 for more trivet ideas. Bake until golden brown. Remove from cooker. Remove foil. Let sit 10 minutes to become more firm. Serve as is, or with a gravy, spaghetti sauce, Cheese Sauce, page 102, Tofu Sour Cream, page 136, or ketchup. After the loaf is chilled it is firm and may be sliced for sandwiches. See photo on page 76.

BAKING TIME ON LOW:
Average Cooker: 4¾-5 hours
Fast Cooker: 4½ hours
Extra Fast Cooker: 4-4¼ hours
(See page 25, #3, for explanation of 3 types of cookers.)

Tips

- The cooker may be plugged into a lamp/appliance timer, page 26, #4, to begin cooking up to 6 hours later.
- Make Ahead: Prepare Steps 1 and 2. Follow Step 3 but refrigerate the baking dish with the recipe in it until ready to bake. Add 45-60 minutes to the baking time, unless waiting at least 2 hours before baking to take the chill off the ingredients.

Lentil Loaf

YIELD: 2½ cups	COOKER SIZE: depends on the size baking dish being used

1ST Lightly boil the following ingredients for 35 minutes in a covered sauce pan. Turn off the burner, but leave the lentils in the pan.

2 cups	water
⅔ cup	lentils

2nd Stir the following ingredients into the lentils.

1¼ cups	quick or rolled oats
½ cup	chopped walnuts or pecans
3 tablespoons	Bragg Liquid Aminos or soy sauce
2 teaspoons	basil

3rd Spray with a food release cooking spray, a dish that will hold 3 cups or more. It may be glass or metal, such as a flat bottom rectangle or round baking dish or a bread pan. Make sure the dish will fit easily into the cooker. This is important, as the dish will be hot when being removed. Pat down the mixture into the dish. Cover with foil. Place the dish on a trivet, such as a canning ring or jar lid, in the cooker. See page 11 for more trivet ideas. Bake until golden brown. Remove from cooker. Remove foil. Let sit 10 minutes to become more firm. Serve as is, or with a gravy, spaghetti sauce, Cheese Sauce, page 102, Tofu Sour Cream, page 136, or ketchup. After the loaf is chilled it is firm and may be sliced for sandwiches. See photo on page 76.

BAKING TIME ON LOW:
Average Cooker: 5-5½ hours
Fast Cooker: 4½-4¾ hours
Extra Fast Cooker: 4¼-4½ hours
(See page 25, #3, for explanation of 3 types of cookers.)

Tips

- The cooker may be plugged into a lamp/appliance timer, page 26, #4, to begin cooking up to 6 hours later.
- Make Ahead: Prepare Steps 1 and 2. Follow Step 3 but refrigerate the baking dish with the recipe in it until ready to bake. Add 45-60 minutes to the baking time, unless waiting at least 2 hours before baking to take the chill off the ingredients.

Recipe titles on page 139

Recipe titles on page 139

Recipe titles on page 139

Recipe titles on page 139

Recipe titles on page 139

Recipe titles on page 139

Recipe titles on page 139

Recipe titles on page 139

Recipe titles on page 139

Recipe titles on page 139

Recipe titles on page 139

Recipe titles on page 139

Recipe titles on page 139

Recipe titles on page 139

Recipe titles on page 139

Recipe titles on page 139

Maple Almond Sweet Potatoes

Smaller Recipe		Larger Recipe
YIELD: 2 cups COOKER SIZE: 2-4 qt.	INGREDIENTS	YIELD: 4 cups COOKER SIZE: 2½-7 qt.

1st Stir the following ingredients into the cooker. Cook until the potatoes are soft.

Smaller Recipe	Ingredient	Larger Recipe
3 cups	peeled, sweet potatoes or yams, cut into ½x1" pieces	6 cups
¼ cup	water	½ cup
3 tablespoons	crushed pineapple	⅓ cup
1½ tablespoons	pure maple syrup	3 tablespoons
¼ + ⅛ teaspoon	salt	¾ teaspoon

2nd Mash the potatoes. Stir in the following ingredients.

Smaller Recipe	Ingredient	Larger Recipe
2 tablespoons	sliced, slivered, or chopped almonds	¼ cup
¾ teaspoon	vanilla	1½ teaspoons

3rd Ready to serve. See photo on back cover.

COOKING TIME ON LOW:

Average Cooker: Smaller Recipe 4-4½ hours OR Larger Recipe 4½-5 hours

Fast Cooker: Smaller Recipe 3¾-4¼ hours OR Larger Recipe 4-4½ hours

Extra Fast Cooker: Smaller Recipe 3½-4 hours OR Larger Recipe 3¾-4¼ hours

COOKING TIME ON HIGH:

Average Cooker: Smaller Recipe 2¼-2½ hours OR Larger Recipe 2½-2¾ hours

Fast Cooker: Smaller Recipe 2-2¼ hours OR Larger Recipe 2¼-2½ hours

Extra Fast Cooker: Smaller Recipe 1¾-2 hours OR Larger Recipe 2-2¼ hours

(See page 25, #3, for an explanation of the 3 types of cookers.)

Tips

- The cooker may be plugged into a lamp/appliance timer, page 11, to begin cooking up to 6 hours later.
- Make Ahead: Peel and chop the potatoes. Refrigerate in a plastic bag. Combine the remaining ingredients in Step 1 and refrigerate until ready to cook. Add 15-30 minutes to the cooking time unless the recipe sits out at least 2 hours before turning on the cooker.
- Reheat on Another Day: Reheat the Smaller Recipe about 1½ hours on low, or the Larger Recipe about 2-2½ hours on low.

Honey Coconutty Sweet Potatoes

Smaller Recipe		Larger Recipe
YIELD: 2 cups COOKER SIZE: 2-4 qt.	INGREDIENTS	YIELD: 4 cups COOKER SIZE: 2-7 qt.

1st Stir the following ingredients into the cooker. Cook until the potatoes are soft.

3 cups	peeled, sweet potatoes or yams, cut into ½x1" pieces	6 cups
⅓ cup	water	⅔ cup
¼ cup	regular, unsweetened, canned, coconut milk (not light)	½ cup
1 tablespoon	pure maple syrup or honey	2 tablespoons
¼ + ⅛ teaspoon	salt	¾ teaspoon

2nd Mash the potatoes. Stir in the following vanilla. Sprinkle the almonds on top.

2 tablespoons	sliced, slivered, or chopped almonds, optional	¼ cup
½ teaspoon	vanilla	1 teaspoon

3rd Ready to serve.

COOKING TIME ON LOW:

Average Cooker: Smaller Recipe 4-4½ hours OR Larger Recipe 4½-5 hours

Fast Cooker: Smaller Recipe 3¾-4¼ hours OR Larger Recipe 4-4½ hours

Extra Fast Cooker: Smaller Recipe 3½-4 hours OR Larger Recipe 3¾-4¼ hours

COOKING TIME ON HIGH:

Average Cooker: Smaller Recipe 2¼-2½ hours OR Larger Recipe 2½-2¾ hours

Fast Cooker: Smaller Recipe 2-2¼ hours OR Larger Recipe 2¼-2½ hours

Extra Fast Cooker: Smaller Recipe 1¾-2 hours OR Larger Recipe 2-2¼ hours

(See page 25, #3, for an explanation of the 3 types of cookers.)

Tips

- The cooker may be plugged into a lamp/appliance timer, page 11, to begin cooking up to 6 hours later.
- Make Ahead: Peel and chop the potatoes. Refrigerate in a plastic bag. Combine the remaining ingredients in Step 1 and refrigerate until ready to cook. Add 15-30 minutes to the cooking time unless the recipe sits out at least 2 hours before turning on the cooker.
- Reheat on Another Day: Reheat the Smaller Recipe about 1½ hours on low, or the Larger Recipe about 2-2½ hours on low.
- Leftover coconut milk may be frozen for later use. Freeze in ¼ or ½ cup amounts.

Tangy Orange Sweet Potatoes

Smaller Recipe		Larger Recipe
YIELD: 1¾ cups COOKER SIZE: 2-4 qt.	INGREDIENTS	YIELD: 3¾ cups COOKER SIZE: 2-7 qt.

1st Stir the following ingredients into the cooker. Cook until the potatoes are soft.

Smaller Recipe	Ingredient	Larger Recipe
3 cups	peeled, sweet potatoes or yams, cut into ½x1" pieces	6 cups
⅓ cup	orange juice	⅔ cup
¼ cup	water	½ cup
1 tablespoon	honey	2 tablespoons
¼ + ⅛ teaspoon	salt	¾ teaspoon

2nd Mash the potatoes. Stir in the vanilla.

Smaller Recipe	Ingredient	Larger Recipe
½ teaspoon	vanilla	1 teaspoon

3rd Ready to serve.

COOKING TIME ON LOW:

Average Cooker: Smaller Recipe 4-4½ hours OR Larger Recipe 4½-5 hours

Fast Cooker: Smaller Recipe 3¾-4¼ hours OR Larger Recipe 4-4½ hours

Extra Fast Cooker: Smaller Recipe 3½-4 hours OR Larger Recipe 3¾-4¼ hours

COOKING TIME ON HIGH:

Average Cooker: Smaller Recipe 2¼-2½ hours OR Larger Recipe 2½-2¾ hours

Fast Cooker: Smaller Recipe 2-2¼ hours OR Larger Recipe 2¼-2½ hours

Extra Fast Cooker: Smaller Recipe 1¾-2 hours OR Larger Recipe 2-2¼ hours

(See page 25, #3, for an explanation of the 3 types of cookers.)

Tips

- The cooker may be plugged into a lamp/appliance timer, page 11, to begin cooking up to 6 hours later.
- Make Ahead: Peel and chop the potatoes. Refrigerate in a plastic bag. Combine the remaining ingredients in Step 1 and refrigerate until ready to cook. Add 15-30 minutes to the cooking time unless the recipe sits out at least 2 hours before turning on the cooker.
- Reheat on Another Day: Reheat the Smaller Recipe about 1½ hours on low, or the Larger Recipe about 2-2½ hours on low.

Baked Sweet Potatoes

Sweet potatoes or yams, baked in a slow cooker, have a rich, bright orange color. They are very moist and flavorful. The clean up is easy!

YIELD: varies	COOKER SIZE: any size

1st Scrub the sweet potatoes or yams. Cut out unwanted blemishes. Do not poke with a fork or knife. The poking leaves dark streaks in the potato. Place them, with the water in the following table, in the cooker. The potatoes may be cut in half for a better fit, if needed, or aluminum foil may be used for the lid. I prefer the bright orange color that comes from baking on high. Baking on low slightly darkens the flesh, but the flavor is still very good. See photo on page 76.

# of Med/Large Sweet Potatoes	Water Added to the Cooker	Baking Time on High
1 potato	½ cup	2-2¼ hours
2 potatoes	½ cup	2½-3 hours
3 potatoes	¾ cup	3-3½ hours

1st The following chart is for a 1½ qt. Rival Crock-Pot. This cooker does not have a high/low heat setting. The potato may be cut in half for a better fit. Aluminum foil may be used for the lid if the potato is too large.

# of Med/Large Sweet Potatoes	Water Added to the Cooker	Baking Time
1 potato	⅓ cup	5 hours

Tips

- The cooker may be plugged into a lamp/appliance timer, page 11, to begin baking up to 6 hours later.
- Make Ahead: Scrub potatoes. Refrigerate in a bag until baking time. Remove blemishes at baking time.

Simple Sweet Potatoes

A recipe using leftover, baked, sweet potatoes.

4 cups	cooked, peeled, mashed sw. potatoes
⅓ cup	regular, unsweetened, coconut milk
2-3 tablespoons	pure maple syrup or honey
1 teaspoon	vanilla, optional
½ teaspoon	salt

1st Stir the ingredients together. Heat and serve as is, or sprinkle chopped almonds on top. A great recipe to make ahead, or even freeze. Reheat in the cooker, on low, for 2-2½ hours. (Thaw before reheating.)

Baked Potatoes

Baked potatoes come out wonderful. They have a firm skin, but are soft and moist on the inside.

YIELD: varies	COOKER SIZE: any size

1st Any variety of potatoes may be used. Scrub the potatoes. Cut out unwanted blemishes. Do not poke with a fork or knife. The poking leaves dark streaks in the potato. Place them, with the water in the following table, in the cooker. I prefer to bake on high. Baking on low slightly darkens the flesh. When the potatoes are done, they will be soft when gently squeezed, but the skin will be firm. See photo on page 72.

# of Potatoes in the Cooker	Water Added to the Cooker	Baking Time on High
1 layer	½ cup	2-2½ hours
½-¾ full	½ cup	2½-3 hours
full cooker	¾ cup	3-3½ hours

2nd Serve with gravy, such as on page 101, Tofu Sour Cream, page 136, or Cheese Sauce, page 102.

Tips

- The cooker may be plugged into a lamp/appliance timer, page 11, to begin baking up to 6 hours later.
- Small potatoes generally take 20-30 minutes less.
- Potatoes may continue to bake an extra 1-1½ hours after they are done. If left much longer the flesh will begin to slightly darken.
- Make Ahead: Scrub potatoes. Refrigerate in a bag until baking time. Remove blemishes at baking time.

Potato Salad

A recipe using leftover, baked potatoes.

3 cups	cooked, peeled, cubed potatoes
1½-2 cups	Tofu Sour Cream, pg 136
1 recipe	Chunky Fried Tofu, pg 136, optional
1 cup	sliced, black olives
¾ cup	finely chopped celery
½ cup	finely chopped onion
2 tablespoons	chopped, fresh parsley (or 1 tbsp. dried)
1 tablespoon	lemon juice
1 teaspoon	onion powder
¼ teaspoon	salt

1st Stir all ingredients together. Chill several hours. Yukon Gold and red potatoes hold their shape the best when cubed, but any variety of potatoes may be used. Try adding pickle relish that is made with lemon juice.

Rustic Potatoes

Smaller Recipe		Larger Recipe
YIELD: 4 cups COOKER SIZE: 2-4½ qt.	INGREDIENTS	YIELD: 6½ cups COOKER SIZE: 3½-7 qt.

1st Stir together the following ingredients in the cooker. Cook until the potatoes are soft. I prefer to cook on high as the potatoes will keep a brighter, white color.

5 cups	peeled potatoes, cut in small, bite size pieces	8 cups
⅔ cup	chopped onion	1 cup
2 tablespoons	chopped, canned pimento or red pepper, for color	¼ cup
2-3 cloves	minced garlic	3-6 cloves
1 tablespoon	olive oil	2 tablespoons
2 teaspoons	onion powder	1 tablespoon
¾ teaspoon	salt	1¼ teaspoons
½ teaspoon	garlic powder	1 teaspoon

2nd Gently stir in the dill weed.

¾ teaspoon	dried dill weed	1½ teaspoons

3rd Ready to serve. May garnish with paprika and fresh, chopped, dill or parsley. See photo on page 73.

COOKING TIME ON HIGH:

Average Cooker: Smaller Recipe 2-2¼ hours OR Larger Recipe 3-3¼ hours

Fast Cooker: Smaller Recipe 2-2¼ hours OR Larger Recipe 2½-2¾ hours

Extra Fast Cooker: Smaller Recipe 1¾-2 hours OR Larger Recipe 2¼-2½ hours

(See page 25, #3, for an explanation of the 3 types of cookers.)

Tips

- The cooker may be plugged into a lamp/appliance timer, page 11, to begin cooking up to 6 hours later.
- Make Ahead: Peel and chop the potatoes, cover with water in a storage container and refrigerate. Combine the remaining ingredients in Step 1 and refrigerate until ready to cook. Add about 15-30 minutes to the cooking time unless the recipe sits out at least 2 hours before turning on the cooker.

Old Fashion Scalloped Potatoes

Smaller Recipe		Larger Recipe
YIELD: 3¾ cups COOKER SIZE: 2½-5 qt.	INGREDIENTS	YIELD: 7½ cups COOKER SIZE: 3½-7 qt.

1st Blend the following ingredients in a blender for 2 minute, until smooth. Pour into the cooker.

Smaller Recipe	Ingredient	Larger Recipe
½ cup	water	⅔ cup
¼ cup	raw cashews or blanched (white) almonds, pg 137	½ cup
3 tablespoons	quick or rolled oats	⅓ cup
4½ teaspoons	McKay's Chicken Seasoning or Chicken Seasoning, pg 136	3 tablespoons
1 tablespoon	olive oil	2 tablespoons
1 tablespoon	lemon juice	2 tablespoons
1½ teaspoons	onion powder	1 tablespoon
½ teaspoon	garlic powder	1 teaspoon
⅛ teaspoon	salt	¼ teaspoon

2nd Rinse the blender with the water in the following table, then stir into the cooker.

Smaller Recipe	Ingredient	Larger Recipe
¾ cup	water	1⅔ cups

3rd Prepare the potatoes, then thoroughly mix with the sauce in the cooker. Cook until the potatoes are tender.

Smaller Recipe	Ingredient	Larger Recipe
4 cups	peeled, thinly sliced potatoes	8 cups

4th Ready to serve. May garnish with paprika and/or fresh, minced parsley. See photo on page 68.

COOKING TIME IF COOKING ON LOW:

Average Cooker: Smaller Recipe 8-8¼ hours OR Larger Recipe 9-9¼ hours

Fast Cooker: Smaller Recipe 4½-4¾ hours OR Larger Recipe 5¼-5½ hours

Extra Fast Cooker: Smaller Recipe 3-3¼ hours OR Larger Recipe 4½-4¾ hours

COOKING TIME IF COOKING ON HIGH:

Average Cooker: Smaller Recipe 3¼-3½ hours OR Larger Recipe 3½-3¾ hours

Fast Cooker: Smaller Recipe 2¾-3 hours OR Larger Recipe 3-3¼ hours

Extra Fast Cooker: Smaller Recipe 2¼-2½ hours OR Larger Recipe 2¾-3 hours

(See page 25, #3, for an explanation of the 3 types of cookers.)

Tips

- The cooker may be plugged into a lamp/appliance timer, page 11, to begin cooking up to 6 hours later.
- In case you noticed that I have commented in previous recipes to cook potatoes on high for a whiter color, and are wondering why I would cook these potatoes on high, or low, well, here is the reason. This recipe has some lemon juice in it. This keeps the potatoes white!
- Make Ahead: Prepare Steps 1 and 2, then refrigerate. Prepare the potatoes, cover with water and refrigerate until ready to cook. Add about 15-30 minutes to the cooking time unless the recipe sits out at least 2 hours before turning on the cooker.

Mashed Potatoes

I put this recipe in because I like to use the slow cooker to reheat mashed potatoes that were made the day before. Use this recipe, or your favorite mashed potato recipe, then reheat in your cooker when ready to serve.

YIELD: 5 cups	COOKER SIZE: 2-5 qt.

1st Boil the following potatoes on the stove until tender. Drain, then place them in a mixing bowl.

5 cups	peeled, chopped potatoes

2nd While the potatoes are cooking, blend the following ingredients until smooth.

¾ cup or ½ box	firm or extra firm Mori Nu tofu
3 tablespoons	water
1½ teaspoons	onion powder
1 teaspoon	salt
½ teaspoon	garlic powder

3rd Mash the potatoes. Stir in the blended ingredients, along with the margarine in the following table. The potatoes are ready to serve, or may be kept warm for an hour in the cooker. They will turn a tan color if left in the cooker too long.

2 tablespoons	non-hydogenated soy margarine, opt.

4th If the potatoes are prepared a day or more ahead of time, then stir in the water from the following table into the potatoes before reheating.

¼ cup	water

5th Serve with gravy, such as on page 101, or Tofu Sour Cream page 136.

REHEATING TIME ON LOW
FOR COLD MASHED POTATOES:
(For a double recipe add 30-60 minutes
to the following time.)
Approximately 2-2½ hours
(See page 25, #3, for explanation of 3 types of cookers.)

Tips
- The cooker may be plugged into a lamp/appliance timer, page 11, to begin cooking up to 4 hours later.
- The recipe may be doubled. Reheat in a 3½-7 qt. cooker.

Roasted Garlic

The aroma of garlic, baking in a slow cooker, is like burning your favorite scented candle! Well, almost...

YIELD: 1 bulb	COOKER SIZE: any size

1st Choose one of the following ways to prepare the garlic. (1) Cut about ½" off the top of the bulb, exposing a small portion of most of the cloves. Peel away the outer, papery skin of the bulb. Place the bulb in a glass bowl. The garlic is ready to bake, or drizzle olive oil, along with a sprinkle of salt and paprika, over the bulb. Cover the dish with foil. Place it on a trivet, such as a canning ring or metal jar lid, in the cooker and bake. I prefer this method because the garlic is easier to peel after it is baked. See photo on front cover. (2) Peel the bulb into individual cloves. Place in a glass bowl. The garlic is ready to bake, or drizzle on olive oil, along with a sprinkle of salt. Cover the dish with foil. Place on a trivet, such as a canning ring or metal jar lid, in the cooker, and bake. See photo on page 72.

Ways to use: Dice and sprinkle over salad, spaghetti, pizza, haystacks, cooked vegetables or beans. Mash and spread on crackers, or just peel, eat and enjoy.

- The cooker may be plugged into a lamp/appliance timer, page 11, to begin baking up to 6 hours later.

BAKING TIME ON LOW:
If bulb is firm: 2½-3 hours for any cooker.
If bulb is older & softer: 2-2½ hours for any cooker.
For cloves, take 15-30 minutes off the time above.
(See page 25, #3, for explanation of 3 types of cookers.)

Roasted Onion Rings

YIELD: ½ cup	COOKER SIZE: any size

1st Peel an onion. Cut in thin slices, ⅛-¼". There is about 1 cup of raw slices in a medium size cooking onion. Separate the rings in a glass bowl. The onion is ready to bake, or drizzle on olive oil, along with a sprinkle of salt and/or other favorite seasonings. Cover with foil. Place on a trivet, such as a metal jar lid, in the cooker, and bake. (More than 1 may be baked.)

BAKING TIME ON LOW:
Average Cooker: 3¼-3½ hours
Fast Cooker: 2½-2¾ hours
Extra Fast Cooker: 2½-2¾ hours
(See page 25, #3, for explanation of 3 types of cookers.)

Butternut, Acorn or Butter Cup Squash or Pie Pumpkin

YIELD: varies	COOKER SIZE: any size

1st Use one or more winter squash. Cut in half, or in smaller pieces. Remove the seeds. Place the squash in the cooker without any water. It may also be baked whole, but will take a little longer. I find it is easier to clean out the seeds before the squash is baked. Cover the cooker with foil if the lid does not fit. Bake until soft. Times may vary from one squash to another do to hardness of the shell.

2nd Try other varieties of squash. Sometimes the color is a little brighter if baked on high.

BAKING TIME ON LOW:
Average Cooker: 5½-6 hours
Fast Cooker: 4½-5 hours
Extra Fast Cooker: 4-4½ hours
BAKING TIME ON HIGH:
Average Cooker: 2-2½ hours
Fast Cooker: 1½-2 hours
Extra Fast Cooker: 1¼-1¾ hours
(See page 25, #3, for explanation of 3 types of cookers.)

Tips
- The cooker may be plugged into a lamp/appliance timer, page 11, to begin cooking up to 6 hours later.
- Serve as desired, or mash and add the following ingredients:

4 cups	cooked, mashed squash
⅓ cup	regular, unsweetened, coconut milk
2-3 tablespoons	pure maple syrup or honey
1 teaspoon	vanilla, optional
½ teaspoon	salt

Roasted Herb Sweet Corn

YIELD: varies	COOKER SIZE: any size

1st Rub the following herbs on about 6 ears of corn, or try your own favorite, fresh or dried, herb combination.

2 tablespoons	fresh, chopped parsley
½ teaspoon	dried basil

2nd Cook as directed under Roasted Sweet Corn. See the recipe on the opposite side of this page.

Baked Spaghetti Squash

YIELD: varies	COOKER SIZE: any size

1st A yellow winter squash, shaped like a football, but round at the ends. The inside looks similar to spaghetti after it is cooked. It is low in calories and has a very mild flavor. Place the squash whole, in the cooker. Cover the cooker with aluminum foil if the lid does not fit. Press the foil tightly around the cooker. Bake until soft. Older squash may have a harder shell and take longer to bake. Serve with a little non-hydrogenated margarine and salt, or use for the pasta when serving spaghetti. It is also good served with Cheese Sauce, page 102.

BAKING TIME ON LOW:
Average Cooker: 7-7½ hours
Fast Cooker: 6-6½ hours
Extra Fast Cooker: 5-5½ hours
BAKING TIME ON HIGH:
Average Cooker: 3¼-3¾ hours
Fast Cooker: 3-3½ hours
Extra Fast Cooker: 2¼-2¾ hours
(See page 25, #3, for explanation of 3 types of cookers.)

Roasted Corn on the Cob

A great way to cook sweet corn. It turns out tender-crisp and sweet. The corn is steamed. No boiling in a big pot of water!

YIELD: varies	COOKER SIZE: any size

1st Place the husked corn in the cooker. Break in half if necessary to fit. If cooking 2-4 ears add ⅓ cup of water to the cooker. If cooking 5-12 ears add ½ cup of water. Cook until tender crisp. See photo on page 76.

COOKING TIME ON HIGH: (Reduce cooking time about 15 minutes if cooking 4 or less ears of corn.)
Average Cooker: 2-2¼ hours
Fast Cooker: 1¾-2 hours
Extra Fast Cooker: 1½-1¾ hours
(See page 25, #3, for explanation of 3 types of cookers.)

Tips
- The cooker may be plugged into a lamp/appliance timer, page 11, to begin cooking up to 6 hours later.
- The cooking time is about 15 minutes longer if the corn was husked, refrigerated and cold before cooking.

Eggplant Garlic Bake

Smaller Recipe		Larger Recipe
YIELD: 3 cups COOKER SIZE: 2-4½ qt.	INGREDIENTS	YIELD: 6 cups COOKER SIZE: 3½-7 qt.

1st Peel and slice the eggplant. Divide it into 3 portions, as equal as possible. Distribute 1 portion of the slices on the bottom of the cooker. Slices may also be cut into bite size pieces, if desired.

Smaller Recipe	Ingredients	Larger Recipe
small size or ½ of medium	peeled eggplant, sliced ¼" thick	medium size, 1-1¼#

2nd Stir together the following ingredients in a mixing bowl. Sprinkle ⅓ cup of the olive mixture over the eggplant for the Smaller Recipe. Sprinkle ¾ cup of the olive mixture over the eggplant, for the Larger Recipe. Follow with a second layer of eggplant, then the same amount of the olive mixture. Distribute the final layer of eggplant, then the remaining olive mixture.

Smaller Recipe	Ingredients	Larger Recipe
¾ cup	sliced, black olives	6 oz. can
¾ cup	chopped onion	1½ cups
3 tablespoons	tahini (sesame seed butter)	⅓ cup
2 tablespoons	cornstarch	¼ cup
2 tablespoons	water	¼ cup
3	minced garlic cloves	6
1 teaspoon	basil	2 teaspoons
½ teaspoon	oregano	1 teaspoon
½ teaspoon	salt	1 teaspoon

3rd Top with the following tomatoes, then cook.

Smaller Recipe	Ingredients	Larger Recipe
¾ cup	drained, chopped or diced, canned tomatoes	1½ cups (14.5 oz. can)

4th Sprinkle with the following parsley.

Smaller Recipe	Ingredients	Larger Recipe
½ teaspoon dried or 1½ teaspoons fresh	dried parsley or fresh, chopped parsley	1 teaspoon dried or 1 tablespoon fresh

5th Ready to serve.

BAKING TIME ON LOW:

Average Cooker: Small Recipe 4½-5 hours OR Large Recipe 7-7½ hours

Fast Cooker: Small Recipe 4-4½ hours OR Large Recipe 5½-6 hours

Extra Fast Cooker: Smaller Recipe 3¾-4¼ OR Large Recipe 4¾-5¼ hours

(See page 25, #3, for an explanation of the 3 types of cookers.)

Tips

- The cooker may be plugged into a lamp/appliance timer, page 11, to begin cooking up to 6 hours later.
- Make Ahead: Prepare the ingredients for Step 2, then refrigerate until ready to bake.

Greens with Veggies

Smaller Recipe		Larger Recipe
YIELD: 3¼ cups COOKER SIZE: 2-4½ qt.	INGREDIENTS	YIELD: 6½ cups COOKER SIZE: 3½-7 qt.

1st Cook the following ingredients in a covered sauce pan for 2 minutes. The greens will be bright green and limp. Empty into the cooker.

approx. ¼# or 2 cups	thinly chopped, packed, fresh collards or kale	4 cups or approx. ½#
¼ cup	water	½ cup water

2nd Stir the following ingredients into the cooker. Cook until the carrots are tender. Carrots usually take the longest to cook. Cook on high for the best flavor.

1 cup	carrots, cut in thin, 2" long strips	2 cups
¾ cup	diced or chopped, canned tomatoes, with juice	14.5 oz. cans or 1¾ cups
¾ cup	potatoes, cut in ½x½" cubes	1½ cups
½ cup	chopped onion	1 cup
2 tablespoons	water	¼ cup

3rd Serve as is, or with Cheese Sauce, page 102, Tofu Sour Cream, page 136, or with a small amount of lemon juice. See photo on page 76.

COOKING TIME ON HIGH:

Average Cooker: Smaller Recipe 3-3½ hours OR Larger Recipe 4½-5 hours

Fast Cooker: Smaller Recipe 2¾-3¼ hours OR Larger Recipe 3½-4 hours

Extra Fast Cooker: Smaller Recipe 2¼-2¾ hours OR Larger Recipe 2¾-3¼ hours

(See page 25, #3, for an explanation of the 3 types of cookers.)

Tips

- The cooker may be plugged into a lamp/appliance timer, page 11, to begin cooking up to 6 hours later.
- Make Ahead: Prepare Step 1, then combine with Step 2, except for the potatoes, and refrigerate. The potatoes may be prepared then covered with water until ready to cook.

Simply Beets

Smaller Recipe		Larger Recipe
YIELD: 3 cups COOKER SIZE: 2-4½ qt.	INGREDIENTS	YIELD: 6 cups COOKER SIZE: 3½-7 qt.

1st Stir together the following ingredients in the cooker. Cook until the beets are tender crisp.

(3-4 med. beets) 4 cups	peeled, raw beets, cut into thin, 1x1" slices	8 cups (7-8 med. beets)
½ cup	water	1 cup
¼ + ⅛ teaspoon	salt	¾ teaspoon

2nd Ready to serve.

COOKING TIME IF COOKING ON LOW:

Average Cooker: Smaller Recipe 5½-5¾ hours OR Larger Recipe 6-6¼ hours

Fast Cooker: Smaller Recipe 4¼-4½ hours OR Larger Recipe 5-5¼ hours

Extra Fast Cooker: Smaller Recipe 3-3¼ hours OR Larger Recipe 3¾-4 hours

COOKING TIME IF COOKING ON HIGH:

Average Cooker: Smaller Recipe 2¼-2½ hours OR Larger Recipe 3-3¼ hours

Fast Cooker: Smaller Recipe 2-2¼ hours OR Larger Recipe 2¾-3 hours

Extra Fast Cooker: Smaller Recipe 1¾-2 hours OR Larger Recipe 2-2¼ hours

(See page 25, #3, for an explanation of the 3 types of cookers.)

Tips

- The cooker may be plugged into a lamp/appliance timer, page 11, to begin cooking up to 6 hours later.
- Make Ahead: Prepare the beets, then refrigerate until ready to cook.

Lemon Beets

After the beets are cooked place them in a bowl. Stir in ¾ cup lemon juice for the Smaller Recipe, or 1⅓ cups for the Larger Recipe. Also stir in ⅓ cup cane juice crystals, sucanat, fructose or sugar for the Smaller Recipe, or ⅔ cup for the Larger Recipe. Refrigerate several hours before serving.

Harvest Vegetable Soup

Smaller Recipe		Larger Recipe
YIELD: 6½ cups COOKER SIZE: 2-5½ qt.	INGREDIENTS	YIELD: 13 cups COOKER SIZE: 4½-7 qt.

1st Combine the following ingredients in the cooker and cook until the vegetables are tender. Carrots take the longest to cook, so cut them small. A food processor is a quick way to chop onions and carrots. The pimento or red pepper is mainly for color. If you do not have it, just leave it out.

Smaller Recipe	Ingredients	Larger Recipe
3 cups	water	6 cups
1½ cups	peeled, butternut squash, cut into 1" cubes	3 cups
1½ cups	peeled, sweet potatoes, cut into 1" cubes	3 cups
1½ cups	finely sliced, chopped or shredded carrots	3 cups
¾ cup	chopped onion	1½ cups
⅓ cup	chopped, canned pimento or chopped, sweet red pepper	⅔ cup
¼ cup	yeast flakes, pg 10	½ cup
1 tablespoon	olive oil	2 tablespoons
2 teaspoons	salt	4 teaspoons

2nd Add the following ingredients to the cooker. Blend the soup smooth in a blender, 2 cups at a time. Pour the soup back into the cooker, or another serving dish, and stir. An immersable blender may also be used. Put it directly into the cooker to blend the soup.

Smaller Recipe	Ingredients	Larger Recipe
1¾ cups or 15 oz. can	cooked, drained, great northern, navy or garbanzo beans	2-15 oz. cans or 3½ cups
1 teaspoon	basil	2 teaspoons

3rd Ready to serve. May add a small amount of water if the soup is too thick. See photo on page 66.

COOKING TIME IF COOKING ON LOW:

Average Cooker: Smaller Recipe 6½-7 hours OR Larger Recipe 8-8½ hours

Fast Cooker: Smaller Recipe 4¼-4¾ hours OR Larger Recipe 6¼-6¾ hours

Extra Fast Cooker: Smaller Recipe 3¾-4¼ hours OR Larger Recipe 5½-6 hours

COOKING TIME IF COOKING ON HIGH:

Average Cooker: Smaller Recipe 3½-4 hours OR Larger Recipe 4½-5 hours

Fast Cooker: Smaller Recipe 2½-3 hours OR Larger Recipe 3¼-3¾ hours

Extra Fast Cooker: Smaller Recipe 2-2½ hours OR Larger Recipe 3-3½ hours

(See page 25, #3, for an explanation of the 3 types of cookers.)

Tips

- The cooker may be plugged into a lamp/appliance timer, page 11, to begin cooking up to 6 hours later.
- When the soup is cooked in an Extra Fast cooker it will be somewhat thicker, and may have a reduced yield of ½-1 cup when compared to using an Average cooker. This is because the Extra Fast cooker cooks at a higher temperature, causing some evaporation of the water while cooking.

Lima Bean Chowder

Smaller Recipe		Larger Recipe
YIELD: 5½ cups COOKER SIZE: 2-4½ qt.	INGREDIENTS	YIELD: 11 cups COOKER SIZE: 3½-7 qt.

1st Combine the following ingredients in the cooker and cook until the beans are soft.

Smaller Recipe	Ingredient	Larger Recipe
3 cups	water	6 cups
2 cups	chopped celery	4 cups
1 cup	rinsed and drained, dried lima beans	2 cups
¾ cup	chopped onion	1½ cups
1 tablespoon	olive oil	2 tablespoons
1¼ teaspoons	salt	2½ teaspoons

2nd Add the tomatoes.

Smaller Recipe	Ingredient	Larger Recipe
½ cup	chopped or diced, drained, canned tomatoes	1 cup

3rd Ready to serve. May garnish with sliced green onion and fresh parsley. May add a small amount of water if the chowder is too thick. See photo on page 77.

COOKING TIME IF COOKING ON LOW:
Average Cooker: Smaller Recipe 8½-9 hours OR Larger Recipe 8½-9 hours
Fast Cooker: Smaller Recipe 6-6½ hours OR Larger Recipe 7½-8 hours
Extra Fast Cooker: Smaller Recipe 4½-5 hours OR Larger Recipe 6-6½ hours
COOKING TIME IF COOKING ON HIGH:
Average Cooker: Smaller Recipe 4-4½ hours OR Larger Recipe 5¼-5¾ hours
Fast Cooker: Smaller Recipe 3½-4 hours OR Larger Recipe 5-5½ hours
Extra Fast Cooker: Smaller Recipe 3-3½ hours OR Larger Recipe 4-4½ hours
(See page 25, #3, for an explanation of the 3 types of cookers.)

Tips

- The cooker may be plugged into a lamp/appliance timer, page 11, to begin cooking up to 6 hours later.
- When the chowder is cooked in an Extra Fast cooker it will be somewhat thicker, and may have a reduced yield of ½-1 cup when compared to using an Average cooker. This is because the Extra Fast cooker cooks at a higher temperature, causing some evaporation of the water while cooking.

Cream of Tomato Vegetable Soup

Smaller Recipe		Larger Recipe
YIELD: 5½ cups COOKER SIZE: 2-5 qt.	INGREDIENTS	YIELD: 11 cups COOKER SIZE: 5-7 qt.

1st Blend the following ingredients very smooth in the blender. Pour into the cooker.

Smaller Recipe	Ingredient	Larger Recipe
½ cup	water	½ cup
¼ cup	raw cashews	½ cup
2 tablespoons	quick or rolled oats	¼ cup

2nd Rinse the blender with the water in the following table, then add to the cooker.

Smaller Recipe	Ingredient	Larger Recipe
1 cup	water	2½ cups

3rd Stir the following ingredients into the cooker. Cook until the soup is lightly boiling around the edges and is slightly thickened throughout.

Smaller Recipe	Ingredient	Larger Recipe
2 cups	canned tomato juice	4 cups
1½ cups or 14.5 oz. can	chopped or diced, canned tomatoes with juice	2-14.5 oz. cans or 3 cups
¾ cup or ½ of a 10 oz. box	frozen spinach, thawed, not drained, see alternatives below	10 oz. box or 1½ cups
⅓ cup	quick (instant) brown rice	⅔ cup

4th Ready to serve.

COOKING TIME IF COOKING ON LOW:

Average Cooker: Smaller Recipe 6½-7 hours OR Larger Recipe 7¾-8¼ hours

Fast Cooker: Smaller Recipe 5¼-5¾ hours OR Larger Recipe 5¾-6¼ hours

Extra Fast Cooker: Smaller Recipe 3½-4 hours OR Larger Recipe 4¼-4¾ hours

COOKING TIME IF COOKING ON HIGH:

Average Cooker: Smaller Recipe 3-3½ hours OR Larger Recipe 5-5½ hours

Fast Cooker: Smaller Recipe 2¼-2¾ hours OR Larger Recipe 3½-4 hours

Extra Fast Cooker: Smaller Recipe 2-2½ hours OR Larger Recipe 2¾-3¼ hours

(See page 25, #3, for an explanation of the 3 types of cookers.)

Tips

Use one of the following in place of the frozen spinach:

- Thinly chop, packed, fresh collard or kale greens. 2 cups for the Smaller Recipe, or 4 cups for the Larger Recipe. Lightly boil the greens with ⅓ cup of water for 2 minutes, until bright green and limp.
- Or, chop 3 cups, packed, fresh spinach for the Smaller Recipe, or 6 cups, packed, for the Larger Recipe. Lightly boil with ⅓ cup of water for 45 seconds, until bright green and limp.
- Or, purchase a 16 oz. bag of frozen spinach. Use 2 cups of unthawed spinach for the Smaller Recipe, or 4 cups for the Larger Recipe.
- The cooker may be plugged into a lamp/appliance timer, page 11, to begin cooking up to 6 hours later.
- When the soup is cooked in an Extra Fast cooker it will be somewhat thicker, and may have a reduced yield of ½-1 cup when compared to using an Average cooker. This is because the Extra Fast cooker cooks at a higher temperature, causing some evaporation of the water while cooking.

Split Pea Chowder

Smaller Recipe		Larger Recipe
YIELD: 5 cups COOKER SIZE: 2½-5 qt.	INGREDIENTS	YIELD: 10 cups COOKER SIZE: 4-7 qt.

1st Combine the following ingredients in the cooker and cook until the split peas and vegetables are tender. Carrots generally take the longest to cook, so cut them thin.

Smaller Recipe	Ingredient	Larger Recipe
3 cups	water	6 cups
1 cup	rinsed and drained split peas	2 cups
1 cup	peeled potatoes, cut in small, bite size pieces	2 cups
1 cup	thinly sliced, chopped or shredded carrots	2 cups
¾ cup	chopped onion	1½ cups
½ cup	chopped celery	1 cup
2	bay leaves	4
1¼ teaspoons	salt	2½ teaspoons

2nd Pre-measure the following ingredients in a small bowl, then stir into the cooker. (You may want to put a sign by the cooker as a reminder to add these ingredients. It is easy to forget them. Otherwise, perhaps put the onion and garlic powder near the cooker.)

Smaller Recipe	Ingredient	Larger Recipe
1 tablespoon	onion powder	2 tablespoons
1 teaspoon	garlic powder	2 teaspoons

3rd Ready to serve. May add a small amount of water if the chowder is too thick. See photo on back cover.

COOKING TIME IF COOKING ON LOW:

Average Cooker: not recommended on low in Average Cooker

Fast Cooker: Smaller Recipe 5-5½ hours OR Larger Recipe 5½-6 hours

Extra Fast Cooker: Smaller Recipe 4½-5 hours OR Larger Recipe 5-5½ hours

COOKING TIME IF COOKING ON HIGH:

Average Cooker: Smaller Recipe 4-4½ hours OR Larger Recipe 5-5½ hours

Fast Cooker: Smaller Recipe 3½-4 hours OR Larger Recipe 4½-5 hours

Extra Fast Cooker: Smaller Recipe 3-3½ hours OR Larger Recipe 4-4½ hours

(See page 25, #3, for an explanation of the 3 types of cookers.)

Tips

- The cooker may be plugged into a lamp/appliance timer, page 11, to begin cooking up to 6 hours later.
- When the chowder is cooked in an Extra Fast cooker it will be somewhat thicker, and may have a reduced yield of ½-1 cup when compared to using an Average cooker. This is because the Extra Fast cooker cooks at a higher temperature, causing some evaporation of the water while cooking.

Lentil Vegetable Soup

Smaller Recipe		Larger Recipe
YIELD: 6½ cups COOKER SIZE: 2½-4½ qt.	INGREDIENTS	YIELD: 13 cups COOKER SIZE: 4½-7 qt.

1st Combine the following ingredients in the cooker and cook until the lentils and vegetables are tender.

Smaller Recipe	Ingredient	Larger Recipe
2½ cups	water	5 cups
1 cup	chopped, shredded or sliced carrots	2 cups
1 cup	peeled potatoes, cut in small, bite size pieces	2 cups
¾ cup	rinsed and drained lentils	1½ cups
½ cup	chopped onion	1 cup
½ cup	chopped celery	1 cup
2	bay leaves	3
1 teaspoon	salt	2 teaspoons

2nd Stir in the following ingredients. Turn off the cooker and let sit 5 minutes.

Smaller Recipe	Ingredient	Larger Recipe
14.5 oz. can or 1½ cups	chopped or diced, canned tomatoes	28 oz. can or 3 cups
⅓ cup	tomato paste	6 oz. can or ⅔ cup
2-3 cloves	minced garlic	3-4 cloves

3rd Ready to serve. May add a small amount of water if the soup is too thick. See photo on page 77.

COOKING TIME IF COOKING ON LOW:

Average Cooker: Smaller Recipe 7½-8 hours OR Larger Recipe 8-8½ hours

Fast Cooker: Smaller Recipe 5-5½ hours OR Larger Recipe 6-6½ hours

Extra Fast Cooker: Smaller Recipe 4-4½ hours OR Larger Recipe 5-5½ hours

COOKING TIME IF COOKING ON HIGH:

Average Cooker: Smaller Recipe 3½-4 hours OR Larger Recipe 6-6½ hours

Fast Cooker: Smaller Recipe 3-3½ hours OR Larger Recipe 5-5½ hours

Extra Fast Cooker: Smaller Recipe 2½-3 hours OR Larger Recipe 4-4½ hours

(See page 25, #3, for an explanation of the 3 types of cookers.)

Tips

- The cooker may be plugged into a lamp/appliance timer, page 11, to begin cooking up to 6 hours later.
- When the soup is cooked in an Extra Fast cooker it will be somewhat thicker, and may have a reduced yield of ½-1 cup when compared to using an Average cooker. This is because the Extra Fast cooker cooks at a higher temperature, causing some evaporation of the water while cooking.

Chili

Smaller Recipe		Larger Recipe
YIELD: 5½ cups COOKER SIZE: 2½-5 qt.	INGREDIENTS	YIELD: 11 cups COOKER SIZE: 4-7 qt.

1st Combine the following ingredients in the cooker and cook until the beans are soft.

Smaller Recipe	Ingredients	Larger Recipe
2¾ cups	water	5½ cups
¾ cup	chopped onion	1½ cups
⅔ cup	rinsed and drained, dried kidney beans	1⅓ cups
1 tablespoon	olive oil	2 tablespoons
1 teaspoon	salt	2 teaspoons

2nd Crush basil and oregano in the following table between fingers. Pre-measure the following dry ingredients in a small bowl. Stir all of the following ingredients into the cooker and continue to cook 10 minutes.

Smaller Recipe	Ingredients	Larger Recipe
1½ cups or 14.5 oz. can	browned, crumbled vegetarian burger, see tip below	2½ cups
1 cup or 8 oz. can	tomato sauce	15 oz. can or 1¾ cups
⅔ cup or 6 oz. can	tomato paste	12 oz. can or 1⅓ cups
1-2 cloves	minced garlic	3 cloves
1½ teaspoons	ground cumin	1 tablespoon
1½ teaspoons	onion powder	1 tablespoon
1 teaspoon	garlic powder	2 teaspoons
½ teaspoon	basil	1 teaspoon
¼ teaspoon	oregano	½ teaspoon

3rd Ready to serve. May add ½ cup of water or more if the Chili is too thick. See photo on page 73.

COOKING TIME IF COOKING ON LOW:

Average Cooker: Smaller Recipe 10-10½ hours OR Larger Recipe 10½-11 hours

Fast Cooker: Smaller Recipe 5½-6 hours OR Larger Recipe 8-8½ hours

Extra Fast Cooker: Smaller Recipe 4-4½ hours OR Larger Recipe 6½-7 hours

COOKING TIME IF COOKING ON HIGH:

Average Cooker: Smaller Recipe 4½-5 hours OR Larger Recipe 6-6½ hours

Fast Cooker: Smaller Recipe 4-4½ hours OR Larger Recipe 5½-6 hours

Extra Fast Cooker: Smaller Recipe 3½-4 hours OR Larger Recipe 4½-5 hours

(See page 25, #3, for an explanation of the 3 types of cookers.)

Tips

Vegetarian burger may come from a variety of sources:

- If using a commercial frozen patty, such as vegan Boca Burgers or Morningstar patties or canned patties, such as from Cedar Lake or Loma Linda, they should be browned then crumbled. Commercial ground burger is also available canned or frozen. Follow package directions for browning.
- Try your homemade gluten or the Tender Gluten, page 58. Cut into small pieces, or chop in a food processor.
- The cooker may be plugged into a lamp/appliance timer, page 11, to begin cooking up to 6 hours later.
- When the soup is cooked in an Extra Fast cooker it will be somewhat thicker, and may have a reduced yield of ½-1 cup when compared to using an Average cooker.

Bean Without the Bacon Soup

Smaller Recipe		Larger Recipe
YIELD: 5½ cups COOKER SIZE: 2½-5 qt.	INGREDIENTS	YIELD: 11 cups COOKER SIZE: 3½-7 qt.

1st Combine the following ingredients in the cooker and cook until the beans are soft.

Smaller Recipe	Ingredients	Larger Recipe
3 cups	water	6 cups
1¼ cups	rinsed and drained, dried, great northern beans	2½ cups
¾ cup	chopped or sliced carrots	1½ cups
¾ cup	chopped onion	1½ cups
1 tablespoon	olive oil	2 tablespoons
1 teaspoon	salt	2 teaspoons

2nd Put the following ingredients into a blender. Add the cooked bean mixture and blend smooth. This will most likely need to be done in two batches. Pour the soup back into the cooker, or another serving dish, and stir.

Smaller Recipe	Ingredients	Larger Recipe
1½ cups or 14.5 oz. can	chopped or diced, canned tomatoes	28 oz. can or 3 cups
2 teaspoons	onion powder	1½ tablespoons
2 teaspoons	Bragg Liquid Aminos	4 teaspoons
¼ teaspoon	Hickory Seasoning Liquid Smoke	½ teaspoon

3rd Ready to serve. May add a small amount of water, tomato juice, or canned tomatoes, if the soup is too thick.

COOKING TIME IF COOKING ON LOW:

Average Cooker: Smaller Recipe 7½-8 hours OR Larger Recipe 10-10½ hours

Fast Cooker: Smaller Recipe 5-5½ hours OR Larger Recipe 8½-9 hours

Extra Fast Cooker: Smaller Recipe 4-4½ hours OR Larger Recipe 7-7½ hours

COOKING TIME IF COOKING ON HIGH:

Average Cooker: Smaller Recipe 4½-5 hours OR Larger Recipe 6-6½ hours

Fast Cooker: Smaller Recipe 4-4½ hours OR Larger Recipe 4½-5 hours

Extra Fast Cooker: Smaller Recipe 3½-4 hours OR Larger Recipe 3½-4 hours

(See page 25, #3, for an explanation of the 3 types of cookers.)

Tips

- The cooker may be plugged into a lamp/appliance timer, page 11, to begin cooking up to 6 hours later.
- When the soup is cooked in an Extra Fast cooker it will be somewhat thicker, and may have a reduced yield of ½-1 cup when compared to using an Average cooker. This is because the Extra Fast cooker cooks at a higher temperature, causing some evaporation of the water while cooking.

Potato Corn Chowder

Smaller Recipe		Larger Recipe
YIELD: 4 cups COOKER SIZE: 2-4 qt.	INGREDIENTS	YIELD: 8 cups COOKER SIZE: 3½-7 qt.

1st Blend the following ingredients in a blender 1-2 minutes, until very smooth. Pour in the cooker.

Smaller Recipe	Ingredient	Larger Recipe
½ cup	water	½ cup
¼ cup	raw cashews	½ cup
3 tablespoons	pimento	⅓ cup
2 tablespoons	yeast flakes, pg 10	¼ cup
1½ tablespoons	quick or rolled oats	3 tablespoons
1½ tablespoons	McKay's Chicken Seasoning or Chicken Seasoning pg 136	3 tablespoons
¼ teaspoon	salt	½ teaspoon

2nd Rinse the blender with the water in the following table, then add to the cooker.

Smaller Recipe	Ingredient	Larger Recipe
1 cup	water	2½ cups

3rd Add the following ingredients to the cooker and cook until the potatoes are tender.

Smaller Recipe	Ingredient	Larger Recipe
1½ cups	peeled potatoes, cut into ½" cubes	3 cups
1 cup	salt free, canned or frozen corn	2 cups
1 cup	finely chopped celery	2 cups
½ cup	chopped onion	1 cup

4th Ready to serve. May garnish with dried parsley or chopped fresh parsley. May add a small amount of soy milk or water if the chowder is too thick.

COOKING TIME IF COOKING ON LOW:

Average Cooker: Smaller Recipe 5¾-6¼ hours OR Larger Recipe 6¾-7¼ hours

Fast Cooker: Smaller Recipe 4½-5 hours OR Larger Recipe 5½-6 hours

Extra Fast Cooker: Smaller Recipe 4-4½ hours OR Larger Recipe 5-5½ hours

COOKING TIME IF COOKING ON HIGH:

Average Cooker: Smaller Recipe 3-3½ hours OR Larger Recipe 3½-4 hours

Fast Cooker: Smaller Recipe 2¼-2¾ hours OR Larger Recipe 2¾-3¼ hours

Extra Fast Cooker: Smaller Recipe 2-2½ hours OR Larger Recipe 2½-3 hours

(See page 25, #3, for an explanation of the 3 types of cookers.)

Tips

- The cooker may be plugged into a lamp/appliance timer, page 11, to begin cooking up to 6 hours later.
- When the chowder is cooked in an Extra Fast cooker it will be somewhat thicker, and may have a reduced yield of ½-1 cup when compared to using an Average cooker. This is because the Extra Fast cooker cooks at a higher temperature, causing some evaporation of the water while cooking.

Boca Beefless Stew

Smaller Recipe		Larger Recipe
YIELD: 4¼ cups COOKER SIZE: 2-4½ qt.	INGREDIENTS	YIELD: 8½ cups COOKER SIZE: 3½-7 qt.

1st Find Boca Burgers in the frozen food section of the supermarket or health food store. Brown the burgers according to the package directions. Break or cut into small, bite size pieces. Other patties may be used in place of the Boca Burgers. Try other commercial patties, your favorite homemade gluten patty, or the Tender Gluten patties, page 58.

Smaller Recipe	Ingredients	Larger Recipe
2	vegan Boca Burgers	4

2nd Combine the following ingredients in the cooker and cook until the vegetables are tender. Carrots take the longest to cook, so slice them thin. The potatoes and carrots will have a brighter color if the stew is cooked on high.

Smaller Recipe	Ingredients	Larger Recipe
1¾ cups	peeled potatoes, cut into ½" cubes	3½ cups
1½ cups	water	3 cups
1¼ cups	thinly sliced carrots	2½ cups
¾ cup	chopped celery	1½ cups
½ cup	sliced or chopped onion	1 cup
2 tablespoons	Bragg Liquid Aminos	¼ cup
½ teaspoon	salt	1 teaspoon

3rd Stir the burgers pieces along with the following onion powder into the cooker.

Smaller Recipe	Ingredients	Larger Recipe
2 teaspoons	onion powder	4 teaspoons

4th Ready to serve. May garnish with fresh dill or parsley. See photo on page 69.

COOKING TIME IF COOKING ON LOW:

Average Cooker: Smaller Recipe 6¾-7¼ hours OR Larger Recipe 8½-9 hours

Fast Cooker: Smaller Recipe 6-6½ hours OR Larger Recipe 8-8½ hours

Extra Fast Cooker: Smaller Recipe 4¼-4¾ hours OR Larger Recipe 5¼-5¾ hours

COOKING TIME IF COOKING ON HIGH:

Average Cooker: Smaller Recipe 3¾-4¼ hours OR Larger Recipe 6¼-6¾ hours

Fast Cooker: Smaller Recipe 3-3½ hours OR Larger Recipe 5¼-5¾ hours

Extra Fast Cooker: Smaller Recipe 2½-3 hours OR Larger Recipe 3¾-4¼ hours

(See page 25, #3, for an explanation of the 3 types of cookers.)

Tips

- The cooker may be plugged into a lamp/appliance timer, page 11, to begin cooking up to 6 hours later.
- When the stew is cooked in an Extra Fast cooker it will be somewhat thicker, and may have a reduced yield of ½-1 cup when compared to using an Average cooker. This is because the Extra Fast cooker cooks at a higher temperature, causing some evaporation of the water while cooking.

Cashew Gravy

Smaller Recipe		Larger Recipe
YIELD: 2½ cups COOKER SIZE: 2-4 qt.	INGREDIENTS	YIELD: 5 cups COOKER SIZE: 2½-7 qt.

1st Blend the following ingredients for 2 minutes in a blender, until very smooth. Empty into the cooker.

Smaller Recipe	Ingredient	Larger Recipe
½ cup	water	1 cup
¼ cup + 2 tablespoons	raw cashews	¾ cup
¼ cup	quick or rolled oats	½ cup
3 tablespoons	Bragg Liquid Aminos, soy sauce or Soy Sauce, pg 136	⅓ cup
1 tablespoon	yeast flakes, pg 10	2 tablespoons
1½ teaspoons	onion powder	1 tablespoon
½ teaspoon	garlic powder	1 teaspoon
⅛ teaspoon	salt	¼ teaspoon

2nd Rinse the blender with the water in the following table, add to the cooker and cook. The gravy should be lightly boiling around the edges and slightly thickened throughout.

Smaller Recipe	Ingredient	Larger Recipe
1¾ cups	water	3½ cups

Ready to serve.

COOKING TIME IF COOKING ON LOW:

Average Cooker: Smaller Recipe 4-4½ hours OR Larger Recipe 5-5½ hours

Fast Cooker: Smaller Recipe 3¼-3¾ hours OR Larger Recipe 4-4½ hours

Extra Fast Cooker: Smaller Recipe 2¾-3¼ hours OR Larger Recipe 3½-4 hours

COOKING TIME IF COOKING ON HIGH:

Average Cooker: Smaller Recipe 2-2½ hours OR Larger Recipe 2½-3 hours

Fast Cooker: Smaller Recipe 1½-2 hours OR Larger Recipe 1¾-2¼ hours

Extra Fast Cooker: Smaller Recipe 1¼-1¾ hours OR Larger Recipe 1½-2 hours

(See page 25, #3, for an explanation of the 3 types of cookers.)

Tips

- The cooker may be plugged into a lamp/appliance timer, page 11, to begin cooking up to 6 hours later.
- Make Ahead: Prepare Step 1 and refrigerate. Mark the container with the amount of water remaining from Step 2 that needs to be added at the time of cooking.
- When the gravy is cooked in an Extra Fast cooker it will be somewhat thicker, and may have a reduced yield of ½-1 cup when compared to using an Average cooker. This is because the Extra Fast cooker cooks at a higher temperature, causing some evaporation of the water while cooking.

Chicken Style Gravy

Leave out the Braggs or soy sauce. The yeast flakes are optional. For the Smaller Recipe, add 1 tablespoon of McKay's Chicken Seasoning or Chicken Seasoning, page 136, and use a total amount of ¾ teaspoon salt. For the Larger Recipe, add 2 tablespoons of Chicken Seasoning and use a total of 1½ teaspoons of salt. See photo on page 65.

White Sauce

Leave out the Braggs or soy sauce and yeast flakes. Use blanched (white) almonds, page 137, instead of the cashews. Use a total of 1¼ teaspoons salt for the Smaller Recipe, or 2½ teaspoons for the Larger Recipe. See photo on page 72.

Cheese Sauce #1

YIELD: 3¼ cups	COOKER SIZE: 2-6 qt.

1st Blend the following ingredients in a blender for 2 minutes, until very smooth. Pour into the cooker.

¾ cup	water
¾ cup	raw cashews
½ cup or 4 oz.	pimento
⅓ cup	quick or rolled oats
¼ cup	yeast flakes, pg 10
3 tablespoons	lemon juice
2 teaspoons	onion powder
1¾ teaspoons	salt
1 teaspoon	garlic powder

2nd Rinse the blender with the water in the following table, then stir into the cooker. Cook until lightly boiling around the edges of the cooker, and thickened throughout.

2 cups	water

3rd Chill to thicken. Use on vegetables, spaghetti, pizza, lasagna, bread or crackers. See photo on page 72.

COOKING TIME ON LOW:
Average Cooker: 4-4½ hours
Fast Cooker: 2¾-3¼ hours
Extra Fast Cooker: 2¼-2¾ hours
COOKING TIME ON HIGH:
Average Cooker: 2-2½ hours
Fast Cooker: 1½-2 hours
Extra Fast Cooker: 1¼-1¾ hours
(See page 25, #3, for explanation of 3 types of cookers.)

Tips

- The cooker may be plugged into a lamp/appliance timer, page 11, to begin cooking up to 6 hours later.
- Cheese should keep a week or longer, but may also be frozen. When ready to use, thaw, then heat cheese until very hot or just to a boil. It will smooth out. Chill.
- Reheat on Another Day: Reheat on low 1½-2 hours for a hot cheese sauce over vegetables, potatoes, spaghetti, rice, haystacks, toast or other ideas.
- Increase the recipe size 1½-2 times and cook in 2½-7 qt. cooker.
- Quick Fix: Instead of using a cooker lightly boil this recipe for 2 minutes, stirring, in a sauce pan, then chill.

Cheese Sauce #2

YIELD: 3⅔ cups	COOKER SIZE: 2-6 qt.

1st Blend the following ingredients in a blender until smooth. Pour into the cooker.

½ cup	water
⅔ cup	quick or rolled oats
½ cup	yeast flakes, pg 10
½ cup or 4 oz.	pimento
3 tablespoons	lemon juice
3 tablespoons	canola oil
1 tablespoon	onion powder
2 teaspoons	salt
1 teaspoon	garlic powder

2nd Rinse the blender with the water in the following table, then stir into the cooker. Cook until lightly boiling around the edges of the cooker, and slightly thickened throughout. It will be about the consistency of thin gravy.

2½ cups	water

3rd Chill to thicken. Use as a topping on vegetables, such as baked potatoes. Serve on haystacks, spaghetti, pizza or lasagna. This cheese also makes a pretty salad dressing. After it has chilled to thicken, combine with cooked macaroni. Reheat for delicious macaroni and cheese.

COOKING TIME ON LOW:
Average Cooker: 3½-4 hours
Fast Cooker: 2¾-3¼ hours
Extra Fast Cooker: 2¼-2¾ hours
COOKING TIME ON HIGH:
Average Cooker: 1¾-2¼ hours
Fast Cooker: 1½-2 hours
Extra Fast Cooker: 1¼-1¾ hours
(See page 25, #3, for explanation of 3 types of cookers.)

Tip

- All of the tips under Cheese #1 apply to this cheese.

Spaghetti Sauce

YIELD: 3 cups	COOKER SIZE: 1½-4½ qt.

1st Stir together the following ingredients in the cooker. (Blend the tomatoes before cooking if a smooth sauce is preferred.) Cook until steaming hot and very lightly boiling in a few places around the edges.

14.5 oz. or 1¾ cups	canned, diced tomatoes with juice
1 cup	water
6 oz. can	tomato paste
2 teaspoons	olive oil
1 teaspoon	sweetener, i.e. honey or sugar
¾ teaspoon	salt

2nd Stir in the following onion and garlic. Crush the herbs between your fingers, then stir into the cooker. Crushing the herbs releases immediate flavor. This is ideal for brief cooking. Turn off the cooker. Let sit 5 minutes.

1½ teaspoons	onion powder
1 teaspoon	dried, granulated garlic
½ teaspoon	basil
¼ teaspoon	marjoram
⅛ teaspoon	oregano

3rd Ready to serve.

COOKING TIME ON LOW:
Average Cooker: 5½-6 hours
Fast Cooker: 3-3½ hours
Extra Fast Cooker: 2-2½ hours
COOKING TIME ON HIGH:
Average Cooker: 1¾-2 hours
Fast Cooker: 1½-1¾ hours
Extra Fast Cooker: 1¼-1½ hours
(See page 25, #3, for explanation of 3 types of cookers.)

Tips
- The cooker may be plugged into a lamp/appliance timer, page 11, to begin cooking up to 6 hours later.
- Reheat on Another Day: Reheat on low 1½-2 hours to serve hot over dishes such as, pasta, haystacks, rice or potatoes.
- Double the recipe and cook in a 2½-7 qt. cooker.

Chunky Pine-Apple Sauce

YIELD: 4 cups	COOKER SIZE: 2½-6 qt.

1st Soak the pineapple in the water for 30 minutes to soften, or lightly boil for 5 minutes. Blend the water and pineapple in a blender until smooth.

1 cup	water
½ cup	chopped, dried pineapple

2nd Thoroughly stir the following apples, with the blended pineapple, in the cooker. The pineapple will keep the apples a light color, otherwise they will darken as they cook. Softer varieties of apples will cook faster than firm, crisp apples. Small pieces will cook faster than large pieces. Cook until soft. Mash to desired consistency.

8 cups	peeled, sliced or chopped apples

3rd Ready to serve. See photo on page 67.

COOKING TIME ON LOW:
Average Cooker: 3½-4 hours
Fast Cooker: 2¾-3¼ hours
Extra Fast Cooker: 2½-3 hours
COOKING TIME ON HIGH:
Average Cooker: 2¼-2¾ hours
Fast Cooker: 2-2½ hours
Extra Fast Cooker: 2-2½ hours
(See page 25, #3, for explanation of 3 types of cookers.)

Tip
- The cooker may be plugged into a lamp/appliance timer, page 11, to begin cooking up to 8 hours later.

Crusty Whole Wheat Bread

This method has become my favorite way to bake bread. The dough may be mixed in a bread machine or by hand.

Smaller Recipe YIELD: 1¼# loaf COOKER SIZE: 5-7 qt.	INGREDIENTS	Larger Recipe YIELD: 1½# loaf COOKER SIZE: 6-7 qt.

1st Stir together the following ingredients. Let sit 8-10 minutes for the yeast to bubble.

Smaller Recipe	Ingredient	Larger Recipe
1 cup	warm water	1¼ cups
1 tablespoon	sweetener, i.e. honey or sugar	1 tablespoon
1 tablespoon	baking yeast	1 tablespoon

2nd Stir the flour before measuring, as it tends to settle as it is stored. Spoon it into a measuring cup. Add the following ingredients to the yeast mixture. Stir vigorously, 1-2 minutes, to develop the gluten in the wheat.

Smaller Recipe	Ingredient	Larger Recipe
1½ cups	whole wheat flour	2 cups
½ cup	white flour	½ cup
2 tablespoons	olive oil	2 tablespoons
1 teaspoon	salt	1¼ teaspoons

3rd Mix in the flour in the following table to create a dough that does not stick to your hands, but remains slightly sticky. Knead 3-4 minutes. Shape the dough into a ball. Use a sharp knife to make a few light cuts on the top of the dough for decoration. A lame may also be used. A lame is a slightly curved razor blade in a safety handle used for cutting a design on bread. It is available in some kitchen stores and online. After making the cuts, lightly dust the top of the dough with flour. If not making the cuts, skip dusting the top with flour.

Smaller Recipe	Ingredient	Larger Recipe
1¼-1½ cups	whole wheat flour	1¾-2 cups

4th Spray the cooker with a food release cooking spray. Place the ball of dough in the middle of the cooker. Cover the cooker with a hand towel that has not been washed with fabric softener (the smell may permeate the bread), or cover with 2 layers of paper towels. Cover with the lid. Bake until the top and sides are lightly browned. Remove with a metal spatula. Place the bread on a cooling rack. The bread will be 1¾-2¾" high. See photos on page 74.

BAKING TIME ON LOW:

Average Cooker: Smaller Recipe OR Larger Recipe 2-2½ hours

Fast Cooker: Smaller Recipe OR Larger Recipe 1¾-2 hours

Extra Fast Cooker: Smaller Recipe OR Larger Recipe 1¾-2 hours

(See page 25, #3, for an explanation of the 3 types of cookers.)

Tips

- The white flour may be replaced with whole wheat. The bread will be very good, just not quite as light.
- Photos on page 74 and 104. Breads can be baked in a variety of pans or oven proof dishes such as ramakins, small or mini bread pans and canapé bread pans. (A full size bread pan doesn't usually work. The bread tends to fall in the middle.) Bake on high, using a trivet, the same as other recipes in this chapter when baking bread in a can or baking rolls. The Larger Recipe, above, may be baked in a large can that holds about 13 cups. These cans are often filled with fruits or vegetables, such as used by restaurants or schools. (Cans are available in supermarkets or restaurant supply stores.) Bake on high according to the directions for Whole Wheat Bread in a Can, page 110.

You may also try different shapes of dough, using the Smaller Recipe, that are laid directly in a 6-7 qt. cooker, such as a braid, see Tips, page 106. Or, roll out the dough, spread with a dried fruit jam, roll up the dough and lay it in a cooker that has been sprayed with a food release spray. Bake on low about 15 minutes less than the times above.

Flax Bread

This method has become my favorite way to bake bread. The dough may be mixed in a bread machine or by hand.

Smaller Recipe		Larger Recipe
YIELD: 1¼# loaf COOKER SIZE: 5-7 qt.	INGREDIENTS	YIELD: 1½# loaf COOKER SIZE: 6-7 qt.

1st Stir together the following ingredients. Let sit 8-10 minutes for the yeast to bubble.

1 cup	warm water	1¼ cups
1 tablespoon	sweetener, i.e. honey or sugar	1 tablespoon
1 tablespoon	baking yeast	1 tablespoon

2nd Stir the flour before measuring, as it tends to settle as it is stored. Spoon it into a measuring cup. Grind the flax to a meal in a coffee grinder or blender. Add the following ingredients to the yeast mixture. Stir vigorously, 1-2 minutes, to develop the gluten in the wheat.

1¼ cups	whole wheat flour	1½ cups
½ cup	white flour	½ cup
3 tablespoons	whole flax seed	¼ cup
2 tablespoons	olive oil	2 tablespoons
1 teaspoon	salt	1¼ teaspoons

3rd Mix in the flour in the following table to create a dough that does not stick to your hands, but remains slightly sticky. Knead 3-4 minutes. Shape the dough into a ball.

1½-1¾ cups	whole wheat flour	2-2¼ cups

4th Spray the cooker with a food release cooking spray. Place the ball of dough in the middle of the cooker. Cover the cooker with a hand towel that has not been washed with fabric softener (the smell may permeate the bread), or cover with 2 layers of paper towels. Cover with the lid. Bake until the top and sides are lightly browned. This recipe will turn out more flat on top compared to all the other bread recipes which have a more rounded top. It is easy to remove the bread with a metal spatula. Place the bread on a cooling rack. The bread will be 1¾-2¾" high. See photo on page 68.

BAKING TIME ON LOW:

Average Cooker: Smaller Recipe OR Larger Recipe 2-2½ hours

Fast Cooker: Smaller Recipe OR Larger Recipe 1¾-2 hours

Extra Fast Cooker: Smaller Recipe OR Larger Recipe 1¾-2 hours

(See page 25, #3, for an explanation of the 3 types of cookers.)

Tips

- The white flour may be replaced with whole wheat. The bread will be very good, just not quite as light.
- The Larger Recipe may be baked in a large can. These cans holds about 13 cups and are often filled with fruits or vegetables, such as used by restaurants or schools. (Cans are available in supermarkets or restaurant supply stores.) Bake on high. Follow directions and baking time for Flax Bread in a Can, page 110.
- See Tips, page 104, for more ideas that can be used for baking this dough.

Old World Black Bread

This method has become my favorite way to bake bread. The dough may be mixed in a bread machine or by hand.

Smaller Recipe YIELD: 1¼# loaf COOKER SIZE: 5-7 qt.	INGREDIENTS	Larger Recipe YIELD: 1⅔# loaf COOKER SIZE: 6-7 qt.

1st Stir together the following ingredients. Let sit 8-10 minutes for the yeast to bubble.

Smaller Recipe	Ingredient	Larger Recipe
¾ cup	warm water	1 cup
¼ cup	molasses	⅓ cup
1 tablespoon	baking yeast	1 tablespoon

2nd Stir the flour before measuring, as it tends to settle as it is stored. Spoon it into a measuring cup. Add the following ingredients to the yeast mixture. Stir vigorously, 1-2 minutes, to develop the gluten in the wheat.

Smaller Recipe	Ingredient	Larger Recipe
1 cup	whole wheat flour	1½ cups
½ cup	rye flour	½ cup
½ cup	white flour	½ cup
2 tablespoons	carob powder	3 tablespoons
2 tablespoons	olive oil	2 tablespoons
1 teaspoon	salt	1¼ teaspoons

3rd Mix in the flour in the following table to create a dough that does not stick to your hands, but remains slightly sticky. Knead 3-4 minutes. Shape the dough into a ball.

Smaller Recipe	Ingredient	Larger Recipe
1-1¼ cups	whole wheat flour	1½-1¾ cups

4th Spray the cooker with a food release cooking spray. Place the ball of dough in the middle of the cooker. Cover the cooker with a hand towel that has not been washed with fabric softener (the smell may permeate the bread), or cover with 2 layers of paper towels. Cover with the lid. Bake until the top and sides are lightly browned. It is easy to remove the bread with a metal spatula. Place the bread on a cooling rack. The bread will be 1¾-2¾" high. See photo on page 74. See note below for making a braid.

BAKING TIME ON LOW:

Average Cooker: Smaller Recipe OR Larger Recipe 2-2½ hours

Fast Cooker: Smaller Recipe OR Larger Recipe 1¾-2 hours

Extra Fast Cooker: Smaller Recipe OR Larger Recipe 1¾-2 hours

(See page 25, #3, for an explanation of the 3 types of cookers.)

Tips

- The white flour may be replaced with whole wheat. The bread will be very good, just not quite as light.
- Braid: In the photo, page 74, the Smaller Recipe bread dough is divided into 3 equal pieces, then rolled into 3 ropes a little longer than the cooker. Braid the ropes, tucking the ends underneath. Bake in a 6-7 qt. cooker that has been sprayed with a food release cooking spray. The baking time for a braid will be about 15 minutes less then the baking times listed above. See Tips, page 104, for more ideas that can be used for baking this dough.
- The Larger Recipe may be baked in a large can. These cans holds about 13 cups and are often filled with fruits or vegetables, such as used by restaurants or schools. (Cans are available in supermarkets or restaurant supply stores.) Bake on high. Follow directions and baking time for Old World Black Bread in a Can, page 111.

Whole Grain Rye Bread

This method has become my favorite way to bake bread. The dough may be mixed in a bread machine or by hand.

Smaller Recipe		Larger Recipe
YIELD: 1¼# loaf COOKER SIZE: 5-7 qt.	INGREDIENTS	YIELD: 1⅔# loaf COOKER SIZE: 6-7 qt.

1st Stir together the following ingredients. Let sit 8-10 minutes for the yeast to bubble.

Smaller Recipe	Ingredient	Larger Recipe
¾ cup	warm water	1 cup
¼ cup	molasses	⅓ cup
1 tablespoon	baking yeast	1 tablespoon

2nd Stir the flour before measuring, as it tends to settle as it is stored. Spoon it into a measuring cup. Add the following ingredients to the yeast mixture. Stir vigorously, 1-2 minutes, to develop the gluten in the wheat.

Smaller Recipe	Ingredient	Larger Recipe
1 cup	whole wheat flour	1½ cups
½ cup	rye flour	½ cup
½ cup	white flour	½ cup
2 teaspoons	caraway seeds, optional	1 tablespoon
2 tablespoons	olive oil	2 tablespoons
1 teaspoon	salt	1¼ teaspoons

3rd Mix in the flour in the following table to create a dough that does not stick to your hands, but remains slightly sticky. Knead 3-4 minutes. Shape the dough into a ball.

Smaller Recipe	Ingredient	Larger Recipe
1-1¼ cups	whole wheat flour	1½-1¾ cups

4th Spray the cooker with a food release cooking spray. Place the ball of dough in the middle of the cooker. Cover the cooker with a hand towel that has not been washed with fabric softener (the smell may permeate the bread), or cover with 2 layers of paper towels. Cover with the lid. Bake until the top and sides are lightly browned. It is easy to remove the bread with a metal spatula. Place the bread on a cooling rack. The bread will be 1¾-2¾" high. See photo on page 74.

BAKING TIME ON LOW:

Average Cooker: Smaller Recipe OR Larger Recipe 2-2½ hours

Fast Cooker: Smaller Recipe OR Larger Recipe 1¾-2 hours

Extra Fast Cooker: Smaller Recipe OR Larger Recipe 1¾-2 hours

(See page 25, #3, for an explanation of the 3 types of cookers.)

Tips

- The white flour may be replaced with whole wheat. The bread will be very good, just not quite as light.
- The Larger Recipe may be baked in a large can. These cans holds about 13 cups and are often filled with fruits or vegetables, such as used by restaurants or schools. (Cans are available in supermarkets or restaurant supply stores.) Bake on high. Follow directions and baking time for Whole Grain Rye Bread in a Can, page 111.
- See Tips, page 104, for more ideas that can be used for baking this dough.

Poppy Seed Bread

This method has become my favorite way to bake bread. The dough may be mixed in a bread machine or by hand.

Smaller Recipe YIELD: 1¼# loaf COOKER SIZE: 5-7 qt.	INGREDIENTS	Larger Recipe YIELD: 1½# loaf COOKER SIZE: 6-7 qt.

1st Stir together the following ingredients and let soak 5 minutes until warm, no longer hot.

Smaller Recipe	Ingredient	Larger Recipe
¾ cup	hot water	1 cup
¼ cup	quick or rolled oats	½ cup
¼ cup	poppy seeds	⅓ cup
¼ cup	coconut	⅓ cup
3 tablespoons	honey	¼ cup
2 teaspoons	lemon flavoring	2 teaspoons

2nd Stir in the yeast and let sit 10 minutes.

Smaller Recipe	Ingredient	Larger Recipe
1 tablespoon	yeast	1 tablespoon

3rd Stir the flour before measuring, as it tends to settle as it is stored. Spoon it into a measuring cup. Add the following ingredients to the yeast mixture. Stir vigorously, 1-2 minutes, to develop the gluten in the wheat.

Smaller Recipe	Ingredient	Larger Recipe
1 cup	whole wheat flour	1½ cups
½ cup	white flour	½ cup
2 tablespoons	mild tasting olive oil or canola oil	2 tablespoons
1 teaspoon	salt	1¼ teaspoons

4th Mix in the flour in the following table to create a dough that does not stick to your hands, but remains slightly sticky. Knead 3-4 minutes. Shape the dough into a ball.

Smaller Recipe	Ingredient	Larger Recipe
1-1¼ cups	whole wheat flour	1¼-1½ cups

Spray the cooker with a food release cooking spray. Place the ball of dough in the middle of the cooker. Cover the cooker with a hand towel that has not been washed with fabric softener (the smell may permeate the bread), or cover with 2 layers of paper towels. Cover with the lid. Bake until the top and sides are lightly browned. It is easy to remove the bread with a metal spatula. Place the bread on a cooling rack. The bread will be 1¾-2¾" high. This bread is especially delicious when toasted. See photo on page 74.

BAKING TIME ON LOW:

Average Cooker: Smaller Recipe OR Larger Recipe 2-2½ hours

Fast Cooker: Smaller Recipe OR Larger Recipe 1¾-2 hours

Extra Fast Cooker: Smaller Recipe OR Larger Recipe 1¾-2 hours

(See page 25, #3, for an explanation of the 3 types of cookers.)

Tips

- The white flour may be replaced with whole wheat. The bread will be very good, just not quite as light.
- The Larger Recipe may be baked in a large can. Follow directions under Tips, page 109.
- See Tips, page 104, for more ideas that can be used for baking this dough.

Oatmeal Raisin Bread

This method has become my favorite way to bake bread. The dough may be mixed in a bread machine or by hand.

Smaller Recipe		Larger Recipe
YIELD: 1⅓# loaf COOKER SIZE: 5-7 qt.	INGREDIENTS	YIELD: 1⅔# loaf COOKER SIZE: 6-7 qt.

1st Stir together the following ingredients and let soak 5 minutes until warm, no longer hot.

Smaller Recipe	Ingredient	Larger Recipe
¾ cup	hot water	1 cup
½ cup	chopped raisins, dried cherries or currants	⅔ cup
½ cup	quick or rolled oats	⅔ cup
2 teaspoons	whole fennel seed, optional	1 tablespoon
1 tablespoon	sweetener, i.e. honey or sugar	1 tablespoon

2nd Stir in the yeast and let sit 10 minutes.

Smaller Recipe	Ingredient	Larger Recipe
1 tablespoon	baking yeast	1 tablespoon

3rd Stir the flour before measuring, as it tends to settle as it is stored. Spoon it into a measuring cup. Add the following ingredients to the yeast mixture. Stir vigorously, 1-2 minutes, to develop the gluten in the wheat.

Smaller Recipe	Ingredient	Larger Recipe
½ cup	whole wheat flour	¾ cup
½ cup	white flour	½ cup
2 tablespoons	mild tasting olive oil or canola oil	2 tablespoons
1 teaspoon	salt	1¼ teaspoons

4th Mix in the flour in the following table to create a dough that does not stick to your hands, but remains slightly sticky. Knead 3-4 minutes. Shape the dough into a ball.

Smaller Recipe	Ingredient	Larger Recipe
1¼-1½ cups	whole wheat flour	1½-1¾ cups

Spray the cooker with a food release cooking spray. Place the ball of dough in the middle of the cooker. Cover the cooker with a hand towel that has not been washed with fabric softener (the smell may permeate the bread), or cover with 2 layers of paper towels. Cover with the lid. Bake until the top and sides are lightly browned. It is easy to remove the bread with a metal spatula. Place the bread on a cooling rack. The bread will be 1¾-2¾" high.

BAKING TIME ON LOW:

Average Cooker: Smaller Recipe OR Larger Recipe 2-2½ hours

Fast Cooker: Smaller Recipe OR Larger Recipe 1¾-2 hours

Extra Fast Cooker: Smaller Recipe OR Larger Recipe 1¾-2 hours

(See page 25, #3, for an explanation of the 3 types of cookers.)

Tips

- The white flour may be replaced with whole wheat. The bread will be very good, just not quite as light.
- The Larger Recipe may be baked in a large can. These cans holds about 13 cups and are often filled with fruits or vegetables, such as used by restaurants or schools. (Cans are available in supermarkets or restaurant supply stores.) Bake on high. Follow directions and baking time for Oatmeal Raisin Bread in a Can, page 112.
- See Tips, page 104, for more ideas that can be used for baking this dough.

Whole Wheat Bread in a Can

The dough may be mixed in a bread machine or by hand.

YIELD: 14 oz.	COOKER SIZE: any size

1st Stir together the following ingredients. Let sit 8-10 minutes for the yeast to bubble.

⅔ cup	warm water
1 tablespoon	sweetener, i.e. honey or sugar
1 tablespoon	baking yeast

2nd Stir the flour before measuring, as it tends to settle as it is stored. Spoon it into a measuring cup. Add the following ingredients to the yeast mixture. Stir vigorously, for 1-2 minutes, to develop the gluten in the wheat.

1 cup	whole wheat flour
⅓ cup	white flour
2 tablespoons	olive oil
¾ teaspoon	salt

3rd Mix in the flour in the following table to create a dough that does not stick to your hands, but remains slightly sticky. Knead 3-4 minutes. Shape the dough into a ball.

¾-1 cup	whole wheat flour

4th Spray a 46 oz. juice can with a food release cooking spray. Place the dough in the can. Place it on a trivet, such as a canning ring or metal jar lid, in the cooker. Cover the can with 2 layers of paper towels. Cover the cooker with aluminum foil (in most cases the lid will not fit on the cooker so foil is used for the lid). Bake until lightly browned. Let the bread cool a few minutes before removing from the can. See photo page 74.

BAKING TIME ON HIGH:
Average Cooker: 2¼-2½ hours
Fast Cooker: 2-2¼ hours
Extra Fast Cooker: 1 hour 50 minutes-2 hours
(See page 25, #3, for explanation of 3 types of cookers.)

Tip

- The white flour may be replaced with whole wheat flour. The bread will be very good, just not quite as light.

Flax Bread in a Can

The dough may be mixed in a bread machine or by hand.

YIELD: 1#	COOKER SIZE: any size

1st Stir together the following ingredients. Let sit 8-10 minutes for the yeast to bubble.

¾ cup	warm water
1 tablespoon	sweetener, i.e. honey or sugar
1 tablespoon	baking yeast

2nd Grind the flax to a meal in a blender or coffee grinder. Stir the flour before measuring, as it tends to settle as it is stored. Spoon it into a measuring cup. Add the following ingredients to the yeast mixture. Stir vigorously, for 1-2 minutes, to develop the gluten in the wheat.

1 cup	whole wheat flour
⅓ cup	white flour
3 tablespoons	whole flax seed
2 tablespoons	olive oil
¾ teaspoon	salt

3rd Mix in the flour in the following table to create a dough that does not stick to your hands, but remains slightly sticky. Knead 3-4 minutes. Shape the dough into a ball.

1-1¼ cups	whole wheat flour

4th Spray a 46 oz. juice can with a food release cooking spray. Place the dough in the can. Place it on a trivet, such as a canning ring or metal jar lid, in the cooker. Cover the can with 2 layers of paper towels. Cover the cooker with aluminum foil (in most cases the lid will not fit on the cooker so foil is used for the lid). Bake until lightly browned. Let the bread cool a few minutes before removing from the can.

BAKING TIME ON HIGH:
Average Cooker: 2¼-2½ hours
Fast Cooker: 2-2¼ hours
Extra Fast Cooker: 1 hour 50 minutes-2 hours
(See page 25, #3, for explanation of 3 types of cookers.)

Tip

- The white flour may be replaced with whole wheat flour. The bread will be very good, just not quite as light.

Old World Black Bread in a Can

The dough may be mixed in a bread machine or by hand.

YIELD: 1#	COOKER SIZE: any size

1st Stir together the following ingredients. Let sit 8-10 minutes for the yeast to bubble.

⅔ cup	warm water
3 tablespoons	molasses
1 tablespoon	baking yeast

2nd Stir the flour before measuring, as it tends to settle as it is stored. Spoon it into a measuring cup. Add the following ingredients to the yeast mixture. Stir vigorously, for 1-2 minutes, to develop the gluten in the wheat.

¾ cup	whole wheat flour
⅓ cup	rye flour
⅓ cup	white flour
2 tablespoons	mild tasting olive oil or canola oil
1½ tablespoons	carob powder
¾ teaspoon	salt

3rd Mix in the flour in the following table to create a dough that does not stick to your hands, but remains slightly sticky. Knead 3-4 minutes. Shape the dough into a ball.

1¼-1½ cups	whole wheat flour

4th Spray a 46 oz. juice can with a food release cooking spray. Place the dough in the can. Place it on a trivet, such as a canning ring or metal jar lid, in the cooker. Cover the can with 2 layers of paper towels. Cover the cooker with aluminum foil (in most cases the lid will not fit on the cooker so foil is used for the lid). Bake until lightly browned. Let the bread cool a few minutes before removing from the can.

BAKING TIME ON HIGH:
Average Cooker: 2¼-2½ hours
Fast Cooker: 2-2¼ hours
Extra Fast Cooker: 1 hour 50 minutes-2 hours
(See page 25, #3, for explanation of 3 types of cookers.)

Tip

- The white flour may be replaced with whole wheat flour. The bread will be very good, just not quite as light.

Whole Grain Rye Bread in a Can

The dough may be mixed in a bread machine or by hand.

YIELD: 1#	COOKER SIZE: any size

1st Stir together the following ingredients. Let sit 8-10 minutes for the yeast to bubble.

⅔ cup	warm water
3 tablespoons	molasses
1 tablespoon	baking yeast

2nd Stir the flour before measuring, as it tends to settle as it is stored. Spoon it into a measuring cup. Add the following ingredients to the yeast mixture. Stir vigorously, for 1-2 minutes, to develop the gluten in the wheat.

¾ cup	whole wheat flour
⅓ cup	rye flour
⅓ cup	white flour
2 tablespoons	olive oil
2 teaspoons	caraway seed, optional
¾ teaspoon	salt

3rd Mix in the flour in the following table to create a dough that does not stick to your hands, but remains slightly sticky. Knead 3-4 minutes. Shape the dough into a ball.

1¼-1½ cups	whole wheat flour

4th Spray a 46 oz. juice can with a food release cooking spray. Place the dough in the can. Place it on a trivet, such as a canning ring or metal jar lid, in the cooker. Cover the can with 2 layers of paper towels. Cover the cooker with aluminum foil (in most cases the lid will not fit on the cooker so foil is used for the lid). Bake until lightly browned. Let the bread cool a few minutes before removing from the can.

BAKING TIME ON HIGH:
Average Cooker: 2¼-2½ hours
Fast Cooker: 2-2¼ hours
Extra Fast Cooker: 1 hour 50 minutes-2 hours
(See page 25, #3, for explanation of 3 types of cookers.)

Tip

- The white flour may be replaced with whole wheat flour. The bread will be very good, just not quite as light.

Poppy Seed Bread in a Can

The dough may be mixed in a bread machine or by hand.

YIELD: 1#	COOKER SIZE: any size

1st Stir together the following ingredients. Let sit 5 minutes.

⅔ cup	hot water
¼ cup	quick or rolled oats
¼ cup	poppy seeds
¼ cup	coconut
3 tablespoons	honey
2 teaspoons	lemon flavoring

2nd Stir in the yeast. Let sit 5 minutes.

1 tablespoon	baking yeast

3rd Stir the flour before measuring, as it tends to settle as it is stored. Spoon it into a measuring cup. Add the following ingredients to the yeast mixture. Stir vigorously, for 1-2 minutes, to develop the gluten in the wheat.

1 cup	whole wheat flour
⅓ cup	white flour
2 tablespoons	mild tasting olive oil or canola oil
¾ teaspoon	salt

4th Mix in the flour in the following table to create a dough that does not stick to your hands, but remains slightly sticky. Knead 3-4 minutes. Shape into a ball.

1-1¼ cups	whole wheat flour

5th Spray a 46 oz. juice can with a food release cooking spray. Place the dough in the can. Place it on a trivet, such as a metal jar lid, in the cooker. Cover the can with 2 layers of paper towels. Cover the cooker with aluminum foil. Bake until lightly browned. Let cool a few minutes before removing bread from the can.

BAKING TIME ON HIGH:
Average Cooker: 2¼-2½ hours
Fast Cooker: 2-2¼ hours
Extra Fast Cooker: 1 hour 50 minutes-2 hours
(See page 25, #3, for explanation of 3 types of cookers.)

Tip
- The white flour may be replaced with whole wheat flour. The bread will be very good, just not quite as light.

Oatmeal Raisin Bread in a Can

The dough may be mixed in a bread machine or by hand.

YIELD: 1#	COOKER SIZE: any size

1st Stir together the following ingredients. Let sit 5 minutes.

⅔ cup	hot water
½ cup	chopped raisins or dried cherries
¼ cup	quick or rolled oats
2 teaspoons	whole fennel seed, optional
2 teaspoons	sweetener, i.e. honey or sugar

2nd Stir in the yeast. Let sit 5 minutes.

1 tablespoon	baking yeast

3rd Stir the flour before measuring, as it tends to settle as it is stored. Spoon it into a measuring cup. Add the following ingredients to the yeast mixture. Stir vigorously, for 1-2 minutes, to develop the gluten in the wheat.

1 cup	whole wheat flour
⅓ cup	white flour
2 tablespoons	mild tasting olive oil or canola oil
¾ teaspoon	salt

4th Mix in the flour in the following table to create a dough that does not stick to your hands, but remains slightly sticky. Knead 3-4 minutes. Shape into a ball.

¾-1 cup	whole wheat flour

5th Spray a 46 oz. juice can with a food release cooking spray. Place the dough in the can. Place it on a trivet, such as a metal jar lid, in the cooker. Cover the can with 2 layers of paper towels. Cover the cooker with aluminum foil. Bake until lightly browned. Let cool a few minutes before removing bread from the can.

BAKING TIME ON HIGH:
Average Cooker: 2¼-2½ hours
Fast Cooker: 2-2¼ hours
Extra Fast Cooker: 1 hour 50 minutes-2 hours
(See page 25, #3, for explanation of 3 types of cookers.)

Tip
- The white flour may be replaced with whole wheat flour. The bread will be very good, just not quite as light.

Whole Wheat Rolls

The dough may be mixed in a bread machine or by hand.

YIELD: 10 oz.	COOKER SIZE: 6-7 qt.

1st Stir together the following ingredients. Let sit 8-10 minutes for the yeast to bubble.

½ cup	warm water
2 teaspoons	sweetener, i.e. honey or sugar
2 teaspoons	baking yeast

2nd Stir the flour before measuring, as it tends to settle as it is stored. Spoon it into a measuring cup. Add the following ingredients to the yeast mixture. Stir vigorously, for 1-2 minutes, to develop the gluten in the wheat.

¾ cup	whole wheat flour
⅓ cup	white flour
2 tablespoons	olive oil
½ teaspoon	salt

3rd Mix in enough of the flour in the following table to create a dough that does not stick to your hands, but remains slightly sticky. Knead 3-4 minutes. Divide the dough into 3 portions. Divide each portion into 3 pieces. Shape each piece into a roll.

½-¾ cup	whole wheat flour

4th Spray an 8" round cake pan with a food release cooking spray. Place the rolls in the pan. Place the pan on a trivet in the cooker. Cover the cooker with a hand towel that has not been washed with fabric softener (the smell may permeate the rolls), or a double layer of paper towels. Do not use a tall trivet, as the rolls may hit the towel as they rise in the cooker. Cover with the lid. Bake until lightly browned. Separate the rolls on a cooling rack.

BAKING TIME ON HIGH:
Most Cookers: 1¼-1½ hours

Tip

- The white flour may be replaced with whole wheat flour. The rolls will be very good, just not as light.

Flax Rolls

The dough may be mixed in a bread machine or by hand.

YIELD: 11 oz.	COOKER SIZE: 6-7 qt.

1st Stir together the following ingredients. Let sit 8-10 minutes for the yeast to bubble.

½ cup	warm water
1 tablespoon	honey
2 teaspoons	baking yeast

2nd Grind the flax to a meal in a blender or coffee grinder. Stir the flour before measuring, as it tends to settle as it is stored. Spoon it into a measuring cup. Add the following ingredients to the yeast mixture. Stir vigorously, for 1-2 minutes, to develop the gluten in the wheat.

¾ cup	whole wheat flour
⅓ cup	white flour
2 tablespoons	whole flax seed
2 tablespoons	olive oil
½ teaspoon	salt

3rd Mix in enough of the flour in the following table to create a dough that does not stick to your hands, but remains slightly sticky. Knead 3-4 minutes. Divide the dough into 3 portions. Divide each portion into 3 pieces. Shape each piece into a roll.

½-¾ cup	whole wheat flour

4th Spray an 8" round cake pan with a food release cooking spray. Place the rolls in the pan. Place the pan on a trivet in the cooker. Cover the cooker with a hand towel that has not been washed with fabric softener (the smell may permeate the rolls), or a double layer of paper towels. Do not use a tall trivet, as the rolls may hit the towel as they rise in the cooker. Cover with the lid. Bake until lightly browned. Separate the rolls on a cooling rack.

BAKING TIME ON HIGH:
Most Cookers: 1¼-1½ hours

Tip

- The white flour may be replaced with whole wheat flour. The rolls will be very good, just not as light.

Old World Black Rolls

The dough may be mixed in a bread machine or by hand.

YIELD: 13½ oz.	COOKER SIZE: 6-7 qt.

1st Stir together the following ingredients. Let sit 8-10 minutes for the yeast to bubble.

½ cup	warm water
2 tablespoons	molasses
2 teaspoons	baking yeast

2nd Stir the flour before measuring, as it tends to settle as it is stored. Spoon it into a measuring cup. Add the following ingredients to the yeast mixture. Stir vigorously, for 1-2 minutes, to develop the gluten in the wheat.

⅓ cup	whole wheat flour
⅓ cup	white flour
⅓ cup	rye flour
2 tablespoons	olive oil
1½ tablespoons	carob powder
½ teaspoon	salt

3rd Mix in enough of the flour in the following table to create a dough that does not stick to your hands, but remains slightly sticky. Knead 3-4 minutes. Divide the dough into 3 portions. Divide each portion into 3 pieces. Shape each piece into a roll.

1-1¼ cups	whole wheat flour

4th Spray an 8" round cake pan with a food release cooking spray. Place the rolls in the pan. Place the pan on a trivet in the cooker. Cover the cooker with a hand towel that has not been washed with fabric softener (the smell may permeate the rolls), or a double layer of paper towels. Do not use a tall trivet, as the rolls may hit the towel as they rise in the cooker. Cover with the lid. Bake until lightly browned. Separate the rolls on a cooling rack.

BAKING TIME ON HIGH: Most Cookers: 1¼-1½ hours

Tip

- The white flour may be replaced with whole wheat flour. The rolls will be very good, just not as light.

Whole Grain Rye Rolls

The dough may be mixed in a bread machine or by hand.

YIELD: 13½ oz.	COOKER SIZE: 6-7 qt.

1st Stir together the following ingredients. Let sit 8-10 minutes for the yeast to bubble.

½ cup	warm water
2 tablespoons	molasses
2 teaspoons	baking yeast

2nd Stir the flour before measuring, as it tends to settle as it is stored. Spoon it into a measuring cup. Add the following ingredients to the yeast mixture. Stir vigorously, for 1-2 minutes, to develop the gluten in the wheat.

⅓ cup	whole wheat flour
⅓ cup	white flour
⅓ cup	rye flour
2 tablespoons	olive oil
1½ teaspoons	caraway seed, optional
½ teaspoon	salt

3rd Mix in enough of the flour in the following table to create a dough that does not stick to your hands, but remains slightly sticky. Knead 3-4 minutes. Divide the dough into 3 portions. Divide each portion into 3 pieces. Shape each piece into a roll.

1-1¼ cups	whole wheat flour

4th Spray an 8" round cake pan with a food release cooking spray. Place the rolls in the pan. Place the pan on a trivet in the cooker. Cover the cooker with a hand towel that has not been washed with fabric softener (the smell may permeate the rolls), or a double layer of paper towels. Do not use a tall trivet, as the rolls may hit the towel as they rise in the cooker. Cover with the lid. Bake until lightly browned. Separate the rolls on a cooling rack.

BAKING TIME ON HIGH: Most Cookers: 1¼-1½ hours

Tip

- The white flour may be replaced with whole wheat flour. The rolls will be very good, just not as light.

Poppy Seed Rolls

The dough may be mixed in a bread machine or by hand.

YIELD: 12 oz.	COOKER SIZE: 6-7 qt.

1st Stir together the following ingredients. Let sit 5 minutes.

½ cup	hot water
3 tablespoons	quick or rolled oats
2 tablespoons	poppy seeds
3 tablespoons	coconut
2 tablespoons	honey
1 teaspoon	lemon flavoring

2nd Stir in the yeast and let sit 5 minutes.

2 teaspoons	baking yeast

3rd Stir the flour before measuring, as it tends to settle as it is stored. Spoon it into a measuring cup. Add the following ingredients to the yeast mixture. Stir vigorously, for 1-2 minutes, to develop the gluten in the wheat.

½ cup	whole wheat flour
⅓ cup	white flour
2 tablespoons	mild tasting olive oil or canola oil
½ teaspoon	salt

4th Mix in enough of the flour in the following table to create a dough that does not stick to your hands, but remains slightly sticky. Knead 3-4 minutes. Divide the dough into 3 portions. Divide each portion into 3 pieces. Shape each piece into a roll.

¾-1 cup	whole wheat flour

5th Spray an 8" round cake pan with a food release cooking spray. Place the rolls in the pan. Place the pan on a trivet in the cooker. Cover the cooker with a hand towel that has not been washed with fabric softener (the smell may permeate the rolls), or a double layer of paper towels. Do not use a tall trivet, as the rolls may hit the towel as they rise in the cooker. Cover with the lid. Bake until lightly browned. Separate the rolls on a cooling rack.

BAKING TIME ON HIGH: Most Cookers: 1¼-1½ hours

Tip

• The white flour may be replaced with whole wheat flour. The rolls will be very good, just not as light.

Oatmeal Raisin Rolls

The dough may be mixed in a bread machine or by hand.

YIELD: 12 oz.	COOKER SIZE: 6-7 qt.

1st Stir together the following ingredients. Let sit 5 minutes.

½ cup	hot water
¼ cup	chopped raisins or dried cherries
2 tablespoons	quick or rolled oats
1 tablespoon	honey
1 teaspoon	whole fennel seed, optional

2nd Stir in the yeast and let sit 5 minutes.

2 teaspoons	baking yeast

3rd Stir the flour before measuring, as it tends to settle as it is stored. Spoon it into a measuring cup. Add the following ingredients to the yeast mixture. Stir vigorously, for 1-2 minutes, to develop the gluten in the wheat.

⅓ cup	white flour
¼ cup	whole wheat flour
2 tablespoons	mild tasting olive oil or canola oil
½ teaspoon	salt

4th Mix in enough of the flour in the following table to create a dough that does not stick to your hands, but remains slightly sticky. Knead 3-4 minutes. Divide the dough into 3 portions. Divide each portion into 3 pieces. Shape each piece into a roll.

1¼-1½ cups	whole wheat flour

5th Spray an 8" round cake pan with a food release cooking spray. Place the rolls in the pan. Place the pan on a trivet in the cooker. Cover the cooker with a hand towel that has not been washed with fabric softener (the smell may permeate the rolls), or a double layer of paper towels. Do not use a tall trivet, as the rolls may hit the towel as they rise in the cooker. Cover with the lid. Bake until lightly browned. Separate the rolls on a cooling rack.

BAKING TIME ON HIGH: Most Cookers: 1¼-1½ hours

Tip

• The white flour may be replaced with whole wheat flour. The rolls will be very good, just not as light.

Focaccia

Smaller Recipe		Larger Recipe
YIELD: 10.5 oz. loaf COOKER SIZE: 5-7 qt.	INGREDIENTS	YIELD: 13.5 oz. loaf COOKER SIZE: 6-7 qt.

1st Stir together the following ingredients. Let sit 8-10 minutes for the yeast to bubble.

Smaller	Ingredient	Larger
½ cup	warm water	⅔ cup
2 teaspoons	sweetener, i.e. honey or sugar	1 tablespoon
2 teaspoons	baking yeast	1 tablespoon

2nd Stir the flour before measuring, as it tends to settle as it is stored. Spoon it into a measuring cup. Add the following ingredients to the yeast mixture. Stir vigorously, 1-2 minutes, to develop the gluten in the wheat.

Smaller	Ingredient	Larger
¾ cup	whole wheat flour	1 cup
¼ cup	white flour, whole wheat flour or whole wheat pastry flour	⅓ cup
1 tablespoon	olive oil	1 tablespoon
¼ teaspoon	salt	½ teaspoon

3rd Mix in enough of the flour in the following table to create a dough that does not stick to your hands, but remains slightly sticky. Knead 3-4 minutes. Lightly flour the counter then roll out the dough to a 6" circle for the Smaller Recipe, or a 7" circle for the Larger Recipe.

Smaller	Ingredient	Larger
½-¾ cup	whole wheat flour	¾-1 cup

4th Spray the cooker with a food release cooking spray. Lay the dough inside. Poke then dough about 10-15 times with a sharp knife or toothpick. Bake as is, or add any of the following optional toppings.

Smaller	Ingredient	Larger
¼ cup	Add one of the following or a combination:	¼-⅓ cup
	chopped or thinly sliced olives	
	thinly sliced, sautéed onion	
	thinly sliced and seeded, fresh tomatoes	
	Cheese Sauce, pg 102, or shredded, nondairy cheese	
1 tablespoon	chopped, canned pimento	1-2 tablespoons

5th If desired, sprinkle with any of the following. (More of these seasonings may be added after baking.)

Smaller	Ingredient	Larger
	fresh or dried, chopped herbs, such as parsley or cilantro	
	paprika or herb seasoning salt	
	onion powder, garlic powder or yeast flakes	

6th Cover the cooker with a hand towel that has not been washed with fabric softener or cover with 2 layers of paper towels. Cover with the lid. Bake until golden brown. See photos on page 65 & 69.

BAKING TIME ON LOW:

Average Cooker: Smaller Recipe OR Larger Recipe 2-2¼ hours

Fast Cooker: Smaller Recipe OR Larger Recipe 1¾-2 hours

Extra Fast Cooker: Smaller Recipe OR Larger Recipe 1½-1¾ hours

(See page 25, #3, for an explanation of the 3 types of cookers.)

Pizza Crust

The dough may be mixed in a bread machine or by hand. This crust is used for fruit or vegetable pizzas.

Smaller Recipe		Larger Recipe
YIELD: 7 oz. crust COOKER SIZE: 5-7 qt.	INGREDIENTS	YIELD: 10 oz. crust COOKER SIZE: 6-7 qt.

1st Stir together the following ingredients. Let sit 8-10 minutes for the yeast to bubble.

⅓ cup	warm water	½ cup
1½ teaspoons	sweetener, i.e. honey or sugar	1½ teaspoons
1½ teaspoons	baking yeast	1½ teaspoons

2nd Stir the flour before measuring, as it tends to settle as it is stored. Spoon it into a measuring cup. Add the following ingredients to the yeast mixture. Stir vigorously, 1-2 minutes, to develop the gluten in the wheat.

⅓ cup	whole wheat flour	½ cup
⅓ cup	white flour or whole wheat flour	½ cup
1 teaspoon	olive oil	1 teaspoon
¼ teaspoon	salt	¼ teaspoon

3rd Mix in enough flour in the following table to create a dough that does not stick to your hands, but is slightly sticky. Knead well for 3-4 minutes. Lightly flour the counter then roll out the dough to the about ⅛" thick. For a thick crust roll the dough to about ¼" thick.

¼-½ cup	whole wheat or whole wheat pastry flour	½-¾ cup

4th Spray the cooker with a food release cooking spray. Lay the dough inside. Cover the cooker with a hand towel that has not been washed with fabric softener (the smell may permeate the crust), or cover with 2 layers of paper towels. Cover with the lid. Bake until the dough is dry and very lightly browned. Place the crust on a cooling rack. Refrigerate or freeze until ready to use for a fruit or vegetable pizza.

BAKING TIME ON LOW:

Average Cooker: Smaller Recipe OR Larger Recipe 1½ hours

Fast Cooker: Smaller Recipe OR Larger Recipe 1¼-1½ hours

Extra Fast Cooker: Smaller Recipe OR Larger Recipe 1¼ hours

(See page 25, #3, for an explanation of the 3 types of cookers.)

Tip

- See page 24 for the fruit pizza. See page 61 for vegetable pizza.

Personal Pizza Crust

The dough may be mixed in a bread machine or by hand. This crust is used for fruit or vegetable pizzas.

Smaller Recipe		Larger Recipe
YIELD: 5.5 oz. loaf COOKER SIZE: 2½-7 qt.	INGREDIENTS	YIELD: 7 oz. crust COOKER SIZE: 5-7 qt.

1st Stir together the following ingredients. Let sit 8-10 minutes for the yeast to bubble.

Smaller Recipe	Ingredient	Larger Recipe
¼ cup	warm water	⅓ cup
1½ teaspoons	sweetener, i.e. honey or sugar	1½ teaspoons
1½ teaspoons	baking yeast	1½ teaspoons

2nd Stir the flour before measuring, as it tends to settle as it is stored. Spoon it into a measuring cup. Add the following ingredients to the yeast mixture. Stir vigorously, 1-2 minutes, to develop the gluten in the wheat.

Smaller Recipe	Ingredient	Larger Recipe
¼ cup	whole wheat flour	½ cup
¼ cup	white flour, whole wheat flour or whole wheat pastry flour	⅓ cup
1 teaspoon	olive oil	1 teaspoon
¼ teaspoon	salt	¼ teaspoon

3rd Mix in enough flour in the following table to create a dough that does not stick to your hands, but is slightly sticky. Knead well for 3-4 minutes. Lightly flour the counter then roll out the dough to a 6" circle for the Smaller Recipe or a 7" circle for the Larger Recipe.

Smaller Recipe	Ingredient	Larger Recipe
¼-⅓ cup	whole wheat flour	¼-½ cup

4th Spray the cooker with a food release cooking spray. Lay the dough inside. Cover the cooker with a hand towel that has not been washed with fabric softener (the smell may permeate the crust), or cover with 2 layers of paper towels. Cover with the lid. Bake until the dough is dry and very lightly browned. Place the crust on a cooling rack. Refrigerate or freeze until ready to use.

BAKING TIME ON LOW:

Average Cooker: Smaller Recipe OR Larger Recipe 1½ hours

Fast Cooker: Smaller Recipe OR Larger Recipe 1¼-1½ hours

Extra Fast Cooker: Smaller Recipe OR Larger Recipe 1¼ hours

(See page 25, #3, for an explanation of the 3 types of cookers.)

Tip

- See page 24 for the fruit pizza. See page 61 for vegetable pizza.

Pock-et & Crock-it Sandwich

Smaller Recipe		Larger Recipe
YIELD: 11 oz. COOKER SIZE: 5-7 qt.	INGREDIENTS	YIELD: 1# COOKER SIZE: 6-7 qt.

1st Prepare the following dough, but use 1 tablespoon of canola oil or mild olive oil instead of 1 teaspoon olive oil as the pizza crust recipe reads. For the Smaller Recipe, roll out the dough to 8x8" on an oiled counter. Roll the Larger Recipe into a 9x9" square.

Smaller Recipe	Personal Pizza bread dough, pg 118	Larger Recipe

2nd Prepare a sandwich spread or individual patties. This may be done a number of ways, such as crumble a loaf, i.e. Tofu Loaf page 63, then moisten with spaghetti sauce, ketchup and/or Cheese Sauce, page 102. May also use patties, such as from the Tender Gluten recipe, page 58, or commercial patties that have been browned, i.e. vegan Boca Burgers. Apply the spread about ½" thick on the bottom half of the dough. Spread to ½" from the edges. Or, lay the patties on the bottom half of the dough. Lay the top half of the dough over the spread or patties. Seal the edges of the dough by pressing down on the dough with a fork, or pinching the dough together with your fingers.

as needed	sandwich spread or patties	as needed

3rd Spray the cooker with a food release cooking spray. Carefully pick up the dough and lay it in the cooker. If the dough is a little too long, gently squeeze it together once it is laying in the cooker. Cover the cooker with a hand towel that has not been washed with fabric softener (the smell may permeate the dough), or cover with 2 layers of paper towels. Cover with the lid. Bake until lightly browned. Remove with a metal spatula. If the sandwich is too heavy to pick up without breaking, then cut it in half before removing. Set on a cooling rack. When preparing to eat the sandwich, cut it in half. Drizzle in a dressing such as Cheese Sauce, page 102, ketchup or Tofu Sour Cream, page 136. Add raw vegetables such as lettuce, tomato and sprouts. See photo on page 72.

BAKING TIME ON LOW:

Average Cooker: Smaller Recipe OR Larger Recipe 2-2¼ hours

Fast Cooker: Smaller Recipe OR Larger Recipe 1¾-2 hours

Extra Fast Cooker: Smaller Recipe OR Larger Recipe 1½-1¾ hours

(See page 25, #3, for an explanation of the 3 types of cookers.)

Melt in Your Mouth Sweet Rolls

Smaller Recipe YIELD: 1¼# COOKER SIZE: 5-7 qt.	INGREDIENTS	Larger Recipe YIELD: 1¾# COOKER SIZE: 6-7 qt.

1st Lightly boil the following ingredients for 5-10 minutes, until the dates are soft. Mash the dates. Let them cool.

¾ cup	packed, chopped dates	1¼ cups
½ cup	water	⅔ cup

2nd Stir the following ingredients in the cooker.

¾ cup	slivered or sliced raw almonds	1 cup
¾ cup	water	1 cup
½ cup	pure maple syrup	⅔ cup
2 tablespoons	mild tasting olive oil or canola oil	2 tablespoons

3rd Prepare the following dough. Roll out the dough to 9x12" on an oiled counter. Spread the dates on the dough. Spread up to 1" from the edge on the 12" sides. Spread up to ½" from the edge on the 9" sides. Roll the dough, making a 12" log. Cut the dough into 8 rolls. To do this use a ruler, mark off 1½" rolls by making a small slit in the dough. The easiest way to cut the rolls is with dental floss. Put the floss under the dough, at one of the cut marks. Cross the floss at the top, then pull both ends of the floss in a criss cross fashion over the dough, like scissors. Lay the rolls cut side down in the cooker. Cover the cooker with a hand towel that has not been washed with fabric softener (the smell may permeate the rolls), or cover with 2 layers of paper towels. Cover with the lid. Bake until lightly browned.

Smaller Recipe	Focaccia bread dough, pg 116	Larger Recipe

4th Let the rolls cool before removing from the cooker unto a plate or storage container. See photo on page 78.

BAKING TIME ON LOW:

Average Cooker: Smaller Recipe OR Larger Recipe 2¾-3 hours

Fast Cooker: Smaller Recipe OR Larger Recipe 2½-2¾ hours

Extra Fast Cooker: Smaller Recipe OR Larger Recipe 2¼-2½ hours

(See page 25, #3, for an explanation of the 3 types of cookers.)

Crunchy Fruit Roll

Smaller Recipe		Larger Recipe
YIELD: 11 oz. COOKER SIZE: 5-7 qt.	INGREDIENTS	YIELD: 1# COOKER SIZE: 6-7 qt.

1st Lightly boil the following ingredients for 5-10 minutes, until the dried fruit is soft. Mash the fruit. Let cool.

Smaller Recipe	Ingredient	Larger Recipe
1 cup	packed, chopped dates or dried fruit of choice	1 cup
⅓ cup	water	½ cup

2nd Prepare the following dough, but use 1 tablespoon of canola oil or mild olive oil instead of 1 teaspoon olive oil as the pizza crust recipe reads. For the Smaller Recipe, roll out the dough to 8x8" on an oiled counter. Roll the Larger Recipe into a 9x9" square.

Smaller Recipe	Ingredient	Larger Recipe
Smaller Recipe	Personal Pizza Crust dough, pg 118	Larger Recipe

3rd Spread the dried fruit jam on the bottom half of the dough. Spread to ½" from the edges. Sprinkle the nuts in the following table over the jam. Lightly press the nuts into the jam. Lay the top half of the dough over the half with the jam. Seal the edges of the dough by pressing down on the dough with a fork, or pinching the dough together with your fingers. Spray the cooker with a food release cooking spray. Carefully pick up the dough. Lay it in the cooker. If the dough is a little too long, then gently squeeze in the sides once it is laying in the cooker. Cover the cooker with a hand towel that has not been washed with fabric softener (the smell may permeate the dough), or cover with 2 layers of paper towels. Cover with the lid. Bake until lightly browned. Remove carefully with a metal spatula. Set on a cooling rack.

Smaller Recipe	Ingredient	Larger Recipe
3 tablespoons	chopped, raw nuts	¼ cup

4th Cut in slices about 1" wide when ready to serve.

BAKING TIME ON LOW:

Average Cooker: Smaller Recipe OR Larger Recipe 2-2¼ hours

Fast Cooker: Smaller Recipe OR Larger Recipe 1¾-2 hours

Extra Fast Cooker: Smaller Recipe OR Larger Recipe 1½-1¾ hours

(See page 25, #3, for an explanation of the 3 types of cookers.)

Oven Fresh Rolls & Bread

YIELD: varies	COOKER SIZE: any size

1st Place whole grain dinner rolls, or a sliced loaf of bread, in a paper lunch bag. Close the bag. Pat 2-3 teaspoons of water around the outside of the bag. Place the bag in the cooker.

WARMING TIME ON LOW: (For ½-¾ full lunch bag. Reduce time a few minutes if the bag is only ¼ full.)
Average Cooker: 1-1¼ hours
Fast Cooker: ¾-1 hour
Extra Fast Cooker: ¾-1 hour
(See page 25, #3, for explanation of 3 types of cookers.)

Garlic Bread

YIELD: varies	COOKER SIZE: any size

1st Slice whole grain rolls, french bread, or even hot dog buns (for a mini french bread). Slice in half horizontally, or in several individual slices. Spread on a layer of olive oil or non-hydrogenated margarine. Follow with a generous sprinkling of your favorite seasonings such as garlic powder, onion powder, yeast flakes, individual herbs, or an herb seasoning mixture. May also add fresh, minced garlic. Close the roll or bread back together. Set rolls or bread side by side, or on top of each other, in a paper lunch bag. Close the bag. Pat 2-3 teaspoons of water around the outside of the bag. Place the bag in the cooker.

WARMING TIME ON LOW: (For ½-¾ full lunch bag. Reduce time about 15 minutes if bag is only ¼ full.)
Average Cooker: 1-1¼ hours
Fast Cooker: ¾-1 hour
Extra Fast Cooker: ¾-1 hour
(See page 25, #3, for explanation of 3 types of cookers.)

Pizza Rolls

YIELD: 1½#	COOKER SIZE: 5-7 qt.

1st Stir together the following ingredients. Let sit 8-10 minutes for the yeast to bubble.

½ cup	warm water
2 teaspoons	sweetener, i.e. honey or sugar
2 teaspoons	baking yeast

2nd Stir the flour before measuring, as it tends to settle as it is stored. Spoon it into a measuring cup. Add the following to the yeast mixture. Stir vigorously, for 1-2 minutes, to develop the gluten in the wheat.

1 cup	whole wheat flour
¼ cup	white flour
1 tablespoon	olive oil
½ teaspoon	salt

3rd Mix in enough of the flour in the following table to create a dough that does not stick to your hands, but is slightly sticky. Knead 3-4 minutes. Divide the dough into 3 portions. Divide each portion into 3 pieces. Shape each piece into a roll.

¼-½ cup	whole wheat flour

4th Stir together the following ingredients in the cooker.

¾ cup	spaghetti sauce
¾ cup	cheese sauce, i.e. pg 102, see tip below
½ cup	water
½ cup	sliced, black olives

5th Place the rolls in the cooker. Cover the cooker with a hand towel that has not been washed with fabric softener (the smell may permeate the rolls), or cover with 2 layers of paper towels. Cover with the lid. Bake until lightly browned. Let cool before removing to a plate or storage container. Serve saucy side up.

BAKING TIME ON LOW:
Average Cooker: 2¾-3 hours
Fast Cooker: 2½-2¾ hours
Extra Fast Cooker: 2¼-2½ hours
(See page 25, #3, for explanation of 3 types of cookers.)

Tip
- See directions in the Tips for Cheese Sauce, page 102. It can be made in a few minutes, if cooked on the stove.

Banana Bread in a Can

YIELD: 1½#	COOKER SIZE: any size

1st Stir together the following ingredients. Let sit 5 minutes.

¾-1 cup	mashed banana (approximately 2)
½ cup	chopped dates
⅓ cup	hot water
⅓ cup	chopped raw nuts
3 tablespoons	honey

2nd Stir in the yeast. Let sit 5 minutes.

1 tablespoon	baking yeast

3rd Stir in the salt.

1 teaspoon	salt

4th Stir the flour before measuring, as it tends to settle as it is stored. Spoon it into a measuring cup. Add the flour to the yeast mixture. Stir vigorously, for 2 minutes, to develop the gluten in the wheat.

2¼ cups	whole wheat flour

5th Spray a 46 oz. juice can with a food release cooking spray. Place the dough in the can. Place it on a trivet, such as a canning ring or metal jar lid, in the cooker. Cover the can with 2 layers of paper towels. Cover the cooker with aluminum foil (in most cases the lid will not fit on the cooker so foil is used for the lid). Bake until lightly browned. Let the bread cool a few minutes before removing from the can. When removing, run a knife around the sides of the can to loosen the bread. See photo on page 67.

BAKING TIME ON HIGH:
Average Cooker: 2¾-3 hours
Fast Cooker: 2½-2¾ hours
Extra Fast Cooker: 2¼-2½ hours
(See page 25, #3, for explanation of 3 types of cookers.)

Date Nut Bread in a Can

YIELD: 1½#	COOKER SIZE: any size

1st Stir together the following ingredients.

2 cups	chopped dates
1 cup	chopped raw almonds, or other nuts
1 cup	coconut
1 cup	apple juice
1	medium, mashed banana, optional
½ teaspoon	salt

2nd Mix in the flour.

1 cup	whole wheat flour

3rd Choose a container that will hold at least 3½ cups, such as a 28 oz. can, a 46 oz. juice can, a canapé bread pan or a baking dish. Spray the container with a food release cooking spray. Add the batter. Place it on a trivet, such as a canning ring or metal jar lid, in the cooker. If using a can cover the top with 2 layers of paper towels. Cover with the lid. If the lid does not fit then cover with aluminum foil. If using a baking dish then cover the cooker with a hand towel (that has not been washed in fabric softener), then cover with the lid. Bake until lightly browned. Let the bread cool a few minutes. When removing, run a knife around the sides of the container to loosen the bread. See photo on page 79.

BAKING TIME ON LOW:
Average Cooker: 5¼ hours
Fast Cooker: 5 hours
Extra Fast Cooker: 5 hours
(See page 25, #3, for explanation of 3 types of cookers.)

Tip

- The cooker may be plugged into a lamp/appliance timer, page 11, to begin cooking up to 8 hours later.

Soy Corn Bread in a Can

YIELD: 1⅓#	COOKER SIZE: any size

1st Soak the following soybeans in the water for at least 8 hours.

⅔ cup	dried soybeans
3 cups	water

2nd Drain the beans. Blend them with the water in the following table until smooth. Empty into a mixing bowl.

1¼ cups	water

3rd Stir the corn meal before measuring, as it tends to settle as it is stored. Spoon it into a measuring cup. Stir in the following ingredients with the blended soybeans.

1½ cups	corn meal, preferably whole grain
⅓ cup	quick or rolled oats
1 tablespoon	sweetener, i.e. honey or sugar
1 teaspoon	salt

4th Choose a can that will hold at least 3½ cups, such as a 28 oz. can or a 46 oz. juice can. Spray it with a food release cooking spray. Place the batter in the can. Put it on a trivet, such as a canning ring or metal jar lid, in the cooker. Cover the can with 2 layers of paper towels. Cover the cooker with the lid. If the lid does not fit then cover the cooker with aluminum foil. Bake until lightly browned. Let the bread cool a few minutes. When removing, run a knife around the sides of the can to loosen the bread. Serve as is, or toasted. See photo on page 77.

BAKING TIME ON LOW:
Average Cooker: 6-6¼ hours
Fast Cooker: 5½-5¾ hours
Extra Fast Cooker: 5-5¼ hours
(See page 25, #3, for explanation of 3 types of cookers.)

Tip
- The cooker may be plugged into a lamp/appliance timer, page 11, to begin cooking up to 6 hours later.

Fruit & Nut Soy Corn Bread in a Can

YIELD: 1¾#	COOKER SIZE: any size

1st Soak the following soybeans in the water for at least 8 hours.

⅔ cup	dried soybeans
3 cups	water

2nd Drain the beans. Blend them with the water in the following table until smooth. Empty into a mixing bowl.

1¼ cups	water

3rd Stir the corn meal before measuring, as it tends to settle as it is stored. Spoon it into a measuring cup. Stir in the following ingredients with the blended soybeans.

1¼ cups	corn meal, preferably whole grain
1 cup	chopped dried fruit
½ cup	chopped raw nuts
⅓ cup	quick or rolled oats
1 teaspoon	salt

4th Spray a 46 oz. juice can with a food release cooking spray. Place the batter in the can. Place it on a trivet, such as a canning ring or metal jar lid, in the cooker. Cover the can with 2 layers of paper towels. Cover the cooker with aluminum foil (in most cases the lid will not fit on the cooker so foil is used for the lid). Bake until lightly browned. Let the bread cool a few minutes. When removing, run a knife around the sides of the can to loosen the bread. Serve as is, or toasted.

BAKING TIME ON LOW:
Average Cooker: 6-6¼ hours
Fast Cooker: 5½-5¾ hours
Extra Fast Cooker: 5-5¼ hours
(See page 25, #3, for explanation of 3 types of cookers.)

Tip
- The cooker may be plugged into a lamp/appliance timer, page 11, to begin cooking up to 6 hours later.

Date Filled Dream Bars

Smaller Recipe		Larger Recipe
YIELD: 1# COOKER SIZE: 2½-5 qt.	INGREDIENTS	YIELD: 2# COOKER SIZE: 5-7 qt.

1st Lightly boil the following ingredients in a covered sauce pan 5-10 minutes, until the dates are soft. Mash the dates.

1 cup	packed, chopped dates	2 cups
¾ cup	water or fruit juice	1⅓ cups

2nd Blend the following ingredients into a coarse flour. Place in a mixing bowl.

½ cup	walnuts	1 cup
¼ cup	quick or rolled oats	½ cup

3rd Blend the following ingredients into a coarse flour. Mix in with the ground walnuts and oats.

1¼ cups	quick or rolled oats	2½ cups
¼ teaspoon	salt	½ teaspoon

4th Use a fork to cut the following honey into the oat mixture. Continue to mix with fingers until crumbly. Drizzle on the water and toss. Reserve ⅔ cup for the Smaller Recipe, or 1¼ cups for the Larger Recipe. Spray the cooker with a food release cooking spray. Press the remaining oat mixture in the bottom of the cooker. Add the date mixture and spread evenly. Sprinkle on the reserved oat mixture, then lightly press. Using a fork, pull the recipe away from the edges of the cooker ½". Cover the cooker with a hand towel that was not washed with fabric softener (the smell may permeate the food), or a double layer of paper towels. Top with the lid. Bake until the top and sides are lightly browned. Score into bars with a knife or spatula. Remove to a cooling rack.

3 tablespoons	honey	⅓ cup
1½ teaspoons	water	1 tablespoon

5th Serve warm or chilled. Serve as is, or with Tofu Cream, page 138. See photo on page 79.

BAKING TIME ON LOW:

Average Cooker: Smaller Recipe 2½-2¾ hours OR Larger Recipe 3-3¼ hours

Fast Cooker: Smaller Recipe 2-2¼ hours OR Larger Recipe 2½-2¾ hours

Extra Fast Cooker: Smaller Recipe 1¾-2 hours OR Larger Recipe 2¼-2½ hours

(See page 25, #3, for an explanation of the 3 types of cookers.)

Tip

- Spray an 8" round cake pan with a food release cooking spray. Assemble the Smaller Recipe in the pan. Place the pan on a trivet in a 6-7 qt. cooker. Cover the cooker with a hand towel or 2 layers of paper towels. Bake 2½-2¾ hours, on low, in an Extra Fast Cooker, until the top is lightly browned. Add 15-30 minutes for Fast or Average cookers.

Polynesian Bars

Replace the dates and water in the Date Filled Dream Bars with the following ingredients. Cook then mash.

Smaller Recipe		Larger Recipe
¾ cup	chopped dates	1½ cups
⅓ cup	crushed pineapple with juice	¾ cup
¼ cup	water or pineapple juice	½ cup

Assemble and bake as above. Serve warm or chilled. Serve as is, or with Tofu Cream, page 138.

Peanut Butter Flax Bars

Smaller Recipe		Larger Recipe
YIELD: ¾# COOKER SIZE: 2½-4½ qt.	INGREDIENTS	YIELD: 1½# COOKER SIZE: 5-7 qt.

1st Stir together the following ingredients.

½ cup	peanut butter or other favorite nut butter	1 cup
⅓ cup	honey	¾ cup
¼ teaspoon	salt	½ teaspoon

2nd Grind the following flax seed to a meal in a blender or coffee grinder, then stir into the peanut butter mixture. Spray the cooker with a food release cooking spray. Press the mixture into the cooker. Using a fork, pull the mixture away from the edges about ¼". Cover the cooker with a hand towel that was not washed with fabric softener (the smell may permeate the food), or a double layer of paper towels. Cover with the lid. Bake until the edges are lightly browned. The consistency will be very soft and somewhat moist on top. The top will dry as it cools. Let cool 30 minutes in the cooker. Score with a sharp knife into bars (clean off the knife as it gets sticky). Remove with a fork to a cooling rack.

¾ cup + 2 tablespoons	brown or golden, whole flax seed	1¾ cups

3rd The bars are chewy and firm when cooled. See photo on page 79 (bars made with brown seeds and golden seeds in the photo).

BAKING TIME ON LOW:

Average Cooker: Smaller Recipe OR Larger Recipe 1½-1¾ hours

Fast Cooker: Smaller Recipe OR Larger Recipe 1¼-1½ hours

Extra Fast Cooker: Smaller Recipe OR Larger Recipe 1-1¼ hours

(See page 25, #3, for an explanation of the 3 types of cookers.)

Tips

- Bake in a Pan Inside the Cooker: Spray an 8" round cake pan with a food release cooking spray. Spread the Smaller Recipe in the pan. Place the pan on a trivet in a 6-7 qt. cooker. Cover the cooker with a hand towel or 2 layers of paper towels. Cover with the lid. Bake 1½-1¾ hours, on low, in an Extra Fast Cooker. Bake until the edges are lightly browned. The top will be a little sticky and somewhat shiny. Let cool 10 minutes. Score with a sharp knife. Remove the bars, with a metal spatula, to a cooking rack. The bars will dry and become more firm as they continue to cool. Add 15-30 minutes for Fast or Average cookers.
- The cooker may be plugged into a lamp/appliance timer, page 11, to begin cooking up to 6 hours later.

Fudgy Carob Brownies

Smaller Recipe YIELD: 1# COOKER SIZE: 2½-4½ qt.	INGREDIENTS	Larger Recipe YIELD: 1¾# COOKER SIZE: 5-7 qt.

1st Stir together the following ingredients.

Smaller Recipe	Ingredient	Larger Recipe
½ cup	chopped walnuts or raw nuts of choice	1 cup
½ cup	honey	1 cup
½ cup	applesauce	¾ cup
2 tablespoons	carob powder	¼ cup
2 tablespoons	canola oil	¼ cup
1 tablespoon	coffee substitute i.e. Roma or Cafix, optional	2 tablespoons
½ teaspoon	salt	1 teaspoon

2nd Stir the flour before measuring, as it tends to settle as it is stored. Spoon the following flour into a measuring cup. Stir it into the mixture. Spray the cooker with a food release cooking spray. Spread the batter in the cooker. Using a fork, pull the mixture away from the edges about ¼". At this time you may sprinkle the top with some additional chopped nuts if desired. Cover with a hand towel that was not washed with fabric softener (the smell may permeate the food), or a double layer of paper towels. Cover with the lid. Bake until the edges are lightly browned. The top will be a little sticky in the center and somewhat shiny. Insert a toothpick into the center. It should come out clean. Let cool 10 minutes. Score with a sharp knife, then remove the brownies with a fork to a cooling rack. The brownies will dry more as they cool but will remain moist.

Smaller Recipe	Ingredient	Larger Recipe
1 cup	whole wheat flour	1¾ cups

3rd Serve as is, or frost with Carob Mocha Frosting, page 138, or a frosting of choice. Or, top with Tofu Cream, page 138. See photo on page 79.

BAKING TIME ON LOW:

Average Cooker: Smaller Recipe OR Larger Recipe 2¼-2½ hours

Fast Cooker: Smaller Recipe OR Larger Recipe 2-2¼ hours

Extra Fast Cooker: Smaller Recipe OR Larger Recipe 1¾-2 hours

(See page 25, #3, for an explanation of the 3 types of cookers.)

Tip

- Bake in a Pan Inside the Cooker: Spray an 8" round cake pan with a food release cooking spray. Spread the Smaller Recipe in the pan. Place the pan on a trivet in a 6-7 qt. cooker. Cover the cooker with a hand towel or 2 layers of paper towels. Cover with the lid. Bake 2¼-2½ hours, on low, in an Extra Fast Cooker. Bake until the edges are lightly browned. The top will be a little sticky in the center and somewhat shiny. Insert a toothpick into the center. It should come out clean. Let cool 10 minutes. Score with a sharp knife. Remove the brownies with a fork or metal spatula to a cooking rack. The brownies will dry more as they cool but will remain moist. Add 15-30 minutes for Fast or Average cookers.

Coconut Crunch Banana Bars

Smaller Recipe		Larger Recipe
YIELD: 1¼# COOKER SIZE: 2½-5 qt.	INGREDIENTS	YIELD: 1¾# COOKER SIZE: 5-7 qt.

1st Stir together the following ingredients.

Smaller Recipe	Ingredients	Larger Recipe
(approx. 1 cup) 2	medium size, mashed bananas	3 (approx. 1½ cups)
2 cups	chopped dates	3 cups
¾ cup	chopped, raw nuts	1 cup
⅓ cup	coconut	½ cup
½ teaspoon	salt	½ teaspoon

2nd Stir in the following oats. Spray the cooker with a food release cooking spray. Press the mixture into the cooker. Using a fork, pull the mixture away from the edges about ¼". Cover with a hand towel that was not washed with fabric softener (the smell may permeate the food), or a double layer of paper towels. Cover with the lid. Bake until the edges are lightly browned and slightly moist on top. Let cool 5 minutes. Cut into bars with a sharp knife. Remove to a cooling rack.

Smaller Recipe	Ingredients	Larger Recipe
¾ cup	quick oats	1 cup

3rd Serve warm or chilled. Serve as is, or with Tofu Cream, page 138.

BAKING TIME ON LOW:

Average Cooker: Smaller Recipe OR Larger Recipe 2-2½ hours

Fast Cooker: Smaller Recipe OR Larger Recipe 1¾-2 hours

Extra Fast Cooker: Smaller Recipe OR Larger Recipe 1¾-2 hours

(See page 25, #3, for an explanation of the 3 types of cookers.)

Tips

- Bake in a Pan Inside the Cooker: Spray an 8" round cake pan with a food release cooking spray. Spread the Smaller Recipe in the pan. Place the pan on a trivet in a 6-7 qt. cooker. Cover the cooker with a hand towel or 2 layers of paper towels. Cover with the lid. Bake 3-3¼ hours, on low, in an Extra Fast Cooker. Bake until the edges are lightly browned. Add 30-60 minutes for Fast or Average cookers.
- The cooker may be plugged into a lamp/appliance timer, page 11, to begin cooking up to 6 hours later.

Carob Clusters

Smaller Recipe		Larger Recipe
YIELD: 24 pieces COOKER SIZE: 1½-5 qt.	INGREDIENTS	YIELD: 48 pieces COOKER SIZE: 5-7 qt.

1st Spread the peanut butter on the bottom of the cooker. Sprinkle on the carob chips and heat.

Smaller Recipe	Ingredients	Larger Recipe
½ cup	peanut butter or nut butter of choice	1 cup
1½ cups	carob chips	3 cups

2nd Stir the chips when they are shiny and are beginning to melt. Stir several times for the chips to become smooth. (If there are still a lot of the chips left whole after stirring, then cover the cooker and continue to heat a few minutes.) Stir in one of the flavorings, if using.

Smaller Recipe	Ingredients	Larger Recipe
1 teaspoon	almond, cherry or maple flavoring, optional	2 teaspoons
2 teaspoons	OR peppermint flavoring, optional	4 teaspoons

3rd Stir in one of the following ingredients or a combination. If using flax seed it should be ground in a blender or coffee grinder.

Smaller Recipe	Ingredients	Larger Recipe
1 cup	chopped or whole, raw nuts	2 cups
1 cup	OR chopped or whole, toasted nuts, pg 137	2 cups
1 cup	OR Brown Rice Crisps or Rice Crispies	2 cups
¾ cup	OR whole flax seed	1½ cups
1¼ cups	OR chopped, dried fruit	2½ cups

4th Cover a cookie sheet or platter with wax paper or parchment paper. Drop the carob on by the spoonful, making each mound about 1½ tablespoons. May garnish tops with a sprinkle of either of the following. May also fill ½ oz. party nut cups with the melted carob.

Smaller Recipe	Ingredients	Larger Recipe
sprinkle	coconut or sesame seeds, optional	sprinkle

5th Chill before serving. Store in the refrigerator or freezer. See photo on page 79.

COOKING TIME ON LOW:

Smaller Recipe 20-35 minutes for most any cooker

Larger Recipe 30-45 minutes for most any cooker

(nonhydrogenated chips generally melt faster than hydrogenated chips)

"Chocolate" Covered Cherry Drops

Melt the carob and peanut butter as directed above. Stir in 1 teaspoon of cherry flavoring for the Smaller Recipe, or 2 teaspoons for the Larger Recipe. Stir in 1¼ cups chopped, dried cherries for the Smaller Recipe, or 2½ cups for the Larger Recipe. Chopped nuts may also be added, using ½ cup for the Smaller Recipe, or 1 cup for the Larger Recipe. Pack the carob mixture into a ¾ oz. cookie scoop, or drop by the spoonful, onto a cookie sheet covered with wax paper or parchment paper. Chill before serving. Store in the refrigerator or freezer.

Carob Pudding

Smaller Recipe		Larger Recipe
YIELD: 4 cups COOKER SIZE: 2-5 qt.	INGREDIENTS	YIELD: 6 cups COOKER SIZE: 3-7 qt.

1st Soften the dates. This may be done in one of two ways. Lightly boil the following dates, with the water, for 5-10 minutes, until soft, then blend smooth. Or, put the dry dates in a blender. Bring the water to a boil and add to the blender. Let sit several minutes for the dates to soften. Blend the dates until smooth. Empty into the cooker.

Smaller Recipe	Ingredients	Larger Recipe
2 cups	chopped dates	3 cups
1½ cups	water	2 cups

2nd Blend the following ingredients in a blender for 2 minutes, until very smooth. Pour into the cooker.

Smaller Recipe	Ingredients	Larger Recipe
1 cup	water	1½ cups
1 cup	raw cashews	1½ cups
¼ cup	carob powder	⅓ cup
2 tablespoons	quick or rolled oats	¼ cup
½ teaspoon	salt	¾ teaspoon

3rd Rinse the blender with the water in the following table. Stir into the cooker. Cook until the pudding is lightly boiling in various places around the edges and thickened throughout.

Smaller Recipe	Ingredients	Larger Recipe
1 cup	water	1¾ cups

4th Stir in the following ingredients. I suggest putting the ingredients, or a sign, near the cooker as a reminder. Adding them is easy to forget.

Smaller Recipe	Ingredients	Larger Recipe
2 teaspoons	coffee substitute, i.e. Cafix or Roma, optional	1 tablespoon
2 teaspoons	vanilla	1 tablespoon

5th Chill. Serve as is, or with Tofu Cream, page 138. See photo on back cover.

COOKING TIME IF COOKING ON LOW:

Average Cooker: Smaller Recipe 3¼-3¾ hours OR Larger Recipe 4½-5 hours

Fast Cooker: Smaller Recipe 3-3½ hours OR Larger Recipe 3-3½ hours

Extra Fast Cooker: Smaller Recipe 1¾-2¼ hours OR Larger Recipe 1¾-2¼ hours

COOKING TIME IF COOKING ON HIGH:

Average Cooker: Smaller Recipe 1¾-2¼ hours OR Larger Recipe 2¼-2¾ hours

Fast Cooker: Smaller Recipe 1½-2 hours OR Larger Recipe 1¾-2¼ hours

Extra Fast Cooker: Smaller Recipe 1¼-1¾ hours OR Larger Recipe 1½-2 hours

(See page 25, #3, for an explanation of the 3 types of cookers.)

Carob Hot Fudge Topping

Prepare the Carob Pudding but serve it hot. If it has been chilled, it may be reheated in a cooker on low. It may also be reheated in the microwave or in a sauce pan. Stir in a small amount of water or soy milk if it is too thick.

Vanilla Pudding

Smaller Recipe		Larger Recipe
YIELD: 2⅛ cups COOKER SIZE: 1½-4 qt.	INGREDIENTS	YIELD: 4¼ cups COOKER SIZE: 2-6 qt.

1st Blend the following ingredients in a blender for 2 minutes, until smooth. Pour into the cooker.

Smaller Recipe	Ingredient	Larger Recipe
¼ cup	water	½ cup
¼ cup + 2 tablespoons	blanched (white) almonds, pg 137	¾ cup
⅓ cup	cane juice crystals, fructose or sugar	⅔ cup
3 tablespoons	quick cooking or granulated tapioca	⅓ cup
¼ + ⅛ teaspoon	salt	¾ teaspoon

2nd Rinse the blender with the water in the following table. Stir it into the cooker. Cook until the pudding is lightly boiling in various places around the edges and is thickened throughout. (The tapioca may be clear before it comes to a boil, but if you stop the cooking at this time, the pudding will not be as thick.)

Smaller Recipe	Ingredient	Larger Recipe
1¾ cups	water	3½ cups

3rd Stir in the vanilla and chill.

Smaller Recipe	Ingredient	Larger Recipe
¾ teaspoon	vanilla	1½ teaspoons

4th Serve as is, or with sliced or chopped, drained, canned or fresh, fruit. The pudding makes a pretty parfait in individual glasses. Layer the pudding with granola and fruit. May also try stirring some juice sweetened jam in with the fruit, or leave out the fruit and just use a thin layer of jam. Or, use the Simple Fruit Topping, page 138.

COOKING TIME IF COOKING ON LOW:

Average Cooker: Smaller Recipe 4¼-4½ hours OR Larger Recipe 5¼-5¾ hours

Fast Cooker: Smaller Recipe 3-3¼ hours OR Larger Recipe 3¼-3½ hours

Extra Fast Cooker: Smaller Recipe 2-2¼ hours OR Larger Recipe 2½-2¾ hours

COOKING TIME IF COOKING ON HIGH:

Average Cooker: Smaller Recipe 1½-1¾ hours OR Larger Recipe 1¾-2 hours

Fast Cooker: Smaller Recipe 1¼-1½ hours OR Larger Recipe 1½-1¾ hours

Extra Fast Cooker: Smaller Recipe 1¼-1½ hours OR Larger Recipe 1½-1¾ hours

(See page 25, #3, for an explanation of the 3 types of cookers.)

Cheese Cake or Banana Cream Pie

- For the cheese cake or the pie prepare a prebaked crust, such as the Crumb Crust, page 138, in a 8-9" spring form pan, or an 8x8" baking dish. Grape Nuts may also be sprinkled in the pan or dish, in a thin layer, for a quick crust.
- For the Banana Cream Pie, slice a banana over the crust before adding the filling.
- Prepare the Larger Pudding Recipe for the cheese cake or pie filling. Use ⅓ cup + 1 tablespoon quick cooking (granulated) tapioca instead of the amount in the pudding recipe. Let the filling cool several minutes. Slowly pour, or spoon, it over the cooled crust. Chill.
- Serve the Cheese Cake with a thickened fruit topping, such as cherries, strawberries or blueberries. Or try the Simple Fruit Topping, page 138. For a quick topping, mix together ½ cup juice sweetened jam and 2-3 tablespoons water. Drizzle over the cheese cake after it has been sliced. See photo on page 78.

Tapioca Rice Pudding

Smaller Recipe		Larger Recipe
YIELD: 2¾ cups COOKER SIZE: 1½-4 qt.	INGREDIENTS	YIELD: 5½ cups COOKER SIZE: 2-7 qt.

1st Blend the following ingredients in a blender for 2 minutes, until smooth. Pour into the cooker.

Smaller	Ingredient	Larger
⅓ cup	blanched (white) almonds, pg 137	⅔ cup
¼ cup	water	½ cup
¼ cup	cane juice crystals, fructose or sugar	½ cup
½ teaspoon	salt	1 teaspoon

2nd Rinse the blender with the water in the following table. Stir it into the cooker.

Smaller	Ingredient	Larger
2¼ cups	water	4½ cups

3rd Stir the following ingredients into the cooker. Cook until the pudding is lightly boiling in various places around the edges and is thickened throughout. (The tapioca may be clear before it comes to a boil, but if you stop the cooking at this time the pudding will not be as thick.)

Smaller	Ingredient	Larger
3 tablespoons	quick cooking or granulated tapioca	⅓ cup
2 tablespoons	quick (instant) brown rice	¼ cup
1 tablespoon	canola oil	2 tablespoons

4th Stir in the following flavorings and chill.

Smaller	Ingredient	Larger
1 teaspoon	vanilla	2 teaspoons
½ teaspoon	cherry flavoring, optional	1 teaspoon

5th Serve as is, or with sliced or chopped, drained, canned or fresh, fruit. The pudding makes a pretty parfait in individual glasses. Layer the pudding with granola and fruit. May also try stirring some juice sweetened jam in with the fruit, or leave out the fruit, and just use a thin layer of jam. Or, use the Simple Fruit Topping, page 138.

COOKING TIME IF COOKING ON LOW:

Average Cooker: Smaller Recipe 4-4½ hours OR Larger Recipe 7-7½ hours

Fast Cooker: Smaller Recipe 3-3½ hours OR Larger Recipe 4-4½ hours

Extra Fast Cooker: Smaller Recipe 2½-3 hours OR Larger Recipe 3-3½ hours

COOKING TIME IF COOKING ON HIGH:

Average Cooker: Smaller Recipe 3-3½ hours OR Larger Recipe 3-3½ hours

Fast Cooker: Smaller Recipe 2½-3 hours OR Larger Recipe 2½-3 hours

Extra Fast Cooker: Smaller Recipe 1½-2 hours OR Larger Recipe 2-2½ hours

(See page 25, #3, for an explanation of the 3 types of cookers.)

Tips

- The cooker may be plugged into a lamp/appliance timer, page 11, to begin cooking up to 6 hours later.
- Make Ahead: Prepare Step 1. Add the water from Step 2 then refrigerate until ready to cook. Add about 15-30 minutes to the cooking time unless the recipe sits out at least 2 hours before turning on the cooker.

Pineapple Upside Down Cake

YIELD: 10 pieces	COOKER SIZE: round, 5-5½ qt.

1st Spray the cooker with a food release cooking spray. Stir together the following first 4 ingredients in the cooker. Add the pineapple, in a circle, then sprinkle on the nuts. (The cake may also be baked in an 8" round pan in the cooker. See the Tip below for directions.)

⅔ cup	pineapple juice or orange juice
⅓ cup	pure maple syrup
2 tablespoons	water
1 tablespoon	canola oil
5	canned, pineapple rings
¼ cup	sliced, slivered or chopped almonds

2nd Stir together the following ingredients in a bowl.

2 cups	whole wheat pastry flour
⅓ cup	cane juice crystals, fructose or sugar
2 teaspoons	Energy Baking Powder
½ teaspoon	salt

3rd Stir in the oil with a fork, then mix in well with fingers.

3 tablespoons	canola oil

4th Quickly stir the water, in the following table, into the flour. Drop around in tablespoon amounts.

½ cup	water

5th Cover the cooker with a hand towel or 2 layers of paper towels. Cover with the lid. Bake until the top is lightly browned. May poke the crust with a toothpick. It should come out clean. Let cool 15 minutes. Run a knife around the edges to loosen. Place a plate over the cooker and quickly, but *carefully*, invert the cooker so that the cake will drop onto the plate. Serve as is, or with Tofu Cream page 138. Warm the cake in the microwave if serving the following day, otherwise the cake is a little dry. See photo on page 66.

BAKING TIME ON LOW:
Average Cooker: 3¼-3½ hours
Fast Cooker: 3-3¼ hours
Extra Fast Cooker: 3-3¼ hours
(See page 25, #3, for explanation of 3 types of cookers.)

Tip

- The cake can also be baked in an 8" round cake pan placed on a trivet inside a 6-7 qt. cooker. Assemble in the pan as the directions read above. Bake on **high** for the same length of time as above. Invert onto a plate.

Fruit Upside Down Cake

YIELD: 10 pieces	COOKER SIZE: 6-7 qt.

1st Use any kind of canned fruit. Cut into small pieces, about ¼" thick. Warm (do not cook) the fruit with the juice, oil and starch in a sauce pan. Pour the mixture in an 8" round cake pan that has been sprayed with a food release cooking spray. Sprinkle on the almonds.

1⅔ cups	chopped, drained, canned fruit
¾ cup	apple juice concentrate
1 tablespoon	canola oil
1 teaspoon	cornstarch
¼ cup	sliced, slivered or chopped almonds

2nd Stir together the following ingredients in a bowl.

2 cups	whole wheat pastry flour
⅓ cup	cane juice crystals, fructose or sugar
2 teaspoons	Energy Baking Powder
½ teaspoon	salt

3rd Stir in the oil with a fork, then mix in well with fingers.

3 tablespoons	canola oil

4th Quickly stir the water, in the following table, into the flour. Drop around in tablespoon amounts.

½ cup	water

5th Place the pan on a trivet in a 6-7 qt. cooker. The trivet will probably need to be at least 1½" high so that the pan will sit on it evenly. Cover the cooker with a towel (that has not been washed with fabric softener) or 2 layers of paper towels. Cover with the lid. Bake until the top is lightly browned. May poke the crust with a toothpick. It should come out clean. Let the cake cool 15 minutes. Run a knife around the edges to loosen the cake. Place a plate over the pan and quickly, but *carefully*, invert so that the cake will drop onto the plate. Serve as is, or with Tofu Cream page 138. Warm the cake in the microwave if serving the following day, otherwise the cake is a little dry.

BAKING TIME ON HIGH:
Average Cooker: 3¼-3½ hours
Fast Cooker: 3-3¼ hours
Extra Fast Cooker: 3-3¼ hours
(See page 25, #3, for explanation of 3 types of cookers.)

Vanilla Ice Cream

YIELD: 4½ cups	COOKER SIZE: 2-6½ qt.

1st Blend the following ingredients until the tofu is smooth. Pour into the cooker.

12.3 oz. box	firm Mori-Nu Tofu
1 cup	cane juice crystals, fructose or sugar
1 cup	water
¼ cup + 1 tbsp.	quick cooking or granulated tapioca
2 tablespoons	canola oil or mild tasting olive oil
½ teaspoon	salt

2nd Rinse the blender with the water in the following table, then stir it into the cooker. Cook until the mixture is lightly boiling in various places around the edges and thickened throughout. The mixture will be thick, like pudding, and may look somewhat like curdled milk or even some foam on top. (The tapioca may be clear before it comes to a boil, but if you stop the cooking at this time the mixture will not be as thick as it should be.)

1½ cups	water

3rd Stir in the following vanilla. Refrigerate overnight.

1 tablespoon	vanilla

4th Proceed to Ways to Freeze in the following column.

COOKING TIME ON LOW:
Average Cooker: 3-3¼ hours
Fast Cooker: 2-2¼ hours
Extra Fast Cooker: 1¾-2 hours
COOKING TIME ON HIGH:
Average Cooker: 2-2¼ hours
Fast Cooker: 1½-1¾ hours
Extra Fast Cooker: 1¼-1½ hours
(See page 25, #3, for explanation of 3 types of cookers.)

Tips

- The cooker may be plugged into a lamp/appliance timer, page 11, to begin cooking up to 4 hours later.
- Double the recipe and cook in a 3-7 qt. cooker.
- Make Ahead: Prepare Step 1. Add the water from Step 2 then refrigerate until ready to cook. Add about 20-30 minutes to the cooking time unless the recipe sits out at least 2 hours before turning on the cooker.
- Quick Fix: Instead of cooking in a slow cooker lightly boil the mixture for 5 minutes on the stove.

Ways to Freeze:

(1) Freeze in an ice cream freezer. Use either the kind where the canister is kept in the freezer until time to use, then it is plugged into an electrical outlet; or the type that uses salt and ice for freezing. After using the ice cream freezer put the ice cream into the freezer for 30-60 minutes for a more firm consistency. It will keep 2-3 hours in the freezer before getting too hard to serve.

(2) Freeze the cooked mixture in a flat container, such as a baking dish or storage container, 1-2" high. When ready to make the ice cream let it sit out at room temperature for 15-30 minutes. Cut it into chunks, then use one of the following two methods:

Blender method: Add 1 cup of chunks to the blender. The chunks should be mostly frozen, but soft enough to blend. Add 1-2 tablespoons of water to blend, if needed. After blending put the ice cream in the freezer for 30-60 minutes, then serve.

Champion Juicer method: Use the solid, "blank" attachment for the juicer. This is used in place of the "screen" attachment, which is used when making juice. Run the chunks through the juicer. You will want to refreeze the ice cream for 30-60 minutes before serving. It will keep 2-3 hours in the freezer before getting too hard to serve.

Leftover Ice Cream:

Leftover, frozen ice cream, that is less than 2 weeks old, may be barely softened in the microwave. Warm it for 15-20 seconds, then stir. Continue to warm one or two more times, if needed.

Otherwise, freeze the ice cream for up to 2 months. Use one of the following methods to prepare it to be served.

(1) Let the frozen ice cream sit out at room temperature for 15-30 minutes. Cut it into chunks. Run it through a blender or Champion Juicer. Follow the same directions that are given under "Ways to Freeze" for the blender and juicer.

(2) A Black & Decker Arctic Twister works great! Let the frozen ice cream sit out at room temperature for 15-30 minutes. Cut it into chunks. Run the chunks through the machine. Comes out like soft serve ice cream with a swirl. Serve immediately, or refreeze for 30-60 minutes for a more firm ice cream. The machine costs about $20.00. It is available where small kitchen appliances are sold.

Variations:

These variations are to give you ideas for making your own creations! Use the Vanilla Ice Cream recipe for the following variations **but leave out the 1 tablespoon of vanilla** and make the following adjustments.

Vanilla Mint Chip Ice Cream

Add the following flavorings after the Vanilla Ice Cream is cooked. The Carob Clusters should be added while using an ice cream freezer. If using a blender or juicer, stir in the Clusters at the end. *To make a small amount of Carob Clusters quickly: Spread 2 tablespoons of peanut butter in a small, glass dish. Sprinkle on ¼ cup of carob chips. Heat in the microwave for about 30 seconds, stir, then continue to heat 10-15 seconds, as needed. Pour onto a piece of wax paper. Chill for 15 minutes, until firm, then chop. You can also use finely chopped carob chips instead of the Clusters but the chips will be harder to chew when frozen. See photo on page 79.

1 teaspoon	vanilla
1 teaspoon	peppermint flavoring
¼ cup	chopped Carob Clusters pg 129*

Carob Mint Chip Ice Cream

Add the following carob powder when blending the ingredients for the Vanilla Ice Cream. Add the peppermint, vanilla and coffee substitute after the ice cream is cooked. The Carob Clusters should be added while using an ice cream freezer. If using a blender or juicer, stir in the clusters at the end. *See note in recipe above for making Carob Clusters quickly.

3 tablespoons	carob powder
1 tablespoon	coffee substitute i.e. Cafix, opt.
1 teaspoon	vanilla
1 teaspoon	peppermint flavoring
¼ cup	chopped Carob Clusters pg 129*

Carob Ice Cream

Add the following carob powder when blending the ingredients for the Vanilla Ice Cream. Add the vanilla and coffee substitute after the ice cream is cooked. See photo on page 79.

3 tablespoons	carob powder
1 tablespoon	coffee substitute i.e. Cafix, opt.
2 teaspoons	vanilla

Cherry Ripple Ice Cream

Add the following vanilla and cherry flavoring after the Vanilla Ice Cream is cooked. The cherries should be added while using an ice cream freezer. If using a blender or juicer, stir in the cherries at the end.

1 teaspoon	vanilla
1 teaspoon	cherry flavoring
⅔ cup	sliced, fresh or frozen cherries

Lemon Sherbert

Add the following ingredients after the Vanilla Ice Cream is cooked.

1 tablespoon	fresh lemon juice
1 teaspoon	lemon flavoring
1 teaspoon	vanilla

Rice Supreme Ice Cream

From the Vanilla Ice Cream recipe: Replace the sugar with the rice syrup. Replace the tapioca and water with what is listed below. Blend the ingredients with ¾ cup of the water. Rinse the blender with the remaining 1 cup of water, add to the cooker. Add the flavoring after the ice cream is cooked.

1¾ cups	water
1 cup	rice syrup
⅓ cup	quick cooking or granulated tapioca
2 teaspoons	vanilla or maple flavoring

Maple Walnut Ice Cream

From the Vanilla Ice Cream recipe: Replace the sugar with the maple syrup. Replace the tapioca and water with what is listed below. Blend the ingredients with 1 cup of the water. Rinse the blender with the remaining 1 cup of water, add to the cooker. Add the flavoring after the ice cream is cooked. Add the nuts during the freezing, or if using a blender or juicer, stir in at the end.

2 cups	water
¾ cup	pure maple syrup
¼ cup	quick cooking or granulated tapioca
2 teaspoons	vanilla or maple flavoring
½ cup	chopped walnuts

Caramel Nut Crunch Ice Cream

Add the nuts to any of the ice creams while using an ice cream freezer. If using a blender or juicer, stir them in at the end. Or, sprinkle them on top of the ice cream.

½ cup	chopped Caramel Nut Crunch pg 137

Chicken Seasoning

YIELD: ¾ cup	Cooker Free Recipe

Blend the following ingredients in a blender until smooth. Store the seasoning in a jar.

1⅓ cups	yeast flakes, pg 10
3 tablespoons	onion powder
3 tablespoons	salt
1½ tablespoons	basil
1 tablespoon	garlic powder
1 teaspoon	oregano
½ teaspoon	turmeric, for color

This seasoning is comparable to using the same amount of McKay's Chicken Seasoning without MSG.

Soy Sauce

YIELD: 2 cups	Cooker Free Recipe

The following sesame seeds may be white (hulled) or brown (not hulled). Toast the seeds in a dry skillet or sauce pan. (Do not use a nonstick pan.) Stir the seeds on medium/low heat, for 5-10 minutes, until the seeds are light, golden brown. Let cool then grind the seeds to a powder in a blender.

¾ cup	sesame seeds

Add the following ingredients to the seeds and blend smooth.

1⅓ cups	lemon juice
1 cup	yeast flakes, pg 10
½ cup	coffee substitute, i.e. Cafix or Roma
6 tablespoons	salt

Add the additional following yeast flakes to the blender. Continue to blend smooth. This is a thick sauce that thickens more when it chills. Store in the refrigerator. It will keep for a few months.

1 cup	yeast flakes, pg 10

This soy sauce has about the same sodium content as regular (not light) LaChoy soy sauce.

Tofu Sour Cream

YIELD: 2 cups	Cooker Free Recipe

Blend the following ingredients in a blender for 2 minutes, until very smooth. Mori Nu tofu will take on a lighter texture with this long blending. Use fresh lemon juice if you have it on hand.

1-12.3 oz. box	firm or extra firm Mori Nu tofu
⅓ cup	raw cashews
⅓ cup	water
1 tablespoon	lemon juice
1 teaspoon	salt
1 teaspoon	onion powder
½ teaspoon	garlic powder

Stir in the following dill. 3-4 tablespoons of fresh dill weed may be used in place of the dried dill weed.

1 teaspoon	dried dill weed, optional

Chill to thicken. See photo on page 71.

Chunky Fried Tofu

YIELD: 1-1½ cups	Cooker Free Recipe

Spray a nonstick skillet with a food release cooking spray. Preheat the skillet on medium heat. Use either the water packed tofu, or the Mori Nu tofu. Using a sharp knife, slice the tofu in various, random, size pieces, ranging from about the size of a nickle to a fifty cent piece. Smaller pieces are fine as well. Cut them ⅛-¼" thick. Place the tofu in the skillet. Sprinkle with the following salt. Use ¼ teaspoon for the Mori Nu tofu, or ½ teaspoon of salt for a 14-16 oz. package of tofu. Sauté the tofu for about 20 minutes to get a dry, somewhat crisp, texture. Gently stir every 3-5 minutes.

12.3-16 oz. box	firm or extra firm tofu
¼-½ teaspoon	salt

Sprinkle the following ingredients over the tofu. Continue cooking and stirring, 1-2 minutes.

1 tablespoon	yeast flakes, pg 10
1 teaspoon	onion powder

Add to many recipes, such as gravy, soup, spaghetti, chili, rice. Add Tofu Sour Cream, page 136, for a delicious sandwich spread. See photo in wrap on page 77.

Garbanzomole

A recipe using leftover, cooked, garbanzo beans.

YIELD: 1¾ cups	Cooker Free Recipe

Stir together the following ingredients.

1-1¼ cups	mashed avocado
1 cup	drained, mashed, garbanzo beans
1 teaspoon	onion powder
¼ teaspoon	garlic powder
¼ teaspoon	salt

Spread on bread or crackers. Add to a salad, Haystacks, page 39, or a sandwich.

Garbanzo Tomato Salad

A recipe using leftover, cooked, garbanzo beans.

YIELD: 2¾ cups	Cooker Free Recipe

Stir together the following ingredients and chill.

1 cup	cooked, drained, garbanzo beans
1 cup	chopped, fresh tomatoes
¾ cup	sliced, black olives
½ cup	finely chopped, fresh parsley
¼-½ cup	chopped, green onions
⅓ cup	lemon juice
1 teaspoon	onion powder
¼ teaspoon	garlic powder
¼ teaspoon	salt

Serve as is, or on a bed of lettuce. See photo on page 65.

Blanched Almonds

YIELD: varies	Cooker Free Recipe

Almonds may be purchased that are white in color, and have been blanched, in order to remove the brown skins. These are usually slivered or sliced almonds. You can easily remove the skins yourself by dropping whole almonds into boiling water. Boil for 30-45 seconds, then drain. Slip the skins off the almonds. Keep blanched almonds in the refrigerator for a few days, or freeze. Blanch almonds ahead and freeze for later use.

Toasted Nuts & Seeds

YIELD: varies	Cooker Free Recipe

Many kinds of raw nuts and seeds can be toasted on the stove, in a skillet or sauce pan (do *not* use a non-stick pan). When toasting on the stove continually stir a thin layer of nuts or seeds.
They may also be done on a cookie sheet in the oven.

Walnuts: Stir over medium-low heat, 5-10 minutes, on the stove, or bake in a single layer for 1¼ hours at 250°.

Sesame Seeds: Stir over medium-high heat, about 5 minutes, on the stove, until lightly golden in color.

Coconut: Stir over medium-low heat, about 5 minutes, on the stove, until lightly golden in color, or bake ¼-½" thick, for 25-35 minutes at 250°.

Almonds: Bake in a single layer for 2 hours at 250°.

Cashews: Bake in 1-2 layers, whole cashews or pieces, for 1½ hours at 250°.

Other nuts can be done with this method, but the time and heat will vary with the nut.

Caramel Nut Crunch

YIELD: ¾ cup	Cooker Free Recipe

Melt the sugar and nuts in a sauce pan over medium heat. This will take 1-2 minutes. When the sugar begins to melt, turn the heat down to medium-low. Continue to stir for 3-4 minutes for the nuts to toast. Immediately empty the nuts into a glass or metal bowl. Stir in the flavoring. Let cool.

¾ cup	chopped, raw nuts or coconut
⅓ cup	cane juice crystals, fructose, brown sugar or sugar
1½ teaspoons	vanilla or maple flavoring

Tips

- Nuts may also be left whole in this recipe. They make an attractive, tasty garnish on desserts or salads. Large, flaked coconut is also pretty.
- Sucanat works fine in this recipe, but the nuts don't look as nice.

Tofu Cream

YIELD: 2 cups	Cooker Free Recipe

Blend the following ingredients in a blender for 2 minutes, until very smooth. Mori Nu tofu will take on a lighter texture with this long blending.

1-12.3 oz. box	Mori Nu firm or extra firm tofu
⅓ cup	raw cashews
¼ cup	cane juice crystals, fructose or sugar
1 teaspoon	vanilla
⅛ teaspoon	salt

Serve immediately, or chill for a little thicker cream. See photo on page 67 on the Blueberry Crumble Crisp and on back cover on the Carob Pudding.

Carob Mocha Frosting

YIELD: 2 cups	Cooker Free Recipe

Soften the dates. This may be done in one of two ways. Lightly boil the following dates with the water for 5-10 minutes, until soft. Or, put the dates in a blender. Bring the water to a boil and add to the blender. Let sit several minutes for the dates to soften.

1 cup	packed, chopped dates
1 cup	water

Add the following ingredients, with the dates, and blend in a blender until smooth.

⅓ cup	peanut butter or other nut butter
2 tablespoons	carob powder
2 teaspoons	coffee substitute, i.e. Cafix, optional
1 teaspoon	vanilla
⅛ teaspoon	salt

Chill for a thicker frosting. Spread on Fudgy Carob Brownies, page 127. See photo on page 79.

Crumb Crust

YIELD: 1 crust	Cooker Free Recipe

Blend the granola and nuts to a coarse flour. Empty into a bowl. Break up the clumps.

1¼ cups	granola
½ cups	walnuts, coconut, or other raw nuts

Mix in the water from the following table. Press into an oiled 8x8" baking dish, or a 9" or 10" pie plate. Cover with plastic wrap. Flatten the dough with a small rolling pin, your hands, or the back of a spoon. Bake at 350° for 9-13 minutes, until golden brown.

2 tablespoons	water

Cool before adding a pie filling. See photo on page 78.

Maple Vanilla Topping

YIELD: 1-1½ cups	Cooker Free Recipe

Lightly boil, stirring, for 1 minute. Serve immediately, or chill for a thicker topping.

½ cup	water
½ cup	pure maple syrup
2 tablespoons	cornstarch
1 teaspoon	vanilla

Serve over Ice Cream, page 134-135, waffles, french toast, Apple Crumble Crisp, page 22, etc.

Simple Fruit Topping

YIELD: 1-1½ cups	Cooker Free Recipe

Lightly boil the juice and starch, stirring, for 1 minute. Drain the fruit. It may be canned or fresh. If using frozen fruit it should be thawed and drained before measuring. Stir the fruit into the thickened juice. Serve immediately, or chill for a thicker topping.

1¼ cups	unsweetened juice concentrate
¼ cup	cornstarch
2-3 cups	berries or fruit cut in small pieces

Serve over the Cheese Cake, page 131, or when making a parfait with the Vanilla Pudding, page 131, or Tapioca Rice Pudding, page 132, or use over waffles, french toast, etc. See photos on pages 78 and 79.

Recipe Titles for Photos

Front Cover
Garden Style Spaghetti pg 51
Tender Gluten Meatballs pg 58
Roasted Garlic (bulb) pg 87

Back Cover
Tofu Loaf pg 63
Maple Almond Sweet Potatoes pg 81

Split Pea Chowder pg 95

Chunky Fried Tofu Gravy & Rice pg 47

Vegetable Lasagna pg 55
Carob Pudding pg 130

Page 65
Sun Seed Roast pg 63
Focaccia pg 116
Garbanzo Tomato Salad pg 137
Chicken Style Gravy pg 101

Page 66
Pineapple Upside Down Cake pg 133

Roast Beef-less pg 59
Harvest Vegetable Soup pg 92

Cuban Black Beans pg 36

Page 67
Stuffed Shells pg 54

Chunky Pine-Apple Sauce pg 103
Blueberry Crumble Crisp pg 22
with Tofu Cream pg 138
Banana Bread in a Can pg 123

Multi Grain Hot Cereal pg 19
Whole Wheat Bread (small bread pan) pg 104

Page 68
Barbecued Sloppy Joes pg 62

Old Fashion Scalloped Potatoes pg 86
Spanish Rice pg 42

Baked Beans pg 37
Flax Bread pg 105

Page 69
Tender Gluten Meatballs pg 58

Boca Beefless Stew pg 100

Pasta Alfredo pg 49
Focaccia pg 116

Page 70
Pizza pg 61

Page 71
Haystacks pg 39
with Instant! Slow Cooked Refried Beans pg 39
with Tofu Sour Cream pg 133

Page 72
Pock-et & Crock-it Sandwich pg 119
Cheese Sauce pg 102
Baked Potato pg 84
with White Sauce pg 101

Chickpea A La King pg 46

Chili pg 97
Roasted Garlic (cloves) pg 87

Page 73
Goulash pg 56

Macaroni & Cheese #1 pg 52

Rustic Potatoes pg 85
Millet Tomato Bake pg 40

Page 74
Breads
2 Whole Wheat Breads (in small pans) pg 104
Old World Black Bread (in a braid) pg 106
Whole Grain Rye Bread pg 107
Whole Wheat Bread (in a ramakin) pg 104
Crusty Whole Wheat Bread pg 104
Poppy Seed Bread pg 108
Whole Wheat Bread in a Can pg 110
Whole Wheat Bread (in a canapé pan) pg 104

Page 75
Garden Style Spaghetti pg 51
Tender Gluten Meatballs pg 58
Roasted Garlic (bulb) pg 87

Page 76
Baked Sweet Potato pg 84
Lentil Loaf pg 64

Roasted Corn on the Cob pg 88
Greens with Veggies pg 90

Mazidra pg 38

Page 77
Whole Wheat Bread pg 104
Harvest Nut Loaf pg 64

Lentil Vegetable Soup pg 96
Soy Corn Bread in a Can pg 124

Lima Bean Chowder pg 93
Wrap with Chunky Fried Tofu and
Tofu Sour Cream pg 133

Page 78
Corn Tamale Casserole pg 41

Cheese Cake pg 131
Crumb Crust pg 138
Simple Fruit Topping pg 138

Melt in Your Mouth Sweet Rolls pg 120

Page 79
Fruit Pizza pg 24

Date Nut Bread in a Can pg 123
Carob Clusters (with Rice Crisps) pg 129
Carob Clusters (with chopped nuts) pg 129
Date Filled Dream Bars pg 125
Peanut Butter Flax Bars (one with golden flax seed,
one with brown flax seed) pg 126

Vanilla Ice Cream pg 134
with Simple Fruit Topping pg 138
Carob Ice Cream pg 135
Vanilla Mint Chip Ice Cream pg 135
Fudgy Carob Brownies pg 127
with Carob Mocha Frosting pg 138

Page 80
Grape Leaf Tofu Rolls pg 57

"Tips" Index

Slow Cooker Tips: Safe Beginnings 6

Slow Cooker Tips: Cooking Tips & Principles
- Your Cooker Temperature Temperament 7
- Cookers Heat From the Sides 7
- Cooker Temperatures 7
- Lid Alternatives 7
- Quick & Easy Clean Up 7
- Herbs 7
- Vegetables 8
- White Potatoes 8
- Sweet Potatoes or Yams 8
- Brown Rice 8
- Pasta 8
- Thickening 8
- Garnishing 8
- Baking 9
- Make A Note 9
- No Peeking 9
- Speed Up The Cooking 9
- Sputtering 9
- Make Ahead 9
- Reheat On Another Day 9
- Adapting Your Recipes 9
- Evaporation in a Slow Cooker 10
- What Size Cooker Do You Have 10
- 1½ Quart Rival Crock-Pots 10
- Programmable Cookers 10
- Buy in Bulk & Save 10
- Measuring Spoons & Cups 10
- What Size Cooker To Get 10

Extra Items for Extra Successful Slow Cooking
- Lamp/Appliance Timer 11
- Liquid Lecithin 11
- Trivets 11
- Baking Containers 11

Definitions
- Yeast Flakes 11
- Tofu 11

Bean Cooking Tips
- Sorting Beans 25
- Soaking Beans 25
- Temperature Temperament-Do You Have an "Average", "Fast" or "Extra Fast" Cooker 25
- What Size Cooker Do You Have 26
- Lamp/Appliance Timer 26
- Cooking with Salt 26
- How Much Salt and Oil to Add 26
- Cooking Old Beans 26
- Water Sputtering from Lid 26
- Not Home-But Beans are Done 26
- Are Beans Well Cooked 26
- Reheating Beans 26
- Ways to Use Leftovers 26
- Oops! 'xcuse Me-Gas Problem 27
- Measuring Beans 27
- Buying in Bulk 27
- Dried, Instant, Refried Beans 27

General Index

A

Acorn Squash 88
Almonds, Blanched 137
All Night Slow Cooked Cereal 16
Apple Crumble Crisp 22
Apple Sauce, Chunky Pine 103

B

Baked Apples & Oats 21
Baked Beans 37
Baked Potatoes 84
Baked Spaghetti Squash 88
Baked Sweet Potatoes 84
Baking Containers 11
Banana Bread in a Can 123
Banana Cream Pie 131
Barbecued Gluten 59
Barbecued Sloppy Joes 62
Beans 28-39
Beans Not Soaked-1½ Quart Rival Crock Pot 32
Beans Soaked-1½ Quart Rival Crock Pot 32
Bean Burritos 62
Bean Cooking Chart 1 28
Bean Cooking Chart 2 29
Bean Cooking Chart 3 30
Bean Cooking Chart 4 31
Bean Cooking Tips 25
Bean Without the Bacon Soup 98
Beets, Lemon 91
Beets, Simple 91
Berries-Wheat, Rye... 12-15
Black (Turtle) Beans 28-32
Blanched Almonds 137
Blueberry Crumble Crisp 22
Boca Beefless Stew 100
Bread Dressing 45
Brownies, Fudgy Carob 127
Butternut Squash 88
Butter Cup Squash 88

C

"Chocolate" Covered Cherry Drops 129
Cake, Fruit Upside Down 133
Cake, Pineapple Upside Down 133
Caramel Nut Crunch 137
Caramel Nut Crunch Ice Cream 135
Carob Brownies, Fudgy 127
Carob Clusters 129
Carob Hot Fudge Topping 130
Carob Ice Cream 135
Carob Mint Chip Ice Cream 135
Carob Mocha Frosting 138
Carob Pudding 130
Cashew Gravy 101
Cashew Rice 44
Cereal Cooking Chart-Large Amount 14
Cereal Cooking Chart-Medium Amount 13
Cereal Cooking Chart-Rival 1½ Quart Crock Pot 15
Cereal Cooking Chart-Small Amount 12
Cheese Cake 131
Cheese Sauce #1 102
Cheese Sauce #2 102
Cherry Ripple Ice Cream 135
Chicken Seasoning 136
Chicken Style Gravy 101
Chickpea A La King 46
Chili 97
Chunky Fried Tofu 136
Chunky Fried Tofu Gravy & Rice 47
Chunky Pine-Apple Sauce 103
Coconut Crunch Banana Bars 128
Collard Leaf Tofu Rolls 57
Corn Bread, Soy 124
Corn Grits 12-15
Corn Meal 12-15
Corn Millet Porridge 17
Corn on the Cob, Roasted 88
Corn, Roasted Herb Sweet 88
Corn Tamale Casserole 41
Cracked Wheat 12-15
Cream of Tomato Vegetable Soup 94
Crisp, Apple Crumble 22
Crisp, Blueberry Crumble 22
Crumb Crust 138
Crunchy Fruit Roll 121
Crust, Crumb 138
Crusty Whole Wheat Bread 104
Cuban Black Beans 36

D

Date Filled Dream Bars 125
Date Nut Bread in a Can 123
Dressing, Bread 45

E

Easy Does It Spaghetti 50
Eggplant Garlic Bake 89

F

Flax Bars, Peanut Butter 126
Flax Bread 105
Flax Bread in a Can 110
Flax Rolls 113
Focaccia 116
Fruit & Nut Soy Corn Bread in a Can 124
Fruit Lasagna 23
Fruit Pizza 24
Fruit Topping, Simple 138
Fruit Upside Down Cake 133
Fudgy Carob Brownies 127

G

Garbanzomole 137
Garbanzo (Chickpea) Beans 28-32

Garbanzo Tomato Salad 137
Garden Style Spaghetti 51
Garlic, Roasted 87
Garlic Bread 122
Gluten: Meatballs, Patties, Strips 58-59
Goulash 56
Grape Leaf Tofu Rolls 57
Gravy, Cashew 101
Gravy, Chicken Style 101
Great Northern Beans 28-32
Great! Great Northerns 33
Great Reasons for Using a Slow Cooker 6
Greens with Veggies 90

H

Harvest Nut Loaf 64
Harvest Vegetable Soup 92
Haystacks 39
Heart Healthy Baked Whole Grains 20
Honey Coconutty Sweet Potatoes 82
Hot Sandwiches-Ready to Go! 62
Hulled Barley 12–15

I

Ice Cream 134-135
Incredibly Delicious Bean Cuisine 25
Instant! Slow Cooked Refried Beans 39

K

Kidney Beans 28-32

L

Lamp/Appliance Timer 6, 11, 26
Lasagna, Fruit 23
Lasagna, Vegetable 55
Lemon Beets 91
Lemon Sherbert 135
Lentil Loaf 64
Lentil Vegetable Soup 96
Lentils 28-32
Lima Bean Chowder 93
Lima Beans 28-32
Liquid Lecithin 11
Loaves 63-64

M

Macaroni & Cheese #1 52
Macaroni & Cheese #2 53
Maple Almond Sweet Potatoes 81
Maple Vanilla Topping 138
Maple Walnut Ice Cream 135
Mashed Potatoes 87
Mazidra 38
Meatballs, Tender Gluten 58
Melt in Your Mouth Sweet Rolls 120
Millet 12-15
Millet Tomato Bake 40
Multi Grain Hot Cereal 19

N

Navy Beans 28-32
Nuts & Seeds, Toasted 137
Nutty Carrot Rice 43

O

Oatmeal Raisin Bread 109
Oatmeal Raisin Bread in a Can 112
Oatmeal Raisin Rolls 115
Oat Groats 12-15
Old Fashion Scalloped Potatoes 86
Old World Black Bread 106
Old World Black Bread in a Can 111
Old World Black Rolls 114
Onion Rings, Roasted 87
Oven Fresh Bread 122
Oven Fresh Rolls 122

P

Pasta Alfredo 49
Pasta Fagioli 48
Patties, Tender Gluten 58
Peanut Butter Flax Bars 126
Personal Fruit Pizza 24
Personal Pizza Crust 118
Pie, Banana Cream 131
Pie Pumpkin 88
Pineapple Upside Down Cake 133
Pinto Beans 28-32
Pita Fruit Pizza 24
Pizza 24, 61
Pizza Crust 117
Pizza Crust, Personal 118
Pizza Rolls 122
Pock-et & Crock-it Sandwich 119
Polynesian Bars 125
Poppy Seed Bread 108
Poppy Seed Bread in a Can 112
Poppy Seed Rolls 115
Potatoes, Baked 84
Potato Corn Chowder 99
Potatoes, Mashed 87
Potatoes, Old Fashion Scalloped 86
Potatoes, Rustic 85
Potato Salad 84
Puddings 130-132

Q

Quick (Instant) Brown Rice 12-15

R

Rice 12-15
Rice, Cashew 44
Rice, Nutty Carrot 43
Rice, Spanish 42
Rice Supreme Ice Cream 135
Rice, Tropical 18
Roasted Garlic 87

Roasted Herb Sweet Corn 88
Roasted Onion Rings 87
Roasted Corn on the Cob 88
Roast Beef-less 59
Rolls 113-115, 120-122
Rustic Potatoes 85

S

Sandwiches, Hot-Ready to Go! 62
Scalloped Potatoes, Old Fashion 86
Seeds, Toasted Nuts & 137
Sesame Tahini Creamy Beans 34
Simple but Simply Delicious Beans 34
Simple Fruit Topping 138
Simple Sweet Potatoes 84
Simply Beets 91
Sloppy Joes, Barbecued 62
Slow Cooker Tips 6
Soups, Stews & Chowders 92-100
Sour Cream, Tofu 136
South of the Border Beans 35
Soybeans 28-32
Soy Corn Bread in a Can 124
Soy Sauce 136
Spaghetti, Easy Does It 50
Spaghetti, Garden Style 51
Spaghetti Sauce 103
Spaghetti Squash, Baked 88
Spanish Rice 42
Split Pea Chowder 95
Steel Cut Oats 12-15
Strips, Tender Gluten 58
Stuffed Shells 54
Sun Seed Roast 63
Sweet Corn, Roasted Herb 88
Sweet Potatoes, Baked 84
Sweet Potatoes, Honey Coconutty 82
Sweet Potatoes, Maple Almond 81
Sweet Potatoes, Simple 85
Sweet Potatoes, Tangy Orange 83
Sweet Rolls, Melt in Your Mouth 120

T

Tangy Orange Sweet Potatoes 83
Tapioca Rice Pudding 132
Tender Gluten 58
Tender Gluten Cooked in Broth 58
Tender Gluten Cooked in Gravy 59
Timer, Lamp/Appliance 6, 11, 26
Tips, Slow Cooker 6-10
Toasted Brown Rice 12-15
Toasted Nuts & Seeds 137
Tofu 11
Tofu, Chunky Fried 136
Tofu Cream 138
Tofu Loaf 63
Tofu Rolls, Collard 57
Tofu Rolls, Grape Leaf 57
Tofu Sour Cream 136
Tortilla Bake 60
Topping, Maple Vanilla 138
Topping, Simple Fruit 138
Trivets 11
Tropical Rice 18

V

Vanilla Ice Cream 134
Vanilla Mint Chip Ice Cream 135
Vanilla Pudding 131
Vegetable Lasagna 55
Vegetarian Burger 50

W

White Sauce 101
Whole Grain Rye Bread 107
Whole Grain Rye Bread in a Can 111
Whole Grain Rye Rolls 114
Whole Wheat Bread in a Can 110
Whole Wheat Rolls 113

Y

Yeast Flakes 11